Competency-Based

Human Resource

MANAGEMENT

Competency-Based

Human Resource

MANAGEMENT

DAVID D. DUBOIS

WILLIAM J. ROTHWELL

With

DEBORAH JO KING STERN

LINDA K. KEMP

Davies-Black Publishing
Mountain View, California

Published by Davies-Black Publishing, a division of CPP, Inc., 1055 Joaquin Road, 2nd Floor, Mountain View, CA 94043; 800-624-1765.

Special discounts on bulk quantities of Davies-Black books are available to corporations, professional associations, and other organizations. For details, contact the Director of Marketing and Sales at Davies-Black Publishing; 650-691-9123; fax 650-623-9271.

Myers-Briggs Type Indicator is a trademark or registered trademark of the Myers-Briggs Type Indicator Trust in the United States and other countries. Sixteen Personality Factor is a trademark and 16PF is a registered trademark of NCS Pearson, Inc. Strong Interest Inventory, Davies-Black, and its colophon are registered trademarks and California Psychological Inventory and CPI are trademarks of CPP, Inc.

Visit the Davies-Black Publishing Web site at www.daviesblack.com.

Printed in the United States of America.
12 11 10 09 08   10 9 8 7 6 5 4

Library of Congress Cataloging-in-Publication Data
Competency-based human resource management / David D. Dubois . . . [et al.].
— 1st ed.
        p. cm.
Includes index.
ISBN 978-0-89106-174-8
1. Personnel management. I. Dubois, David D.
HF5549.C7115 2004
658.3—dc22

2003023886

FIRST EDITION
First printing 2004

To the life and memory of my late mother, Edith M. Dubois, who inspired me to persevere in the face of seemingly impossible obstacles, to love when it was difficult to do so, to care when others did not, and to have the courage to stand alone when it was correct to do so.

—David D. Dubois

To my wife, Marcelina Rothwell, and daughter, Candice Rothwell. Without them, my life would not have the same meaning.

—William J. Rothwell

To my mother and father, Verna and Floyd D. King.

—Deborah Jo King Stern

To my teachers and friends, Dr. Lee J. Richmond, professor at Loyola College, Maryland, and Richard W. Bolles, author of What Color Is Your Parachute?

—Linda K. Kemp

Contents

Figures and Forms ix

Preface xi

Acknowledgments xv

Part One: Finding a New Focus

Chapter 1   Why a Focus on Jobs Is Not Enough *3*

Chapter 2   An Overview of Competency-Based HR Management Practices *15*

Part Two: Understanding Competency-Based HR Management

Chapter 3   A Need for Implementing Competency-Based HR Management *43*

Chapter 4   Competency-Based HR Planning *61*

Chapter 5   Competency-Based Employee Recruitment and
                Selection   *95*

Chapter 6   Competency-Based Employee Training   *125*

Chapter 7   Competency-Based Performance Management   *141*

Chapter 8   Competency-Based Employee Rewards   *163*

Chapter 9   Competency-Based Employee Development   *183*

Part Three: Transitioning to Competency-Based HR Management

Chapter 10   The Transformation to Competency-Based
                HR Management   *219*

Chapter 11   Competency-Based HR Management: The Next Steps   *233*

Appendixes

              A: Frequently Asked Questions About Competency-
                 Based HR Management   *241*

              B: Further Suggestions on Employee Development   *247*

              C: Examples of Life-Career Assessment Exercises   *251*

              D: Employee Development and Succession Management
                 255

Notes   257

References   263

Index   281

Figures and Forms

Figures

1   Comparison of Traditional and Competency-Based HR Management *11*

2   A Model to Guide the Implementation of Strategic HR Management *54*

3   Implementing Competency-Based HR Planning *76*

4   Dynamic Relationships *85*

5   Summary of Competency Inventory Data Useful for HR Planning *93*

6   Traditional Recruitment Process *97*

7   Traditional Selection Process *100*

8   Competency-Based Employee Recruitment and Selection *113*

9   Competency-Based Performance Management *147*

10   Implementing Competency-Based Performance Management *156*

11   Competency-Based Employee Reward Process *175*

12   The Three-Step Process for Choosing the Correct Work *190*

13   Implementing Competency-Based Employee Development *200*

14   A Model for Transforming the HR Function *222*

15   An Example of the Use of Kemp's Life-Career World Wheel *252*

Forms

1   Job Description and Job Specification (Sample) *7*

2   Traditional Worker Skills Inventory Questionnaire *68*

3   Worker Competency Inventory Questionnaire *70*

4   Assessing the HR Function *223*

5   Selecting Which HR Functions Should Become Competency Based *224*

6   Expected Roles, Competencies, and Outputs *226*

7   Educating Key Stakeholder Groups on Competency-Based HR Management *227*

8   Important HR Practitioner Competencies and Associated Behaviors *229*

9   Assessing the Competency-Based HR Practitioner *230*

Preface

Human resource (HR) management is undergoing a major transformation in today's organizations. Once upon a time—and not all that long ago—HR management practitioners were expected to be the traffic cops of their organizations. It was their responsibility to note legal noncompliance or departures from organizational policies and then punish transgressors, just as traffic cops watch for and issue tickets to drivers who exceed speed limits. As a direct consequence of this compliance orientation, some HR management practitioners became risk averse—and some remain so to this day. They oppose innovative actions taken to leverage the talents of organizational members for the simple reason that treading on new ground means taking new risks, which could possibly cause deviations from external legal requirements or internal policy standards.

The new role of HR management demands an outlook that differs considerably from the compliance mind-set. HR management practitioners are expected to be experts on leveraging human talent within their organizations for the purpose of achieving competitive advantage. They must demonstrate new sensitivity to the full range of human capabilities (including emotional intelligence), align HR efforts with strategic objectives, and integrate various HR activities so that people are consistently encouraged to achieve desired results.

For many practitioners, traditional writings on HR management do more to stand in the way of progress than to facilitate it. One reason is that traditional college textbooks on the field continue to define "jobs," "job descriptions," and "work analysis" as making up the foundation for most HR efforts. That view persists even as the work of Bill Bridges and others who have noted that "jobs are dead" is described in the same books. Traditional textbooks on HR management, although important because they build expectations among HR professionals about the nature of their role, do not address the critical importance of individual differences, which create *exemplary performers,* who may be many times more productive than others with the same job titles, education, and experience. And yet the importance of individual characteristics, or competencies, is well known to CEOs, operating managers, and others. Recognizing critical differences in individual productivity implies that more work might be done by fewer people, or that better work might be done by the same number of people. Of course, that can only happen if HR practitioners become more savvy about finding the best-in-class performers, discover what makes them different from their fully successful counterparts, and reorient HR toward recruiting, selecting, training, developing, rewarding, appraising, and otherwise managing these exceptional people.

This book offers a guide to the process of reinventing HR so that it focuses on identifying those stellar individual characteristics and then aligns all HR activities around them. The purpose of HR management is thus not to describe "jobs" and find people to fit into boxes on organizational charts. Instead, its goal is to achieve quantum leaps in productivity and in competitive advantage by unleashing the power of exemplary performers, discovering their characteristics, and building those characteristics into all aspects of HR.

Any person with an interest in effectively managing human resources through a competency-based system is part of the audience for this book. Such individuals might include HR leaders and practitioners, organizational effectiveness and development managers, trainers, employee or career development practitioners and facilitators, operations managers of all types, executive officers and their staffs, college or university professors in fields related to human resources and executive education, college or university administrators committed to improving the use of human talent in their institutions, and others who are interested in utilizing human talent for maximum benefit.

Contents of This Book

Over the years, early thinkers and writers such as David McClelland and Richard Boyatzis and others including Daniel Goleman, Patricia McLagan, and Lyle and Signe Spencer have contributed to the field's wide knowledge base. Further, the models for adopting individual competency-based HR management functions are supported, at least in part, by recently published case reports that attest to the validity of the approaches in specific settings. As others try out the (sometimes untested) suggestions in this book, they will discover the best methods for implementing competency-based HR management. We hope this new knowledge, shared with others, will be used to raise the state of the art and of the practice.

Part 1, which comprises the first two chapters, explains the background and presents a rationale for reinventing HR management with a competencies rather than a jobs foundation. In this sense, the book is revolutionary in its approach to HR management.

Chapter 1 presents and analyzes several vignettes that illustrate the necessity of shifting HR management to a competency foundation in most organizations. Chapter 2 contains an overview of competency-based HR management practices. Key terms are defined in the context of their use in later chapters. This chapter also explains the business needs that are met through competency-based HR management and the ways in which the use of competencies can be aligned with business plans, objectives, and needs.

Part 2 is composed of seven chapters and will help the reader to understand the details of competency-based HR management on a function-by-function basis.

Chapter 3 presents a model for the establishment of a competency-based HR management function. The model is positioned as a response to conclusions drawn from a vignette and the discussion of six trends affecting businesses and organizations. Chapters 4 through 9 offer models—presented in a step-by-step format—for developing competency-based HR planning, employee recruitment and selection, employee training, performance management, employee reward processes, and employee development. The chapters offer suggestions for implementing each model. In addition, we take a frank look at the advantages and challenges of using a competency-based approach for each HR management function and provide criteria by which to determine whether the area should become competency based or be managed traditionally.

Part 3, which consists of chapters 10 and 11, is devoted to helping readers understand how to handle the transition from a jobs-based to a competency-based HR management system.

Chapter 10 presents a model for transforming HR into a competency-based department and explains the process of applying that model. The chapter concludes by addressing a critical question, namely, "How can HR practitioners become competent in the new approach?" The answers are essential to a successful transition to competency-based HR management.

Chapter 11, the final chapter, examines the next steps for competency-based HR management by discussing its future direction and anticipated innovations. The chapter concludes by reviewing methods of adoption and use as well as some of the challenges involved in applying competency-based practices to traditional jobs-based organizations.

Acknowledgments

With each new book project, we are reminded over and over that the support of others is essential to achieving a successful result. This project is no exception.

David Dubois acknowledges those colleagues and clients—far too many to thank individually here (but they know who they are)—who encouraged him to write this book. Remembering their words helped him to tackle this work and to urge the other authors to make this book a reality despite the obstacles they all faced. He acknowledges the monumental efforts of Connie Kallback, developmental editor, and the numerous contributions and encouragement she offered along the way.

Linda Kemp and David Dubois acknowledge the influence of Drs. Anna Miller-Tiedeman and David Tiedeman on the development of the "life-career" concept, which affected the thinking behind the employee development practices in this book. They also thank Dr. Lee J. Richmond for her unselfish efforts—over many years—to bring us (and others) together in forums that enabled us to gain a deeper understanding of the "life-career" paradigm and its significance for employee development. Thanks to all!

Deborah Jo King Stern extends a most sincere "thank you" to family, friends, and colleagues for their support. She especially wishes to thank the co-authors for their many contributions and for leading this project to fruition. She also expresses her gratitude to her husband and children for their understanding, to her mother for the constant words of encouragement and never-ending faith, and to her father for his belief in her. She thanks her sister for always being there. A warm thank-you, too, goes to those she has met along the way and who have offered much inspiration.

Finally, the authors wish to thank those individuals at Davies-Black Publishing who contributed their time and talents to this project.

Part One

FINDING A
New Focus

CHAPTER 1

Why a Focus on Jobs
Is Not Enough

This chapter describes the challenges facing today's human resource (HR) practitioners and offers justification for a new way of thinking about human resource management. The following five vignettes portray HR situations in fictitious organizations. Readers are prompted to write down a solution to the problem presented in each vignette; then the vignettes are analyzed. Next, we discuss the problems that result when organizations focus on jobs as the criterion for matching employees with the work that is essential to organizational success. The chapter closes with an answer to the question, What are the major HR management subsystems in organizations today?

Five Vignettes

First, take out a sheet of paper. Next, read over each of the following vignettes. As you read each vignette, record what you believe should be done to solve the problem described.

Vignette 1

John Parks, director of HR for Acme Corporation, is upset. He remarks to his secretary, "It seems like the only thing we do in this department is look for people to hire. We're always churning people. We don't have time to stem the turnover by taking a proactive approach to human resources. Instead, we are always looking for warm bodies to fill the latest vacancies."

Vignette 2

The senior vice president of operations has just been informed by the CEO that he must let go of 20% of his staff within 30 days in order to cut costs. He sends a memo to his direct reports, instructing them to reduce their work units by 20% of the committed working hours. He then leaves for a 3-week vacation. His direct reports are left guessing as to how to implement the order and how to handle the consequent fallout. The senior vice president is not available to consult for advice.

Vignette 3

The CEO and the director of marketing approach an international organization with a proposal to provide services in an area outside the company's core business. They do not expect to win the business, but much to their surprise, they are awarded the contract. At this point, they begin to wonder how they will staff for the work. The first person they call is the director of HR; she is told to recruit five different specialists who must report within 6 weeks. The director of HR is given little information to guide the search.

Vignette 4

The director of HR in a large organization of more than 20,000 employees examines the projected retirement dates of the senior executive group. To their chagrin, the executives learn that 80% of their key group is eligible for retirement within 2 years. The CEO assigns the vice president of HR the task of preparing a succession plan for building an internal talent pool sufficient to meet the expected shortfall of executive talent.

Vignette 5

The Axeljocanda Corporation has a long history of preparing and using high-quality strategic business plans. In this organization, the HR department operates as an administrative, paper-pushing work unit. The department has performed job analysis and job performance assessment on only a few key jobs in the organization, leaving the rest unexamined.

In Axeljocanda's corporate culture, department managers commonly do not compare notes with their peers about initiatives in their departments. As a direct consequence, the compensation manager has never met with the training director or with the director of employee relations. Furthermore, the vice president of HR has never been invited to participate in strategic business planning retreats with the other senior executives.

Analysis of the Vignettes

Think for a moment about what happened in these vignettes. In Vignette 1, the HR department is too busy churning people to focus on results and determine how best to achieve them. In Vignette 2, middle managers find themselves facing the difficult task of reallocating work responsibilities simply to achieve short-term cost savings. In Vignette 3, the organization is experiencing a need for talent and does not know how to get it. In Vignette 4, a highly competent vice president of HR faces the challenges of developing, in the short term, a plan to meet long-term requirements. In Vignette 5, the HR department is neither vertically aligned with organizational strategy nor horizontally aligned among its own functions.

The Problem With Focusing on Jobs Alone

The vignettes described in the previous section dramatically underscore some of the problems facing HR professionals and their organizations today.

Traditionally, job analysis—the process of identifying the work that people do—has been the foundation of HR department activities. According to a classic treatment by Walker (1980), a job analysis has four possible purposes. Each purpose provides a view of the job from a different angle; therefore, each is identified by a slightly different approach. One purpose is to discover what people do in their jobs. This approach takes a close look at the reality of the jobs. A second purpose is to find out what people think job incumbents do in their jobs. This approach seeks to gather perceptions about the jobs. A third purpose is to ascertain what people or their immediate supervisors believe job incumbents should be doing at their jobs. This approach determines the job norms. A fourth purpose is to determine what people or their supervisors believe job incumbents are doing or should be preparing to do in their jobs in the future should changes occur in their workplace. This approach to job analysis emphasizes planning for changes (Rothwell & Kazanas, 1994, 1998).[1]

A *job description,* which tells what the incumbent does, and a *job specification,* which clarifies the minimum requirements necessary to qualify for a job, are major outputs of job analysis. Job descriptions and job specifications, in turn, are key to such HR functions as employee recruitment, selection, training, and performance management.

One problem with traditional job descriptions is that they are written only to clarify those activities job incumbents are supposed to perform and may not clearly describe measurable worker outputs or results that meet the requirements for organizational success. If you doubt that, examine Form 1, Job Description and Job Specification (Sample), which contains a typical job description from an organization. Note that the example does not list the desired outputs or results under the description of responsibilities.

Outputs or *results* are the products or services that workers produce and deliver to others; recipients might include coworkers, constituents, customers, or persons or organizations external to the workers' organizations. Outputs or results should be produced to a level of quality that meets or exceeds the receiver's expectations.

Another problem with traditional job descriptions is that they quickly become outdated. In today's dynamic organizations, work activities do not remain the same for long. Job descriptions, however, rarely keep pace with changes in work requirements. That leads to much confusion as people try to figure out whether a job description is current or outdated.

Form 1: Job Description and Job Specification (Sample)

PART I: JOB DESCRIPTION	
Job title	Job analyst
Purpose of job	Conducts studies of work performed. Prepares job descriptions and other information requested by managers and HR practitioners.
Number of people supervised	None
Responsibilities	• Collects, analyzes, and prepares work information for personnel, administrative, and management functions. • Consults with management to determine the purpose, range, and type of prospective studies. • Studies the organization's current work data and compiles the necessary background information. • Observes work processes and interviews workers and supervisors to determine job and worker requirements. • Analyzes work data and develops written summaries. Uses developed data to evaluate methods and techniques for worker-related programs; improves them if necessary. May specialize in classifying positions to meet civil service requirements. • Performs other assigned duties.
PART II: JOB SPECIFICATION	
Minimum education required	Bachelor's degree with a specialty in HR management, general management, or a related field
Minimum experience required	None
Other essential qualifications	Patience, perseverance

Cornell University professors Patrick Wright and Lee Dyer conducted a study on how the HR profession will change because of technology. According to their preliminary findings, there is a possibility that the job description will be "one of the first institutional fixtures of the profession" to become obsolete (Leonard, 2000). Job descriptions will not only be out-of-date before they are even written due to rapid change, but may become obstacles for HR professionals who are trying to effect organizational change. Leonard further noted that job descriptions are carefully written to meet legal requirements and to list the organization's expectations for an employee but lack the flexibility needed today.

Again, examine the job description shown in Form 1. Assume you are the supervisor of the person in the described position and ask yourself the following questions:

- How will I know if this worker demonstrates successful performance?
- How do I know that the job description is current?

Unfortunately, workers often have the same questions. They are left to guess about the measurable outputs or results they are expected to produce, in what form, at what level of quality, and on what schedule.

Sometimes workers are not alone in playing this guessing game. When they put those questions to a supervisor they might be greeted with a blank stare or given answers too vague to make sense. Frustrated, workers continue doing what they have always done—or what they have seen others do—without knowing for certain whether they are achieving desired outputs. But when customers, supervisors, or managers do not receive the products or services they expected on time or of sufficient quality, they blame the worker. This raises yet another question: What is the supervisor's responsibility for this dilemma?

This scenario illustrates a possibly three-fold problem. First, there might be a mismatch between workers' capabilities and the outputs or results they are required to produce. Second, the information provided could be inaccurate or incomplete. Third and finally, the expected outputs might not conform to traditionally defined jobs that are rigid, compact, and inflexible.

The point is that job descriptions are not enough. Yet the findings of one survey, sponsored by the American Compensation Association and conducted with a sample of 1,000 members and 219 respondents, seem to indicate that "even though work design endeavors have created changes in the way work is done, most respondents still apply traditional job analysis to jobs to get information for compensation and other human resources management purposes" (Fay, Fisher, & Mahony, 1997, p. 21). Joinson (2001, p. 12) suggested that "one option is moving away from skills-based descriptions and toward 'job roles,' focused on broader abilities, that are easier to alter as technologies and customer needs change."[2] Although it is true that well-prepared job descriptions can be a powerful tool, keeping them clear and current is a major challenge that exceeds the grasp of many organizations today. As a consequence, the mismatches described in the previous paragraph are all the more likely to occur.

The Major HR Management Subsystems in Organizations Today

There are several ways to conceptualize the structure and means for organizing the HR system in an organization.

The first, and perhaps most familiar, is the *functional method* (Rothwell, Prescott, & Taylor, 1998). In this approach, HR management is organized into units such as employee relations, training, compensation and benefits, and payroll. Each is considered a function because it bears specific responsibilities for the organization's total HR system.

A second way of structuring HR management is the *point of contact method*. With this approach, which is much rarer than the functional approach, HR is organized around meeting the needs of its clients, stakeholders, and community. There are separate functions for worker input (such as recruitment, placement, and orientation), maintaining workers (such as payroll, training, compensation, and employee relations), and output (such as decruitment and retirement).

A third way to think about HR management has become popular in recent years. This method divides those who do the work of the HR function into two groups. One group handles transactions, such as processing payroll, making name changes on benefit forms, and updating employee records. A second group extends the people management expertise of the HR function to line management groups, offering on-the-spot, real-time consulting advice to managers and workers who may be dealing with "people challenges."

There are, of course, other ways of organizing the HR function. Basically, the HR subsystems of most organizations include recruitment, selection, performance management, job analysis and evaluation, compensation, payroll, development and improvement, and career and succession planning. But regardless of whether you are an HR specialist or generalist in one of today's organizations, you should be aware of how competency-based HR management differs from traditional work-based HR management. Figure 1 summarizes the differences in the two approaches. Competency-based HR management focuses attention on the people who do the work rather than on the work done by those people. We will examine this important distinction in the next chapter.

Summary

This chapter opened with vignettes that underscore differences between the traditional work-based approach and a new competency-based approach to HR. It went on to discuss some of the problems associated with the work-based approach and described key issues facing HR practitioners today. A focus on jobs is no longer enough. HR practitioners need to explore a new approach as a foundation for their work, an approach called *competency-based human resource management.*

Figure 1: Comparison of Traditional and Competency-Based HR Management

	Traditional HR Management	Competency-Based HR Management
Foundation	Work analysis and job descriptions form the foundation of traditional HR management. Work analysis becomes the basis for recruiting, selecting, orienting, training, rewarding, appraising, and developing people. The job description delineates work activities. It does not state expected work results in measurable or observable terms.	Competencies are the traits that individuals use for successful and exemplary performance. The identification, modeling, and assessment of competencies form the foundation of competency-based HR management. The HR function seeks to discover worker traits that lead to fully successful and exemplary performance and configures HR activities around cultivating them.
Chief reasons for using the approach	The approach is a known quantity and is geared toward achieving compliance. It categorizes individuals on organizational charts so they can be assigned identifiable tasks for which they can be held accountable. U.S. college textbooks on HR management are devoted exclusively to traditional HR management.	The approach stimulates productivity and uses human talent to the best competitive advantage. It recognizes differences in individual abilities to achieve work results. Exemplary performers are significantly more productive than their fully successful counterparts. If the organization finds or develops exemplary performers, it could be more productive with the same size workforce.
Major challenges	• Work changes rapidly, and job descriptions quickly become outdated. • The approach is rarely successful in providing leadership on using human talent to greatest advantage.	• The meaning of the term *competency* is not clearly and consistently understood. • Identifying the competencies that distinguish exemplary from fully successful performers is labor-intensive and can be expensive and time-consuming. • Much inexpert competency work is being done in today's organizations.

Figure 1: Comparison of Traditional and Competency-Based HR Management (continued)

	Traditional HR Management	Competency-Based HR Management
Role of HR function	• Ensures compliance with laws, rules, regulations, and organizational policies and procedures.	• Takes the lead in achieving breakthrough competitive advantage by selecting and developing more people who can achieve at the measurable productivity levels of exemplary performers. • Continues to fulfill its compliance responsibilities in a competency-based environment.
HR planning subsystem	• Concentrates on head count and HR expenses. • Makes forecasts based on the assumption that the future will be like the past and that the same number of people are needed to achieve predictable, measurable work results. • Favors quantitative methods for workforce planning.	• Concentrates on talent and the value HR brings to the organization. • Does not assume that the future will be like the past or that the same head count is needed to achieve predictable results. • Favors the use of qualitative planning methods.
Employee recruitment and selection	• Consults the usual external and internal sources. • Finds candidates to match the qualifications outlined in job specifications. • Assumes that education, experience, and other qualifications are equivalent to the ability to perform assigned work activities.	• Tries to identify patterns that indicate past sources of exemplary performers and recruits through those or similar sources. • Makes selection decisions based on demonstrated ability to perform or evidence of results. • Compares applicants' talents to competency models that define the traits of fully successful or exemplary performers in their work areas.

Figure 1: Comparison of Traditional and Competency-Based HR Management (continued)

	Traditional HR Management	Competency-Based HR Management
Employee training subsystem	• Distinguishes training needs from management needs. • Builds employee knowledge, skill, and attitude to conform with the organization's expectations.	• Focuses attention on roadblocks to individual productivity that are created by the organization and management's responsibility to eliminate those obstacles. • Builds individual competencies in line with measurable fully successful or exemplary performance.
Performance management subsystem	• Keeps costs at a minimum while providing performance feedback to individuals. • Makes decisions about pay raises, promotions, and related issues.	• Periodically assesses individuals against competency models for their current work and their aspirations. • Provides feedback to individuals to help them move toward exemplary performance.
Employee reward processes subsystem	• Attracts and retains people who perform the work of the organization.	• Attracts and retains people whose measurable contributions demonstrate their ability to perform at an exemplary level.
Employee development subsystem	• Process is either vague or ambiguous.	• Process is designed to help individuals to discover their own competencies, help the organization to identify the talent it has available, and cultivate talent as work is being accomplished. • Recognizes that 98% of all efforts to build competencies occurs through work experiences. • Places equal emphasis on work results and on the work process as a means of building bench strength by exposing individuals to new experiences.

CHAPTER 2

An Overview of Competency-Based HR Management Practices

This chapter lays the foundation for the book by answering the following key questions:

- What are competencies?
- What is the difference between fully successful and exemplary performers, and why does it matter?
- What are competency models?
- How are competencies identified?
- What is human resource (HR) management?
- What is competency-based HR management?
- What business needs are met through the use of competency-based HR management practices?
- How are competencies aligned with business plans, objectives, and needs?

Competencies

Think for a few minutes about the best supervisor you ever had. Take a moment to identify three or four of this person's most significant characteristics, which, used appropriately and consistently, led you to select him or her as your best supervisor. Perhaps this person behaved in some of the following ways:

- Always trusted you to do your work well.
- Gave you immediate feedback on your work.
- Was incredibly and brutally honest—but in a very positive way.
- Showed concern for others when their personal problems affected their work.

From this exercise, you have just learned the meaning of the word *competency*. Your best supervisor probably had anywhere from 12 to 15 traits or characteristics that affected his or her behavior and, therefore, work performance.

Competencies, then, are characteristics that individuals have and use in appropriate, consistent ways in order to achieve desired performance. These characteristics include knowledge, skills, aspects of self-image, social motives, traits, thought patterns, mind-sets, and ways of thinking, feeling, and acting.

Competencies form the foundation of competency-based HR management practices. Interpretations of the meaning of competencies are quite varied. A brief look at the history of the competency movement will perhaps provide you with a better understanding of the term as it has been defined and is used in HR management.

Background

Several key developments laid the early groundwork for the competency movement and contributed significantly to the field. First, in 1954, John C. Flanagan devised an approach he called the *critical incident technique,* which was used to examine what people do (Flanagan, 1954). He defined the technique as "a set of procedures for collecting direct observations of human behavior in such a way as to facilitate their potential usefulness in solving practical problems and developing broad psychological principles. The critical incident technique outlines procedures for collect-

ing observed incidents having special significance and meeting systematically defined criteria." An incident is an observable human activity that is
complete enough on its own to allow inferences and predictions to be
made about the individual performing the act. For an incident to be critical, it "must occur in a situation where the purpose or intent of the act
seems fairly clear to the observer and where its consequences are sufficiently definite to leave little doubt concerning its effects" (p. 327).

Flanagan noted that the foundation for the critical incident technique originated in the studies of Sir Francis Galton in the late 1800s
and in later developments such as time sampling studies pertaining to
recreational activities, controlled observation tests, and anecdotal
records. It is specifically rooted, however, in studies conducted in the
United States Army Air Forces' Aviation Psychology Program. The
Aviation Psychology Program was founded in the summer of 1941 to
create selection and classification procedures for aircrews.[1]

The concept of human competence reached the forefront of human
resource development with the concurrent work of the psychologists
Robert White and David C. McClelland. White (1959) identified a
human trait that he called *competence*. McClelland (1973) originated an
approach for predicting competence that was notably different from
widely accepted intelligence tests of the time. He suggested that although
intelligence influences performance, personal characteristics, such as an
individual's motivation and self-image, differentiate successful from
unsuccessful performance and can be noted in a number of life roles
that include job roles. McClelland and his associates conducted the first
tests associated with this new approach with U.S. State Department
Foreign Service information officers (McClelland & Dailey, 1973, in
Spencer, McClelland, & Spencer, 1994).[2]

McClelland (1973, 1976), who is often credited with coining the
term *competency,* defined it as a characteristic that underlies successful
performance. Over the years, many writers, including key thinkers and
leaders in the field, have defined and refined the word *competency* and
related terms.[3]

Zemke (1982) set out to ascertain the precise attributes of a competency and conducted a number of interviews with experts in the field.
He determined from the interviews that there is no complete and total
agreement on what is and is not a competency:

> Competency, competencies, competency models, and competency-based
> training are Humpty Dumpty words meaning only what the definer
> wants them to mean.—The problem comes not from malice, stupidity or
> marketing avarice, but instead from some basic procedural and philo-
> sophical differences among those racing to define and develop the con-
> cept and to set the model for the way the rest of us will use competencies
> in our day-to-day training efforts. (p. 28)

McLagan (1989) suggested that a competency is "an area of knowledge or skill that is critical for producing key outputs." She also noted
that people may express these capabilities in a "broad, even infinite,
array of on-the-job behaviors" (p. 77).

George Klemp (1980) defined a *job competency* as "an underlying
characteristic of a person which results in effective and/or superior performance in a job" (in Boyatzis, 1982, p. 21). He also noted that "competencies are characteristics that are causally related to effective or superior
performance in a job" (p. 23). Expanding on that definition, Spencer and
Spencer (1993) described a competency as "an underlying characteristic
of an individual that is causally related to criterion-referenced effective
and/or superior performance in a job or situation" (p. 9). They explained
that competency characteristics include these five types: motives, traits,
self-concept, knowledge, and skill.

Dubois (1993) adapted Boyatzis's 1982 interpretation of the term
and defined a competency as an underlying characteristic that "leads to
successful performance in a life role" (p. 5). This definition varies
according to the context of its application and the differences in procedure and philosophy. Flannery, Hofrichter, and Platten (1996) noted
that competencies "add value and help predict success" (p. 93). Dubois
and Rothwell (2000) described competencies as tools used by workers in
a variety of ways to complete units of work, or job tasks.

Knowledge and skills are the more obvious competencies employees
use to achieve the expected outputs or results. Some of the more abstract
worker competencies, however, are those that have been associated with
successful completion of select types of work; such competencies
include patience, perseverance, flexibility, and self-confidence. Note that
competencies have less to do with assigned tasks (work activities) and
more to do with personal qualities. This critical dimension is largely
missing or not well represented in traditional definitions of jobs.

There are two schools of thought concerning differences in the interpretation of competency. One school of thought maintains that competency implies knowledge or skill. The second interprets competency as any characteristic that supports performance. In the latter interpretation, competency can include knowledge or skill as well as any number of other characteristics such as levels of motivation and personality traits. Central to the second school of thought is the philosophy that the focus should be on the people who do the work, not on the work those people do.

There are different types and levels of competencies, and they are classified or organized in different ways. They can also be subdivided repeatedly, and very often are, but are frequently grouped as either organizational or individual. Within the category of individual competencies, there are different types of competencies, such as technical and personal functioning. Some practitioners simply make the distinction between technical and nontechnical competencies: Technical competencies are specific to certain roles, and nontechnical competencies are more generic in nature (Rothwell, Hohne, & King, 2000). Byham and Moyer (1998) classified competencies as organizational, job- or role-related, and personal.

In addition to the term *competencies,* with its range of definitions, some organizations use the term *dimensions.* Data on the behaviors, motivations, and knowledge related to job success or failure can be reliably described and grouped under both terms.

The language used in association with competency-based HR management practices is often referred to as a *behavioral language.* A behavioral language can be used to describe the actions necessary to achieve organizational goals, and it affords the opportunity to understand further what has been done in the past, what is occurring in the present, and what needs to occur in the future (Green, 1999). After the terms associated with competency-based practices are defined, competencies can provide a common language across an entire organization.[4] A common language is very useful for discussing the workforce and its skills, performance, impact, and much more.

Competency Measurement Methods

A competency may be demonstrated in many ways. One method of identifying the typical ways that competencies are demonstrated is to identify the behaviors or tangible results (outcomes) produced by their use in the context of the work performed. A *behavior* is an observable action that is taken to achieve results or that contributes to an accomplishment. Green (1999) defined behavior as an action that can be observed, described, and verified. Competencies could be measured by using *behavioral indicators.* A behavioral indicator is a statement of an action, or set of actions, that one would expect to observe when a person successfully uses a competency to perform work.

The Crucial Role of Corporate Culture

It is worth emphasizing here that appropriate behaviors linked to a competency may differ, depending on the corporate culture in which that competency is grounded. *Corporate culture* refers to the unspoken beliefs held in common by the people in an organization about the right and wrong ways to behave. Schein (1992) defined the culture of a group as follows:

> A pattern of shared basic assumptions that the group learned as it solved its problems of external adaptation and internal integration, that has worked well enough to be considered valid and, therefore, to be taught to new members as the correct way to perceive, think, and feel in relation to those problems. (p. 12)

Hence, the demonstration of a competency is tied to the unique corporate culture in which it appears in much the same way that national culture determines the demonstration of success factors. For instance, to be successful in a tribe of headhunters, one must collect the most heads, and to be successful in a capitalist society, one must collect the most money.

Corporate cultures are embodiments of organizational values, and values are the underpinning of management decisions. Views about the equivalents to success are grounded in the culture. And so it is with behavioral indicators. The "right" and—by implication—the "wrong" behaviors differ across such disparate corporate cultures as those, for example, of the American Red Cross, Ford Motor Company, Intel, and the Internal Revenue Service. In short, one competency model for the same work does not fit all corporate cultures. The difference might be not in the statement or definition of the competency, for example, but how it is successfully demonstrated within the context of organizational culture, values, or strategic settings.

Outputs Versus Activities

In the discussion on outputs and results in chapter 1, we defined the term *outputs* as the goods or services (results) that workers produce and turn over to clients or constituents. A *job output* is a product or service delivered to others by an individual, a team, or a group. Job outputs can be measured through metrics associated with quantity, quality, time, cost, and requirements related to customer service (Rothwell & Kazanas, 1998).

Several other terms related to outputs and work activities in organizations are appropriate for discussion here. Work activities in most organizations include the performance of a series of tasks or units of work that generate outputs or results. The term *task* means an activity with a distinguishable beginning, middle, and end. The more specific term *job task* refers to a unit of work that contributes to the job outputs expected of an employee. A group of completed job tasks that produces job outputs is a *job activity. Job competence* is an employee's capacity to at least meet, if not exceed, job requirements by producing outputs or results at an expected level of quality within the constraints of the organizational environment.

In today's world of work, knowing and measuring the outputs or results that workers must produce, and the circumstances surrounding their production, is key to understanding organizational success. Workers achieve the desired results by carrying out job tasks. But what are the personal characteristics in the domains of thoughts, feelings, and actions that workers use to perform their tasks? These characteristics are their competencies. Therefore, competencies are essential to achieving work of any kind. This leads to a simplistic reduction: no competencies, no outputs, no organization.[5]

The Difference Between Fully
Successful and Exemplary Performers

The view that all people are created equal is commonplace in U.S. culture. In reality, however, it is not true. If all people were equal, then everyone could produce mathematical results like Einstein's or write plays equal to those of Shakespeare.

People may be treated equally by the government, but that does not mean talent is equally distributed among them. Some individuals excel in certain spheres of human effort. We call those people *exemplars*. They are the best-in-class performers. Research indicates that they may be as much as 20 times more productive in achieving work results or outputs compared to other experienced job incumbents who have the same job titles, carry out the same duties and activities, and probably earn the same compensation.

One goal of looking at competencies is to discover the differences between the exemplary performers and the fully successful performers, those incumbents who meet job standards but are not outstanding. Why does this distinction matter? If we can pinpoint those differences in operational terms, we may be able to select more people who function at the exemplar's level or help others to develop that capability. Such an achievement would enable an organization to become dramatically more productive with the same staff. Exemplary performance is perhaps best understood as an ideal, a desired future performance level that is more than minimally adequate or the best performance currently possible. It signifies a goal that can be achieved through an infinite number of possible behaviors and activities.

While it is not possible to turn every worker into an exemplary performer—owing to what educators term "individual differences"—it is possible to develop select individuals who possess enhanced abilities in some areas or to build competence closer to the level of the exemplar. In addition, the information gained from identifying the competencies (traits or characteristics) used by exemplary performers helps all workers to improve their performance. Even modest improvement can significantly increase overall productivity. The concepts and practices described in this book are based on this key principle.

Given the cost and resources needed to rigorously identify and isolate the competencies of exemplary performers from those of their fully successful peers, we realize that not every organization can afford the endeavor. In other words, some organizations will be satisfied to identify and use, for HR management purposes, the baseline competencies of all fully successful workers without differentiating the competencies of exemplary performers. Organizations that make this decision will still achieve performance improvement benefits because the competencies of fully successful workers will be available for designing their HR practices.

Let's take a moment to learn about the desirable actions of exemplary performers and the organizational factors that affect them. Research reported by Fuller (1999) revealed that exemplary performers customize their work agendas, either eliminating unnecessary steps or entire processes or adding undocumented steps to their processes. Exemplary performers seek out the data and documentation they need from sources that might not be known to others in their organizations. They also create their own highly effective job aids based on their individual experience. Exemplary performers have passion for the work they do and are willing to "go the extra mile" to locate and acquire work tools for themselves. It is largely for this reason that the work tools of exemplary performers are better than those of their counterparts in the organization.

Fuller (1999) also discovered that exemplary performers tend to receive frequent coaching and better feedback from their managers. They are offered different incentives, since their managers generally understand the importance of recognition and rewards. Training did not appear to be a major contributor to exemplary performance; instead, emphasizing other HR management components enabled organizations to have greater impact on performance. Finally, when managers removed barriers, performance improved dramatically.

Competency Models

A *competency model* is a written description of the competencies required for fully successful or exemplary performance in a job category, work team, department, division, or organization. Competency identification and modeling can be a beginning point for strategic development plans linked to organizational and individual needs.

As you might expect, organizations express competency models in somewhat different ways. These variations reflect their different constraints, preferences, practices, values, business objectives, and reasons for using competencies. Competency models may also vary by type. Many organizations do not distinguish among competency models that underscore the differences between exemplary and fully successful performers, those that identify minimum requirements for job success, or so-called derailment studies that indicate the likely causes of failure. In general, then, the structure of a competency model, the way in which it is communicated to workers, and the manner of its use reflect the values of the organization's decision makers and leaders.

Research on the characteristics included in competency models is of much interest today. In one study with 300 respondents conducted by Arthur Andersen, Schoonover, and SHRM, the following categories were reported as included in competency models: technical skills, knowledge areas, performance behaviors, personal attributes, metrics/results, and key experiences (Schoonover, Schoonover, Nemerov, & Ehly, 2000, p. 7).

Competency Identification

We often advise clients in our consulting practice to ask for a quick definition from anyone who uses the term *competency*. There is good reason to do so. Not everyone uses the word in the same way, as you learned earlier in this chapter. Because there is confusion with the terms involved in competency work, establishing clear definitions is an important part of the field.[6] And to complicate matters, not everyone uses the same approach to discovering the competencies linked to job success, a process known as *competency identification*.

Confronting the Challenges of Competency Identification

Striking a balance between speed and rigor is perhaps the chief challenge of competency identification work. *Speed* refers to how quickly the competencies for a targeted group can be identified. *Rigor* refers to the validity and reliability of the competency modeling results. A very rigorous methodology for competency modeling may require such an extended time frame that the results are useless by the time they are delivered to impatient clients. This impatience on the part of clients is often warranted, as their production cycles may be short and must be modified to accommodate revised work methods.

Many other challenges await those who undertake competency identification. An organization may have difficulty matching the resources needed to conduct competency identification with the resources available to carry out the task. Decision makers are not always easily convinced that competency modeling efforts are worth the necessary effort and cost. Yet another challenge involves deciding whether to devote time and resources to producing culture-specific competency models or to find and use models from other sources.

Pickett (1998) mentioned challenges such as difficulty identifying competencies, not enough time allotted for the project, resistance from staff, and lack of management support and commitment. As the reasons for problems, he suggested poor communication, not enough background information made available, and unmet expectations. Cooper (2000) further noted challenges such as less than total commitment throughout the organization, an unawareness of the benefits, and a culture that does not support competency practices.

According to Lucia and Lepsinger (1999), lack of commitment is often caused by failure to clearly articulate the purpose for using a competency model, not enough stakeholders involved, and fear of changes, limited choices, and extra work. They suggested other issues that are critical to identify in the development stage of an action plan, such as conflicts related to time, influence of different individuals and key stakeholders, power and politics, availability of resources, resistance, and skill.

We should comment here, however, that a competency-based approach to HR management provides a method of dealing with each issue. Several research studies on competency-based HR management have addressed the topic of challenges and barriers and provided suggestions for meeting and overcoming them. Here is a brief look at the some of the results.

- From a survey on competency systems, both their design and use, conducted with 134 people, Green (1999) indicated that the findings suggest five broad categories of challenges: gaining buy-in, involvement, and participation; developing reliable and valid forms of measurement; addressing the challenge of negative feedback through introduction of acceptable and representative performance measurement; ensuring job relevance; and seeking methods of cost effectiveness.

- More than 130 HR executives were interviewed for a study during late 1999 and early 2000. The results indicated the following barriers to using competencies: no buy-in or visible commitment from top management; organizational unreadiness; lack of time and resources needed to develop and validate credible, useful models that could withstand legal challenge; insufficient time and resources for creating reliable, valid evaluations with which to guide follow-up steps (Rahbar-Daniels, Erickson, & Dalik, 2001).

- The Society for Human Resource Management sponsored a study in late 1999 and early 2000 that involved 300 organizations. The results suggested that barriers to success include lack of expertise, insufficient staff and financial resources, limited support, and conflicting priorities (Schoonover et al., 2000). Identifying realistic outcomes, determining resources needs and time requirements, and consistently using best practices were noted as contributors to positive outcomes (Schoonover et al., 2000).

- In 1998, researchers Cook and Bernthal Development Dimensions International conducted a study of 292 members of the HR Benchmark Group. The survey included a number of different questions about competencies and their use in organizations. One of the topics was barriers to the effective use of competencies. The findings suggested difficulties in the following areas: making resources available for job analyses, developing strategies for using competencies, linking competencies to organizational strategy, securing management support, identifying competencies, adapting to changing jobs and roles, assigning responsibility for competency identification, and providing clear, accurate definitions (Cook & Bernthal, 1998).

Professionals who work with competencies often have very good suggestions for addressing problems associated with competency projects. A few of these suggestions are briefly described here.

Representatives of organizations with competency-based HR management practices offered a number of approaches that include applying a consistent method of competency identification and using the same language across the organization, communicating and teaching competencies more effectively; obtaining involvement of the HR staff who need to apply competencies at the beginning and throughout the process, devoting sufficient time to implementation, and maintaining alignment of competencies with corporate strategy (Dewey, 1997). Lucia and Lepsinger (1999) had these suggestions for increasing the likelihood of positive outcomes with competency projects: establish ongoing communication, do not develop competency models in isolation, but rather in keeping with the business needs and job environment, and remain focused on original objectives.

Some organizations continuously seek ways of facilitating competency projects. For example, the Public Service Commission of Canada, collaborating with the Treasury Board Secretariat, conducted a survey that involved 57 organizations of the federal Public Service to ascertain interest in the use of competency-based human resource management. Members of the project team reported a number of practices that worked well in introducing the concept of competency-based HR management, including identifying a champion for a pilot of the competency project; creating a committee in some organizations for HR disciplines in order to establish a connection between competencies and the potential applications; inviting internal and external clients to participate in validating and assessing employee competency profiles; inviting unions to participate in the identification and validation of competency profiles; developing self-assessment guides with development tools; designing a manager's guide for facilitating the use of competency profiles; developing an information kit for distribution to all employees; using consultants to develop some expertise among personnel; and establishing a competency assessment center for employees (*Competencies in the Public Service,* 1998).

Yet, many HR practitioners who undertake competency identification efforts find themselves between the figurative rock and the hard place: they are expected to perform rigorous studies without the time and resources they need to do so. Under those circumstances, rigor is often sacrificed to expediency, and the competencies identified are neither valid nor reliable. Consequently, the identified competency model has no credibility with decision makers, who then become unenthusiastic about future competency modeling efforts. It is therefore very important that those who plan to pursue competency identification and modeling are clear about the time and other resources required to produce high-quality results. Decision makers should be informed about the relationship between resource availability or unavailability and the quality of the results they will receive.[7]

Competency Identification Methods

Competency identification is a means of clarifying key requirements for a job category or department and should be completed only after the dimensions of the work (for example, activities, tasks, setting, and tools) are identified. While it is not possible here to provide detailed descriptions of all competency identification methods, the following summary of common approaches will help those who are unfamiliar with the key methods.[8] Each approach has it costs, limitations, and strengths. It is essential to remember, however, that the selection of an appropriate competency identification method is a strategic decision.

The Job Competence Assessment Method (JCAM)

JCAM was one of the first competency identification methods created to provide information on workers and the work they perform, and it can lead to the development of a highly valid and reliable competency model when the model is carefully applied. Harvard psychologist David McClelland originated the process, which is generally used to identify the abstract, or less obvious, competencies with which workers achieve exemplary and fully successful performance.[9]

The method relies on the collection and analysis of data obtained through a process called *behavior event interviewing*. The behavioral event interview (BEI) is a technique developed by McClelland and Charles Dailey (1973). It combines Flanagan's (1954) critical incident technique with other data based on more than 30 years of McClelland's (1985) studies on motivation, called the Thematic Apperception Test (TAT). In the BEI, the interviewer asks a series of detailed questions about actions performed in the work setting that workers perceive to be successful or unsuccessful and the thoughts, feelings, and outcomes that accompanied them (Spencer, McClelland, & Spencer, 1994). Isolating the characteristics unique to exemplary performers is a common goal of this approach.

Through the use of BEIs, exemplary and fully successful workers are first identified and then interviewed about critical events in their work experience. The interviewer asks participants to provide detailed descriptions of both successful and unsuccessful work experiences. Respondents are prompted to fully describe their thoughts and feelings, the actions they took, and the circumstances surrounding or influencing each work event. After obtaining permission from the person being interviewed, the session is taped, and the researcher later has a verbatim, written transcript prepared. In most cases, researchers require at least 6 to 12 individual interviews for each job they are modeling. Once the interviews have been collected and the transcripts prepared, interviewers work together to identify the characteristics (which are potential competencies) that were revealed during the interviews. Key themes from the transcripts are subjected to coding with appropriate qualitative data analytical methods (Miles & Huberman, 1994). The persons doing the coding, usually the interviewers, do not know whether the transcript represents an interview with an exemplary or a fully successful worker.

The data are tabulated and subjected to rigorous statistical analyses. Three sets of characteristics are identified: those used by only the exemplary performers, those used by both exemplary and fully successful performers, and those cited by the fully successful but not the exemplary performers. The worker competencies that distinguish performance are represented by the first of the preceding sets; the minimum worker competencies are represented by the second set; and the characteristics of the third set are discarded, as they are not used by the exemplary performers even to achieve at least fully successful performance. Consequently, the characteristics, or *traits*, in this third group are not competencies. A trait emerges as a competency only when it is shown to be *required* for fully successful or exemplary work performance.

Although BEIs produce rich and comprehensive work-related data, they do have limitations. First, they cannot be used to identify competencies for future work. After all, the interviews rely on the experiences of the respondents. Second, BEIs require skilled interviewers and statistical support services. For that reason, an organization might need to contract with outside sources to complete many of the tasks required for this approach. Third, key employees must be available for interviews, which does result in lost work time. It is easy to see why conducting BEIs can be a costly and time-consuming process. (For a further review of behavioral event interviewing, including the advantages and challenges, see Spencer & Spencer, 1993, pp. 97–99.)

The Competency Menu Method
The *competency menu method* is becoming increasingly popular as a means of identifying competencies. It relies on competency lists obtained

from sources in the private and public domains. Practitioners create menus from the lists and then use the menus to identify the competencies necessary for a work role or traditional job in an organization. Many vendors have made competency menus available; they can also be found through a quick search of the World-Wide Web.

As a starting point for developing an organization-specific competency model, competency menus tend to be less costly than the Job Competence Assessment Method we described earlier. But there is a trade-off. Competency menus from external sources may be of questionable value to an organization, although menus of high quality have been devised from credible research conducted by professional associations or government agencies. The real question is this: How did a vendor create the competency menu?

To be both useful and defensible, a competency menu must be comprehensive for the work it embraces. It must also represent the current state of the art and state of the practice for its work area. These factors affect the validity and reliability of the competency models derived from a menu. *Validity* refers to the measurement of the competencies needed to bring about desired business results, and *reliability* refers to the means of measurement that accurately reflects the actual competency levels of employees (Cooper, 2000). Accordingly, practitioners should carefully examine the origins of the competency menus they have found.

Competency models built from competency menus can be organized in a variety of ways, depending on the needs or preferences of the user. Competencies can be organized around work roles, traditional jobs, or work outputs or results. Flexibility is one of the key selling points for competency menus, especially in organizations that must accommodate frequent change.

A competency menu must be modified—a process that some call "tailoring"—to meet the needs of a unique corporate culture. Modifications may be accomplished in several ways, such as by using card sorts, focus groups, surveys, or a combination of the three. Each approach has its advantages and challenges.

A card sort activity is easy to design. Competency statements (taken verbatim or edited from a menu) are placed on index cards. A respondent group is identified, and group members meet to sort the cards. Members may be instructed, for example, to sort the cards to identify not more than 15 competencies that they believe job incumbents must be able to demonstrate in order to perform their jobs successfully. The objectives of the activity will dictate the procedures that are used. The resulting list may be further refined if desired.

Focus groups also can be used to identify competencies from a menu. With focus groups, researchers must take care to avoid groupthink and grandstanding. *Groupthink* refers to a situation in which a majority of participants have the same ideas or opinions and dissenters are reluctant to speak their minds. As a result, the group becomes focused on one train of thought. *Grandstanding* occurs when dominant personalities in a focus group exercise too much influence. Traditional focus groups alone, used without comprehensive competency menus available to them at the time of competency identification, are predicted to identify only about 40% of the key competencies for a targeted job category.

Printed surveys are composed of a competency menu (or elements of one) and a scale with which respondents rate the importance of each competency. This method can be problematic for several reasons. First, long questionnaires may produce a response set in which participants rate all the competencies as having the same importance or value. Second, managers may delegate completion of the questionnaires to less informed subordinates.

In summary, the way in which a competency menu is used dramatically influences the quality of the results obtained.[10]

The Modified DACUM Method
The *modified DACUM method* is based on the "Developing A CurriculUM" (DACUM) method (Norton, 1997). DACUM is a popular job analysis process that relies on a disciplined, focus group approach for information collection, analysis, and presentation of results. Dubois and Rothwell (2000) extended the DACUM process to include the identification of abstract competencies (for example, patience) that are frequently difficult to identify and verify.

The modified DACUM method begins by assembling work experts. These experts may be exemplary performers, managers, supervisors, team leaders, and possibly customers if they are highly informed about the work to be profiled. The experts are asked to describe the work activities people perform daily to achieve the necessary results. These work activities become the basis for discovering the underlying competencies essential to achieving work outputs or results.

Application of the modified DACUM method increases understanding in the following areas: organizational business needs and the effects of project outcomes on meeting those needs; work outputs, activities, and tasks; and the nontask or abstract competencies required for successful performance of the work.

Other Aspects of Competency Identification

Competency identification also requires consideration of other factors.

Sources

Regardless of the method, data about competencies are dependent on sources, whether internal, external, or both. Practices regarding the types and number of sources vary from one organization to another.

The Job/Role Competency Practices study conducted by researchers Cook and Bernthal (1998) received responses from 292 members of the HR Benchmark Group, Development Dimensions International. One of the topics in the survey was sources of data used in competency identification practices. Results of the group surveyed showed that 85% or more of the organizations responding depend on information from managers and job incumbents in defining job and role competencies. Input from HR staff, while not as extensive, was nevertheless common. Other, less frequently used sources were "senior leaders, incumbents in similar positions, external consultants, direct reports, outside publications, and external customers" (p. 7). Another finding of this study on the subject of sources indicated that 86% of organizations collect job and role competency data from three to seven sources and that consulting additional sources "gains buy-in from various groups and helps make the competency selection and definition process more accurate and comprehensive" (p. 7).

Experience

Research indicates that the use of competencies in HR management practices is enhanced with experience. Schoonover et al. (2000) pointed out that "more experienced and sophisticated end users developed richer and more encompassing competency frameworks" (p. 7).

HR Management

Human resource management has been defined in various ways. But essential to any definition is the understanding that effective organizations must be able to find, use, keep, and develop human beings in order to achieve results. HR management is the process of helping organizations do just that.

The manner in which organizations manage their people is a potential source of sustained competitive advantage. As Sherman, Bohlander, and Snell (1998) noted, "the term 'human resources' implies that people have capabilities that drive organizational performance (along with other resources such as money, materials, information, and the like). Other terms such as 'human capital' and 'intellectual assets' all have in common the idea that people make the difference in how an organization performs" (p. 4).

The Nobel Prize–winning economist Theodore W. Schultz was the first to use the term *human capital* in the article "Investment in Human Capital," which appeared in the *American Economic Review* in 1961 (Davenport, 1999). The four elements of human capital investment can be seen in this human capital equation: (ability + behavior) × effort × time" (p. 22).

Jac Fitz-enz, a leader in human capital performance benchmarking, pointed out that

> The knowledge, skills, and attitudes of the workforce separate the winning companies from the also-rans. It is a complex combination of factors. Still, people per se are not the only force behind the inherent power of human capital. If the key to wealth creation were only a head count, then the dullest, lowest-level person would be as valuable as the brightest, highest-level person. In actuality, it is the information that the person possesses and his or her ability and willingness to share it that establish value potential. Data and people are inexorably linked as never before. Either one without the other is suboptimized. (Fitz-enz, 2000, p. 6)

Fitz-enz (2000) also suggested that "the key to sustaining a profitable company or a healthy economy is the productivity of the workforce, our human capital" (p. 1).

Human capital is the topic of much discussion in organizations today. It has also been the subject of a number of research studies. The term *human capital* is interpreted differently, however, depending on the viewpoint. For example, Ulrich, Zenger, and Smallwood (1999) incorporated the distinction they see between what employees can do and will do into the following measurable definition of human capital: employee capability multiplied by employee commitment.

Competency-Based HR Management

In chapter 1, we saw that it is no longer enough to focus on work activities and jobs. Work-based HR management cannot keep up with the pace of change. In addition, a focus on work activities does not direct management attention to desired performance or results, nor does it enable the organization to capitalize on the high productivity of exemplary performers.

In contrast, competency-based HR management concentrates first on the person and then on his or her outputs or results. Competencies are enduring, while work activities and specific work tasks are transitory. Competency models can supplement traditional job descriptions and become the foundation for an entire HR system. When that happens, an organization is using competency-based HR management.

Competency-based HR management views the needed outputs and the organization's work roles or requirements from a person-oriented rather than a job-oriented perspective. This approach makes competencies the foundation for the entire HR management function. Competencies drive recruitment, selection, placement, orientation, training, performance management, and workers' rewards. With all aspects of HR management integrated through competencies, rather than through traditional notions of jobs or work activities, the organization has a competency-based HR system.

Exemplary, not fully successful, performance is the goal of most organizations with competency-based systems. Competencies must therefore be both valid and reliable in differentiating exemplary and fully successful performers.[11]

Meeting Business Needs Through Competency-Based HR Management

Used properly, competency-based HR management has the potential to meet many business needs. It can, for example, be of value to organizations that seek to achieve the following goals:

- Enhance competitive advantage
- Develop better quality in products and services
- Increase productivity
- Position the organization for future growth
- Facilitate culture change and transformation
- Assist with large-scale organizational change
- Foster positive outcomes with customers or suppliers
- Increase financial performance
- Establish systematic linkages and integration among HR management practices
- Align HR management practices with the mission, vision, values, or the business strategies or objectives of the organization

In addition to pursuing the actions listed above, organizations adopt competency-based HR management practices for several key reasons.

Pritchard (1997) saw competencies as a way to integrate HR strategy with business strategy, thus adding performance value to the organization. He explained that the use of competencies empowers individuals and teams and frees management from complex HR processes.

Cooper, Lawrence, Kierstead, Lynch, and Luce (1998) noted some of the positive outcomes produced by valid and reliable competency-based HR management models. These include linking individual competencies directly to the organization's strategies and goals; developing profiles for positions or roles and matching individuals to the task sets and responsibilities; affording the opportunity to continuously monitor and refine competency profiles; facilitating the selection and evaluation of employees as well as the training and development; assisting with the hiring of individuals with unique competencies that are costly and not easily developed; assisting organizations in the ranking of competencies for both compensation and performance management.

Lucia and Lepsinger (1999) mentioned these additional business needs that can be addressed through the use of competency models: providing clarification for both job and work expectations, assisting in creating effective hiring practices, enhancing productivity, creating effective processes for 360-degree feedback, providing a tool that can assist in meeting today's needs as well as assist with changing needs, and aligning behaviors with strategies of the organization and its values.

Some of the most frequently given reasons for the introduction of competencies are to improve organization performance, increase the ability to be competitive, support culture change, enhance training and development effectiveness, improve processes associated with recruitment and selection, reduce turnover, clarify managerial roles and specialist roles, increase emphasis on business objectives, aid in career and succession planning, analyze skills and be able to identify the current and projected deficiencies in skills, improve workforce flexibility, support the integration of overall HR strategies, and provide a basis for compensation and reward programs (Pickett, 1998). Research studies reveal more reasons for using competency-based HR management. Cook and Bernthal (1998) asked respondents in the Job/Role Competency Practices study of the HR Benchmark Group, Development Dimensions International, to rate the performance of their organization compared to 1997 as it related to the following success indicators: "retention of quality employees, customer satisfaction, quality of products and services, employee satisfaction, productivity, and financial performance" (pp. 12–13). The results suggest that improved organizational performance and improvements to the bottom line can occur when competencies support even a few HR systems. Nine out of ten organizations indicated overall improvement when job/role competencies support six HR systems, and with support from competencies in four HR systems or more, the percentage of organizations that experience improvement almost doubles.

The use of competencies is appealing because it enables HR systems to concentrate on the factors that contribute directly to the organization's success (*Raising the Bar*, 1996). The practice of identifying, defining, and applying competencies helps employees to understand the areas in which their efforts will improve their performance, and this in turn helps the entire organization. The American Compensation Association (ACA), in cooperation with Hay Group, Hewitt Associates LLC, Towers Perrin, and William M. Mercer, Inc., conducted a study about competency-based HR applications, distributing 19,016 fax-back questionnaires to 19,016 North American companies. A total of 426 companies responded, and the identification of 1,257 competency-based applications was made.

Five different questions were developed and distributed to the respondents and other organizations that were known by the researchers to be in the development stages, in an effort to gather information about the applications. At this stage of the study, 217 companies responded, indicating 247 competency-based applications either in place or in the process of development. There were many findings as a result of this study, a few of which are listed here. The study results suggest that some of the reasons that companies use competency-based human resource management include "raising the bar" and enhancing employee performance, providing a focus on the culture and values of an organization, and facilitating the integration of HR applications by providing a framework (p. 7). Other findings from the study include that information about competencies is obtained from a number of sources and business strategy plays an important role in the development; competencies emphasize the ways in which performance results are achieved; applications for competencies are "evolutionary, not revolutionary"; compensation is the less frequently used and newest application; and the newness of some of the applications mean that it's too soon to determine their effectiveness (p. 7).

Researchers associated with the ACA study participated in a roundtable discussion noting that the study results of the previous year were fairly reflective of the practices of the following year as well. The researchers noted that performance, values, and culture continue to be drivers of competencies, with business strategies playing an important role in the competencies found in the best applications. The discussion served as a year in review about competencies and their applications in the year following the study.

In *Competencies and the Competitive Edge* (1998), Watson Wyatt researchers reported the results of a 1997 study in which they examined trends and explored people strategies. The study was based on survey responses from 1,020 North American organizations, in-depth case studies conducted with 17 companies, and on-site evaluations and interviews. The role of competencies was one of the areas reviewed. Noting that competencies can define and convey an organization's strategy and its meaning and assist employees in understanding the strategy and achieving its goals, the report suggests the roles of competencies in organizations, including articulating organizational values; providing a common language in which to describe value creation; creating a new paradigm for the programs in HR (organizational levers); emphasizing the development of individuals instead of the organization's structure; connecting pay, promotions, and growth to what the organization deems to be of value; and guiding employees and managers concerning expectations as well as how value is defined during change and restructuring. The results indicated that competency-based practices contribute positively to the bottom line, and that contributions to the organization are related to the roles of individuals rather than to their jobs. In addition, results suggest that endeavors designed to further employee commitment have the potential to generate positive returns, and that training and development are viewed as drivers of future success.

The 300 respondents participating in an electronic survey conducted in 2000 by Schoonover et al. (2000) on competency-based HR applications were queried on their reasons for applying competencies. The results of these findings indicated that enhanced performance expectations and integrating the HR processes were the major causes with 33% of respondents specifying the first reason and 20% specifying the second. Other goals for competency-based practices were to align behavior with core values (11%); provide a career framework and create bands of competence or levels of competence (both 8%); focus on the way in which work gets done and support exemplary performance (both 7%); and communicate generic leadership skills and develop specific roles (both 2%).

In an interview with several practitioners in the field, the subject of competency models was discussed (Johnson Brackey, 1998). After the skills of the best performers are known, the competency model provides value and usefulness both for training and motivation and as the basis for acquiring the competencies the organization needed to change. Included in the interview were the following comments about competency models. There is a growing interest in competency models because of an increased focus on the individual since the workforce is becoming more knowledge based and businesses are more technology based, according to Sandra O'Neil Gaffin. Also, the process involved with creating a model often places a strong focus on the company's resources and goals, according to Edward J. Cripe. Incorrect, noted Maxine Dalton, are companies that devote their efforts to the development of the model but then do not seriously implement it.

Competency-based HR management practices produce significant benefits to organizations and their employees. The value of using competencies to help meet business needs cannot be overemphasized.

Aligning Competencies With Business Plans, Objectives, and Needs

Business plans identify the organization's competitive targets. Key decision makers formulate a strategic plan for the purpose of clarifying the organization's long-term direction. A *business strategy* expresses the way in which the organization plans, implements, and evaluates its competitive process. It is basically a means to a desired end.

With the goal of meeting business needs, organizations are adopting strategies and practices that nurture competence. Competencies have value when there is a strategy to apply and align them with organizational objectives (Cook & Bernthal, 1998). HR is often held accountable for changing workforce competencies, and it is vital to adopt an effective strategy (McDowell, 1996). "The alignment of workforce capabilities with business strategies must be strategic, collaborative and business-focused to be successful" (p. 6).[12]

HR plays a significant role in creating business strategy. The HR department should have a list of technical knowledge and skills in the organization and should be able to supply information about the organization's cultural strengths and weaknesses. HR practitioners should be able to suggest methods for determining the kind of culture that will maximize opportunities and must also be prepared to provide the reasons for their suggestions (Brockbank, 1997). *Business objectives* are the measurable targets to be achieved. When business objectives are expressed in measurable terms, they can be linked to worker results and, therefore, to the competencies those workers must possess and use in order to produce those results.

Do not confuse worker competencies, or job/role competencies as they are often called, with organizational core competence. In their seminal work, Prahalad and Hamel (1990) suggest that "core competencies are the collective learning in the organization," and that "if core competence is about harmonizing streams of technology, it is also about the organization of work and the delivery of value." Core competence is also "communication, involvement, and a deep commitment to working across organizational boundaries." Further,

> Core competence does not diminish with use. Unlike physical assets, which do deteriorate over time, competencies are enhanced as they are applied and shared. But competencies still need to be nurtured and protected; knowledge fades if it is not used. Competencies are the glue that binds existing businesses. (p. 81)

An organization's core competence is built on its core competencies. An *organizational core competency* is an organization's strategic strength. It is what the organization does best and what it should never outsource. Organizational core competencies—the unique resources of an organization—affect many products and services and provide a competitive advantage in the marketplace (Green, 1999).

Employee core competence could have two possible meanings. In one sense, an employee core competency is a characteristic that an employee has and uses in ways that contribute to the organization's core competence. In a second sense, an employee core competency could be regarded as an individual strategic strength when compared to other persons.

Frequently Asked Questions

When we talk and listen to others about competency-based HR management, we receive numerous questions from intrigued listeners who had thought about this topic. We present the most frequently asked questions and our responses to them in Appendix A. We hope our readers will find that reading this appendix will enrich their understanding of the concepts.

Summary

In this chapter, we defined the meanings of *competency, competency model, human resource management,* and *competency-based human resource management.* We explained the differences between fully successful and exemplary performers. We examined the process of identifying competencies and aligning them with an organization's business plans, needs, and objectives. And finally, we explained the business needs that are met through the use of competency-based HR management.

Part Two

UNDERSTANDING
Competency-Based
HR Management

CHAPTER 3

A Need for Implementing Competency-Based HR Management

The following real-life vignette portrays the dilemma of a CEO who must contend with the challenges of competency-related issues within a typical organization. Conclusions drawn from the vignette provide an overview of the competence needs of most organizations today and suggest approaches by which an HR department could address those needs. We then briefly explore six trends that affect organizations and explain their influence on the need for competency-based HR management applications. The chapter concludes with the presentation and discussion of the generic model for the conceptualizing and planning of customer-driven, competency-based HR management applications.

A Revealing Vignette

"Dr. Rothwell, I have a problem," began the CEO of a small high-tech company. "I'm calling you because my HR department is broken."

"Really?" said Rothwell. "Tell me more."

"It all began a few years ago. I hired an HR director from a multinational company. His former employer described him to me as someone who could 'walk on water,' in terms of HR. I invited him to join my explosive growth firm and head up our first HR department. After 12 years, we have 400 employees, and our business has been growing an average of 100% per year. It was time to establish a department to bring order out of the chaos of our HR activities."

"Yes, please give me more background," Rothwell said.

"Well, it's a simple thing. My director of HR has a written contract, which is due to be renegotiated, and I have to decide what to do. Our turnover is atrocious, and it seems to take entirely too long to fill positions. We have no salary system, no employee recognition and reward processes, and no new-hire orientation. Our workers want to unionize, and I'm hearing complaints from all departments that HR is not doing its job. Could you come in here and take a look?"

"Certainly," replied Rothwell, "but I'd like to see some documents before I arrive. Could you send me a copy of your job descriptions, company performance appraisal system, personnel policy manual, employee handbook, and strategic business plan?"

"I'd be happy to," responded the CEO, "if we had all of that. But we don't. In fact, we've never been able to agree on job descriptions, and when we tried to implement a performance appraisal system, it was a complete disaster."

Following this discussion, Rothwell visited the company and interviewed numerous managers and new hires. He learned that internal customers of the HR function were most unhappy with the quality of candidates recruited for vacant positions. Managers, in attempts to get the work out, selected the best from among the undesirable (in their opinion) applicants. The organization, Rothwell learned, was experiencing a crisis of competence in several departments. Further investigation revealed that the director of HR and his staff had not requested adequate information about the competencies required of workers who could successfully fill those positions. Consequently, competencies that could not be easily learned on the job were not considered during recruitment and selection. Interview questions lacked focus and instead covered such topics as an applicant's strengths and weaknesses or reasons for applying for a job. Accordingly, the persons selected and placed in strategic positions were not capable of producing the outputs or results needed for organizational success.

Many of the managers interviewed for the HR department audit insisted that they had repeatedly requested the HR department's assistance with competency development for their employees. The consultant discovered that the HR department largely ignored such requests because it did not know how to design, develop, deliver, and evaluate competency-based training.

Drawing Conclusions From the Vignette

Although several conclusions could be drawn from this real-life vignette, we can make two critical observations. First, the HR director failed to understand the importance of several key trends affecting the high-tech industry. And second, the explosive growth nature of the organization created an environment in which he was pressured to find somebody—anybody—to fill immediate vacancies. The HR director had worked with a multinational firm, but in that setting, he enjoyed the support and assistance of a large, competent HR staff.

Details of the vignette give the impression that the organization's managers wanted competency-based HR management. The HR director should have initiated the following steps:

- Determine short-term and long-term worker competency needs
- Assess existing worker competency needs in at least those areas most critical for long-term organizational success
- Establish competency modeling applications and a structured and disciplined approach to competency identification
- Develop competency-based position, role, or work plan descriptions for key work areas
- Implement competency-based recruitment and selection for key work areas
- Empower workers at the lowest levels of the organization
- Provide for competency assessment, individual development planning, and competency-based performance improvement opportunities for workers, prioritized at least in part according to the relationship between the work and the organization's strategic business objectives

- Provide employee career planning and development activities based on relationships among competencies
- Design a competency-based performance management and appraisal system that incorporates employee and management input
- Align compensation, reward, and recognition efforts with the performance management system and achievement of the organization's business or other objectives
- Develop and publish an employee handbook and establish a new-hire employee orientation program

It is quite clear that the CEO's concerns were largely about developing or acquiring the competencies needed for organizational success and the HR director's failure to do so. Virtually nothing can be achieved without human competence, even in an organization that has an impressive array of modern technology at its disposal.

Next, we examine key trends that affect businesses and organizations, including the one described in the vignette.

Six Trends Affecting Businesses and Organizations

Many business publications today contain references to trends that are predicted to affect businesses or organizations in the future. Whatever factors affect a business, it is certain that they will ultimately affect its human resources and the HR function.

A study conducted by Rothwell (1996), and jointly sponsored by the Society for Human Resource Management (SHRM) and CCH, identified the most important trends that will affect organizations and their HR management over the next 10 years. The study specified six key trends, pinpointed their causes, listed their possible consequences, suggested organizational best practices to address them, and recommended essential leadership competencies that will help organizations anticipate the effects of the trends.

These trends were examined further by Rothwell, Prescott, and Taylor (1998), who prioritized them as follows:

- Technological change
- Increased globalization

- Continued cost containment
- Accelerated speed in market change
- Growing importance of knowledge capital
- Increased rate and magnitude of change

In the following pages, we briefly explain each trend and its influence on the need for competency-based HR management.

Technological Change

Technology is more than gizmos. The word *technology* refers to any tools that are essential to achieving work results. It also includes the human know-how needed to make the tools work. As such, technology affects the skills that workers must have in order to perform.

More new technology has been unveiled since the dawn of the 20th century than in all the centuries before it, and technological change continues to occur at an accelerating pace. The HR function is just at the beginning of a learning curve in that respect. As noted by Ulrich (1997), "Managers and HR professionals responsible for redefining work at their firms need to figure out how to make technology a viable and productive part of the work setting. They need to be ahead of the information curve and learn to leverage information for business results" (p. 13).

There are six categories of technology that represent important components of this trend. The first five are information technology, communications technology, industry and product technology, process technology, and revolutionary or evolutionary technology (Rothwell et al., 1998). The sixth category is "human know-how, which links human creativity, knowledge, and ability to the other five technologies" (pp. 43–44).

Technology confers a competitive advantage only when human beings are capable of using it. Hence, organizational decision makers should structure their thinking around the competencies that enable individuals to make the best use of both existing and emerging technologies. Competency-based HR management, unlike traditional work- or job-related approaches, helps to identify exemplary performers and can be used to develop and select others to match the exemplary performer's ability to achieve results.

Increased Globalization

Globalization refers to commerce without borders. The emergence of a worldwide marketplace was perhaps the single most important development of the 1990s (Rothwell, Prescott, & Taylor, 1999). In addressing this trend, managers and HR practitioners must collaborate across national cultures as they seek solutions to international management problems. Some HR experts have noted that this trend will likely require more attention to diversity, open thinking, constant willingness to embrace change, use of different distribution channels, and more robust global labor organizations (Rothwell et al., 1998).

Ulrich (1997) described the impact of globalization as follows:

> *Globalization* dominates the competitive horizon. The concept is not new, but the intensity of the challenge to get on with it is. Globalization entails new markets, new products, new mindsets, new competencies, and new ways of thinking about business. In the future, HR will need to create models and processes for attaining global agility, effectiveness, and competitiveness. (p. 2)

Kerr and Von Glinow (1997) suggested that as the impact of globalization intensifies, HR will be called upon to help prepare people for international assignments and the numerous aspects of doing business away from home.

Globalization will lead to increasingly fierce competition on a worldwide scale. Nations where labor is cheap will enjoy a comparative advantage over economically developed nations where labor costs are much higher. Economically developed nations that intend to remain competitive must tap the creative talent of their workforces. Competency-based HR management can help by identifying exemplary performers and pinpointing their capabilities. And, indeed, there is keen interest globally in competencies and their value for remaining competitive through superior talent management.

Continued Cost Containment

Cost containment means making products or delivering services at the lowest possible cost. HR experts cited the following consequences of an organization's attempts to contain costs: more emphasis on establishing strategic relationships; use of outsourcing, which allows the organization to focus on its key business strengths; and demand for new technology that can reduce costs (Rothwell et al., 1998). To those ends, organizations must manage their people-related expenses and their talent needs more effectively. That will mean, in one sense, that decision makers must do a better job of fitting work to the people rather than fitting people to the work, a goal with which competency-based HR management is well suited to assist.

Accelerated Speed in Market Change

Speed in market change means that customer expectations are changing more quickly than ever and that customers expect their needs and desires to be instantly gratified. Organizations that intend to thrive in this environment must respond more rapidly to consumers' wishes. Markets in many sectors are unstable, and the first company to get there with the desired products or services will be in the best position to capture market share. Customers have come to expect a faster cycle of new products or services, and they tend not to tolerate quality or quantities that do not meet their expectations.

What can be done to adapt to this trend? Organizations should prepare for new markets before they emerge and use their market data before the information becomes outdated. They should establish strategic partnerships. Those that are leading the market must be able to recognize their position and capitalize on it. Organizations should also stay in touch with their customers, monitor the performance of their products or services, and take action when correction is needed. It is also important to understand that work stress will increase along with the need for reduced cycle time to create more new products and services (Rothwell et al., 1998).

Under these conditions, decision makers will be pressured to respond to customer expectations faster and with higher quality goods and services. To that end, they must unleash the creative power of workers. Competency-based HR management can be helpful in that respect, since it develops the strengths of individual workers in anticipation of future need.

Growing Importance of Knowledge Capital

To an increasing degree, organizations must pay close attention to their knowledge capital. To effectively manage intellectual capital, an organization must create or acquire the critical knowledge and then organize, analyze, disseminate, and apply it toward producing the desired results. Intellectual capital is frequently associated with a core capability. (For further information, see Green, 1999, or Greene, 2000a, 2000b.)

Rothwell et al. (1998) defined *knowledge capital* as the "collective economic value of an organization's workforce" (p. 180), which comprises institutional memory, the talent pool, and creativity. *Institutional memory* refers to the preserved collective experience of the organization. It is composed of everything that people remember about the organization's past actions and includes lessons learned from that experience. The *talent pool,* or *competency pool,* as it is often called in this book, is the know-how that is currently available in an organization.[1] *Creativity* means the ability of the workforce to produce innovative solutions and breakthrough ideas.

HR experts noted that the growing significance of knowledge capital created additional needs for organizations. These include a need to distinguish between the technical and management competency, an ever-growing business and worker mobility, and a rising need for training.

It is also important to develop ways of measuring intellectual capital. Ulrich (1997) suggested that measurement methods change with the process of securing intellectual capital.

> Traditional measures of success, focused on economic capital (for example, profitability or financial performance), must now be coupled with measures of intellectual capital. Seeking, finding, and using such measures will be among the primary challenges facing the HR professionals of the future. (p. 14)

Competency-based HR management is an especially appropriate response to the growing importance of knowledge capital. After all, the competency-based approach strives to achieve the greatest competitive advantage by identifying and developing exemplary performers and bringing fully successful performers closer to exemplary performance.

Increased Rate and Magnitude of Change

From a business perspective, change is challenging because it means many things to those who experience it. Employees of organizations that have been part of a regulated business environment or otherwise stable industry often react in a chaotic manner when faced with change. By

functioning with expertise in the significant area of change management, HR practitioners can be of great value in facilitating organizational change.

Yeung, Woolcock, and Sullivan (1996) reported on a research study
based on interviews with 10 senior HR executives. The study was com-
missioned by The California Strategic Human Resource Partnership, a
consortium of senior-level HR leaders from 31 leading California companies. The interviewees identified the capacity to facilitate and implement change as a key competency for senior HR generalists at both
corporate and business levels.

Unmanaged change can have negative effects, including reduced
productivity, burnout, loss of quality in products and services, damaged
customer relations, and lower employee morale (Bennett, 2001). "Resistance to change also contributes to longer-term resistance to future
change, making it more difficult to smoothly implement the next restructuring, be it a technology update, a merger or acquisition, or a leadership transition" (p. 3). The findings of a 1997 research study of more
than 2,000 senior executives from 23 countries, including 455 from the
United States, indicate that organizational culture is the greatest barrier
to promoting desired change (*Competing in a Global Economy,* 1997).

Researchers Bernthal, Percuric, and Wellins (1998) explored workforce development practices in a 1998 survey that included responses
from 171 organizations of Development Dimensions International's HR
Benchmark Group. The respondents, primarily HR directors or vice
presidents (67%), were asked to name two skill areas that were most in
need of development. The results suggested that the greatest need for
skill development is focused on skills for effectively approaching the
challenges that accompany a work environment experiencing rapid
change.

SHRM sponsored a research project that analyzed data from multiple sources and provided thematic analysis of the interviews and feedback from focus groups in order to identify functional challenges and
develop definitions for the critical roles in human resources as well as for
competencies and behaviors that support each of the roles. Results indicated that one of the significant functional challenges for the human resources community is managing rapidly evolving change. Issues
involved with this challenge include "early detection of and response to

key competitive issues, identification and initiation of change/innovations required for preempting competition, leadership in process improvement and re-engineering initiatives, and facilitation of continuous change initiatives (to overcome team process barriers and accelerate the pace of change)" (Schoonover, 1998, p. 17).

Lawler and Mohrman (2000) noted that change results from a number of key trends, such as the rapid deployment of information technology, globalization of the economy, and the increasingly competitive, dynamic business environments in which corporations operate. Beer (1997) explained that the transformation of HR management is due primarily to competition, globalization, and continuous change in markets and technology. He suggested that because of these forces, organizations are undergoing a revolution in organizing and managing people that will last well into the 21st century.

If HR practitioners are to help organizations react to, and even anticipate, change, they must be able to assemble a team of individuals capable of dealing with the challenges posed by the external environment. For that reason, they must become more adept at establishing and maintaining competency inventories that link individual capabilities to the rapid and robust solution of organizational problems and strategic issues. Competency-based HR management consequently becomes a competitive necessity, since it offers the only means of converting the traditional focus on work activities into an approach based on individual competencies.

Implementing Competency-Based HR Management

The implications of the six trends just described can be summarized in just a few words. HR practitioners must assume responsibility for leading the way in their organizations to add value. The use of competency-based HR management techniques provides the single most useful approach to position the HR function in a leadership position so they can provide this value.

After a decision has been made to initiate one or more competency-based HR management applications, HR professionals must develop a conceptual plan to implement the application. The success of a competency project depends somewhat on its project plan. "An action plan is the primary tool to manage the workload, review and appraise project progress, and communicate with project team members and key stake-holders about the work to be done" (Lucia & Lepsinger, 1999, p. 56). It will also be a useful tool for identifying resource requirements—people, time, money, and technological tools—needed to complete the project (p. 57).

Figure 2 depicts a useful model for achieving that purpose. The steps are not intended to be rigid. Practitioners should use this model to plan at the macro level, rather than the micro level, regarding which compe-tency-based HR management applications they will create later. We pro-vide detailed implementation plans for each competency-based HR management application in other chapters.

Step 1: Identify organizational business objectives and HR customer needs

Begin the process of implementing strategic HR leadership by deter-mining the organization's business objectives and ensuring that they are communicated clearly to the customers of the HR function.

A good place to start is to ask HR customers, such as line managers, to identify their goals for a competency-based HR management applica-tion—for example, improved employee retention, succession planning or management, or improved individual development. These goals should relate to the application results, and the results must be in line with business objectives.

The customer may need to complete an operational analysis in order to pinpoint focal areas. An *operational analysis* is an assessment of the organization's environment, strategies, and resources. A set of writ-ten guidelines along with a brief example of the application in use are generally enough, but if the customer needs assistance, a collaborative effort works well. This first level of analysis must be completed before proceeding to meet a customer's need.

Steps 2 and 3: Conduct environmental scanning and identify sectors of chief concern to the HR customer

Environmental scanning is the process of identifying and assessing trends or issues in the organization's external environment that might suggest that the HR customer could possibly benefit from using a competency-based HR management approach. Environmental scanning, which focuses on the future, has numerous benefits. Assessing trends that affect the future of the customer's application can help decision makers to

Figure 2: A Model to Guide the Implementation of Strategic HR Management

Step 1 Identify organizational business objectives and HR customer needs.
Step 2 Conduct environmental scanning.
Step 3 Identify sectors of chief concern to the HR customer.
Step 4 Align organizational business objectives with HR customer needs and define project objectives.
Step 5 Ensure HR customer endorsement of the project objectives.
Step 6 Decide on the next steps.
Step 7 Develop a project management plan to guide long-term implementation.
Step 8 Implement the project management plan.
Step 9 Conduct formative and summative evaluations.

avoid costly investments in competency-based applications that are of limited use. The trends and issues discussed in chapters 1 and 2 are the primary references for environmental scanning work. Other valuable resources include information published by trade, professional, labor, or other organizations or available at Internet sites.

Benchmarking, which addresses recent past and present approaches to solving or managing problems, contributes to identifying innovative, competency-based solutions with long-term value to the HR customer and the organization. It can also identify useful practices and the success factors that affect them.

Both environmental scanning and benchmarking help HR practitioners and their customers to determine which sectors will benefit from competency-based applications. It often is not necessary to focus on every sector. HR practitioners and their line management customers therefore should not hesitate to commit appropriate resources to the completion of Steps 2 and 3.

Step 4: Align organizational business objectives with HR customer needs and define project objectives

Aligning an organization's business objectives or strategies with HR customer needs might appear to be a complex or abstract process, but it is not.

Competencies provide a means of characterizing an organization's human capital. Effectively selecting and rewarding the needed competencies in employees should have an impact on organizational success (Orr, 1998). Linking competency applications to strategic requirements is an important step in the model.

Use a straightforward approach to establishing alignment between the organization's business objectives and the HR customer's project objectives. The process includes researching and verifying answers to several questions and then triangulating the answers to clarify how much and what kind of alignment is necessary.

Here are some recommended questions:

- What are the expected or planned organizational outputs or results now and in the future?

- What are the planned outputs or results for the HR project?

- How are the outputs or results of the HR customer project related to those of the organization and the trends that affect the organization?

- What would be the impact on the organization if the planned project objectives are not met or the project is canceled?

- What would be the impact on the organization and its outputs or results if the HR project is not completed as planned?

Objectives for the competency-based HR management application are defined as soon as both the customer and the HR practitioner see clearly that alignment exists. Outcomes for the application should be expressed in observable and measurable terms, as shown in the following example:

- The HR department and the marketing department will collaborate to design, develop, and pilot test a competency-based performance management system specific to the needs of the marketing department; the pilot test will be completed and evaluated in at least two of the five branches of the marketing department within 1 year of inception of fully committed work on the project.

- The competency-based performance management system described earlier will be fully implemented and operational in at least two of the five branches of the marketing department within 2 years of inception of fully committed work on the project.

Without clearly stated objectives for the projects, and without the understanding and agreement of all parties involved, difficulties can—and most probably will—arise.

Steps 5 and 6: Ensure HR customer endorsement of the project objectives and decide on the next steps

If the HR practitioner has been actively involved with his or her customer up to this point, obtaining customer endorsement should proceed smoothly for both parties.

There are times, however, when the HR function, the customer, or both are unable to deliver all the envisioned results. Possible reasons include legal restrictions, limited time and resources, and constraints imposed by organizational or external environmental factors. In cases such as these, the HR practitioner must keep the customer informed and seek ways (sometimes with customer support) to remove the constraints when possible.

After addressing the obstacles, the HR practitioner and the customer will have enough information to decide whether to complete the project as it was envisioned or to adopt a modified form of it. We refer to this as making a "go" or "no go" decision. Allowing major projects to remain in limbo for too long compromises the possibility of successful completion.

It is very important that the HR practitioner avoid committing to completion of a competency-based HR management project under the following conditions: the decision-making time frame is extended excessively and without credible explanation; the customer is reluctant to accept project terms that are known to lead to success; the customer does not allocate the resources defined as necessary for use in implementing the project; the expertise within the HR function *and* within the customer's control is not sufficient to complete the project successfully; or the organization is in a state of turmoil that can be predicted to affect achievement of the project objectives. Other circumstances could be mentioned, but these are the primary ones that practitioners frequently encounter. Timely action by HR practitioners is an important factor in the success of all competency-based HR management projects.

Step 7: Develop a project management plan to guide long-term implementation

A project management plan is an essential requirement for a successful competency project.[2] Several software tools that support the development and maintenance of project management plans are currently available. The choice of which tool to use is a matter of personal or organizational preference.

In our experience, the following elements are a necessary part of every competency project management plan:

- A list of project deliverables, outputs, or results. These should be identified at the outset of the project management planning process and should include descriptions of deliverables for each project step.
- A roster of project participants that includes the employees or contract workers who will participate in the project. The roster should include the e-mail address and other contact information for each person.
- A list of tasks that must be completed in order to achieve the project deliverables, outputs, or results. The dependencies among the tasks should be made clear.
- The names and organization affiliations of the persons who will be responsible for completing each project task and any deliverable, output, or result of the task.
- A target date for completion of each deliverable, output, or result.

Additional information may be required for successful use of certain software packages. Regardless of the software and its requirements, however, a less than perfect plan is better than no plan at all.

Step 8: Implement the project management plan

After a project management plan has been developed and endorsed by HR and the HR customer and adequate resources have been committed to the project, implementation can begin.

We offer the following suggestions to increase the likelihood of successful implementation:

- Inform everyone involved in the project about its objectives, outputs, or results.
- Provide information to others before and in the early stage of project implementation. The more information disseminated about competency-based HR management projects, the better the chance of buy-in.
- If the project has sweeping or broad implications within the organization or with its customers or clients, form an advisory panel of key persons to assist with design, evaluation, and implementation.
- Remember that change is the only constant. Obtain HR customer agreement to project plans that are flexible and suited to rapid or constant change.
- Ensure that employees who will be most affected by the project are involved in its design and in the implementation of results that will most affect them. Involvement leads to commitment.
- Keep senior managers informed through in-person, electronic, or printed briefings as the project moves toward implementation.
- Be honest and realistic in portraying project situations, outputs or results, and their impact.
- Do not oversell the project or its benefits. Avoid creating rising expectations for outcomes that may not be achievable, given the scope of the project.

Step 9: Conduct formative and summative evaluations

Astute managers know that evaluation of any project begins in the planning stage. Evaluations of competency-based HR management project inputs, processes, materials, and interim outputs are called *formative eval-*

uations and are made from the inception of the project—usually through testing out the project through a small-scale pilot project. Every step, product, and process in a project should be subjected to rigorous evaluation. For example, learning about inappropriate data collection procedures early in the initial stages of a project provides the opportunity to correct deficiencies before they become problems. The effective use of formative evaluation is key to successful project development and implementation.

Assuming the project underwent adequate formative evaluations and the changes made had a positive effect on outcomes, it is time for an evaluator to conduct a summative project evaluation. A *summative evaluation* assesses the overall results of a project after it is completed. The evaluator explores many fundamental issues. Did the project achieve its expected objectives? Were the objectives fully or only partially achieved? For what reasons? What were the effects of the results or outputs on the organization? Were these effects the desired ones? How did the outputs or results affect achievement of the organization's business objectives and business strategies? Were there unintended effects? Were they beneficial or detrimental? What could have been done differently during various project phases to improve the likelihood of successful results or inputs beyond the project objectives?

Both formative and summative evaluations are essential for the long-term success of competency-based HR management projects. A formative evaluation is particularly useful in decision making, and a summative evaluation is helpful in assessing the overall results of a project and maintaining accountability.[3]

Summary

This chapter opened with a vignette that portrayed the dilemma of the CEO of a typical organization and highlighted the organization's competency challenges. In drawing conclusions from the vignette, we developed an overview of the competence needs of most organizations today and the HR function's response to those needs. Six trends affecting organizations and their need for competency-based HR management were presented and discussed. We concluded by presenting and briefly explaining a nine-step model for planning and implementing a customer-driven competency-based HR management project.

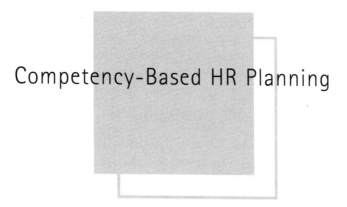

CHAPTER 4

Competency-Based HR Planning

Human resource planning is a necessary first step for aligning HR with the organization's strategic goals and objectives. HR planning assesses the supply of existing human talent, determines current needs, and forecasts future demand for talent in the organization. By comparing current supply to both current need and future demand, the HR professional can discern the gap between the organization's people and the competencies needed to achieve the organization's strategic goals and objectives in the present and the future. These gaps guide the development and performance of HR department activities as well as suggest the HR responsibilities of operating managers.

This chapter provides an overview of HR planning and addresses the following key questions:

- What is HR planning?
- How is HR planning traditionally carried out?
- How can HR planning become competency based?
- What are the advantages and challenges of a competency-based approach to HR planning?

- When should HR planning be competency based, and when should it be handled traditionally?
- What model can guide competency-based HR planning, and how is it implemented?

By addressing these questions, this chapter explains how traditional HR planning efforts can be transformed through a competency-based approach. Such an approach is not always appropriate, however, and we will review situations in which a change is suitable and what it involves.

HR Planning Defined

HR planning has traditionally been defined as "the process of anticipating and making provision for the movement of people into, within, and out of an organization" (Sherman, Bohlander, & Snell, 1998, p. 124). The purpose of HR planning is to effectively utilize the resources represented by these people in order to realize the organization's goals.

The traditional view of HR planning is that the organization should forecast, based on history, the head count needed to replace the people who leave the organization. HR planning as traditionally practiced focuses attention on *quantity*, the number of people, rather than the *quality*, or underlying characteristics (that is, the talents or competencies), of people.

In a different sense, it is also possible to understand HR planning as the strategic business plan that guides the HR department or function, which clarifies the mission and purpose of the department or function, its goals and objectives, current strengths and weaknesses, possible threats and opportunities, and long-term strategy (Rothwell & Kazanas, 2003). HR planning serves as a guide for an organization's HR policies, programs, and procedures; it is an important part of the organization's overall business plan. Combining strategy and HR planning creates a greater capacity for change (Ulrich 1992). The challenge, however, as Brockbank (1999, in Kesler, 2000) pointed out, continues to be identifying ways in which to link HR plans and business strategy.

Interest in HR planning has increased greatly in recent years. Rothwell and Sredl (2000) suggest reasons such as the importance of people and their competencies to an organization, challenges created as people affect plans that apply to them; and the wide effect of HR plans on the entire organization. HR planning cannot effectively be accomplished if it is aligned or linked with the business, yet done in isolation as separate human resource efforts (Walker, 1994). Widespread downsizing has prompted growing attention to the qualitative difference in people, since some people are, for instance, simply more creative or productive than others.

It should be emphasized, however, that HR leadership is essential no matter how HR planning is defined. The top HR official, usually a vice president, plays a role in ensuring that the organization adopts a proactive, rather than a reactive, stance in winning the war for talent (Rothwell, Prescott, & Taylor, 1998). Competency-based HR planning can play an important part in giving the HR leader what he or she needs in order to exert that important leadership role.

Traditional HR Planning

HR planning has its roots in military personnel planning. Initially, the U.S. military faced the challenge of ensuring stable staffing levels as some people concluded their tours of duty and left the military and others advanced through the ranks. The goal at that time was to determine the quantity of people sufficient to meet replacement needs and thereby maintain staffing levels in different job categories, at different levels of the organization, and in different locations.

Defense contractors adopted this military focus on head count. They carried over the philosophy of equating head count to production levels and, in turn, linking production levels to competitive success as measured by achievement of the organization's measurable strategic goals and objectives. This approach seemed to work well until the 1960s. At that time, three trends began to emerge that affected the success of traditional HR planning:

1. **Changing technology:** Technology is continuously changing. Organizations often undergo technological change in the hope of achieving breakthroughs in productivity. With cutting-edge technology, fewer people may be able to produce the same or greater outputs as were produced with traditional means.

2.   **Decreasing correlation of head count to outputs and success:** A widening gap began to develop between the number of people employed by an organization, the output levels achieved by those people, and the organization's competitive success. There has never been an easy or particularly effective way to correlate the organization's head count with productivity and, in turn, with competitive success in a dynamic marketplace.

3.   **Increasing inaccuracy of labor forecasts:** Labor forecasts based on historical ratios between head count and competitive success have been growing less accurate. Traditional forecasting bases predictions of the future on the past or present. But as most businesspeople are now keenly aware, tomorrow's workplace may be radically different from the workplaces of yesterday and today. We should note, too, that individuals are not machines. One person's production level is not necessarily the same as another's. Hence, historical forecasts not only are often useless in predicting outputs or competitive success but may mislead decision makers by presenting them with inaccurate conclusions.[1]

The traditional approach to HR planning begins with an assessment of the current supply of people at each level and of the current demand at each level and then proceeds to balancing supply and demand. The HR function performs balancing through such actions as recruitment, hiring, development, and reduction. The traditional focus of HR planning, however, has been on taking action with people rather than on achieving results.

To make the point more dramatically, and perhaps controversially, many organizations operate as if they were simply recruiting to "fill slots" or maintain the head count as vacancies occur. Recruiters concentrate on sourcing people whose perceived competencies appear to match the qualifications in job specifications and whose work experience and education make them appear qualified to carry out the work activities listed on a job description for a targeted job opening.

Making HR Planning Competency Based

Transforming HR planning to a competency basis requires a major paradigm shift in the way HR planners think about organizations and people. They must rethink what they are doing, why they are doing it, and how they should do it.

Putting a competency-based HR planning system in place begins with building the awareness of the organization's decision makers. Since they control the organization's resources, they must be convinced that the benefits of competency-based HR planning will outweigh the costs associated with the change. Often, that requires a simple leap of faith. After all, if Edison had waited to see a lightbulb before he invented one, we would all still be in the dark. If decision makers demand solid cost-benefit projections or evidence that other organizations achieved competitive success by moving to competency-based HR planning, then the effort may be dead. There are few published case studies of organizations that achieved this switchover for all aspects of HR. (And those who have them would have a valuable secret weapon they would not be willing to share.)

As a part of the larger ACA research study on competency-based human resource management practices, 60 organizations with and in the process of developing staffing applications that were competency based provided details related to their practices on a separate questionnaire. Asked if they had a formal workforce planning process directed toward organizational needs, assessing, forecasting, and deploying the workforce, 59% indicated that such a planning process was in place. Of those who used formal planning processes, 69% responded that competencies were used in making decisions associated with the planning (*Raising the Bar*, 1996).

In a study conducted by Schoonover, Schoonover, Nemerov, and Ehly (2000), 29% of the 300 respondents rated the use of competencies in their strategic HR planning as either "effective" or "very effective"; however, there was a correlation between the level of sophistication of the implementers and the level of perceived effectiveness.

Competency-based HR planning requires, as a first step, that decision makers articulate the organization's strategic goals or business objectives. Every organization exists for at least one purpose. For instance, a business exists to make a profit; a government agency exists to meet a social need; and a charitable organization exists to offer services that other organizations do not offer. The organization's goals or objectives must be translated into desired organizational outputs or results.

Workers support the achievement of their organization's strategic goals or business objectives. Competency-based HR planning requires practitioners to determine the quantity and quality of work that must be performed to support achievement of their organization's strategic goals or business objectives, the conditions and methods of work performance, who should perform it, and what worker characteristics will result in successful performance.

To move to a competency-driven HR planning process, planners must establish and maintain a human resource management system in which to store, update, and, most important, instantaneously access information about workers' competencies. An information management system must display clearly the expertise available in the organization. It should go beyond the old-style "skill inventory" and become a "competency inventory" that catalogs and enables easy access to what people can do and the results they can achieve, not, for example, as in many skill inventories, their educational credentials. After all, educational credentials may not be directly related to organizational results.

Companies are developing methods of tracking competencies and then using the information and models created with software programs and human capital development applications, spreadsheets, and even paper when making important business decisions involving HR functions such as recruiting, training, and succession planning. Virtual Inc., a small integrated management-marketing firm based in Wakefield, Massachusetts, developed a matrix of skills and competencies to assist in hiring and training to meet the specific and continuously changing needs of the organization (Greengard, 2001).

After decision makers determine the organization's required competencies, they must compare their needs to the current workforce and develop a plan to acquire the competencies that are lacking (Gendron, 1996). PepsiCo India uses a model that tracks the competencies for each position through a period of 3 years, so that individuals who are hired have the needed competencies at the time of hiring, but also have the ability to acquire the competencies that will likely define their positions in the future (Chowdhury, 1999).

The Advantages and Challenges of Competency-Based HR Planning

There are several key advantages to creating and using a competency-based approach to HR planning.

First, competencies are the most important foundational requirement for human performance. It thus makes increasing sense in today's business world to think in terms of competencies—which speak to a qualitative view of talent—rather than in terms of head count or work activities. People are unique. People's talents vary, and some people are simply more talented at some things than other people. It makes sense for the decision makers in an organization to know where to find that unique talent when they need it on short notice to address real-time, unique business needs or problems.

Second, a competency-based approach improves the specificity of HR planning. Quantitative approaches, based on head count, do not direct attention to the sought-after results. Quantitative approaches focus on the accoutrements associated with ability—academic degrees, certifications, credits, or job titles and responsibilities—not on the measurable *results* people have achieved or have the potential to achieve in the future. Form 2 illustrates the traditional information included in a skill inventory. Compare that to the information included in a competency inventory, as shown in Form 3.

Of course, when an organization's decision makers decide to pursue a competency-based approach to HR planning, they face unique challenges.

First, leaders must understand the costs and benefits associated with implementing and maintaining a competency-based HR system. They will usually want to know what immediate payoffs or benefits can be derived from a competency-based approach that could not be obtained from a traditional one.

Second, leaders must commit the resources needed to identify the organization's strategic objectives, outputs, or results and the outputs, results, characteristics, work activities, and tasks performed by its workers. That usually requires devoting staff time to the effort. External consulting may also be necessary.

Form 2: Traditional Worker Skills Inventory Questionnaire

Employee's name	
Employee's work location	
Current position	
Current job title	
Telephone number	
E-mail address	
PART I: WORK DUTIES AND RESPONSIBILITIES	
Job title	
Duties	
Date position held (from/to)	
PART II: EDUCATION AND TRAINING	
Education and training completed (summarize briefly here)	
High school	
Undergraduate education, college or university	
Degree earned	
Majors	
Minors	
Other education or training completed (list all)	

Form 2: Traditional Worker Skills Inventory Questionnaire (continued)

PART III: PROFESSIONAL CERTIFICATIONS	
Certifications held	
Certifying body	
Date granted	
Expiration date	
State	
County	
City	
Licenses held	
Licensing body	
State	
County	
City	

PART IV: CAREER OBJECTIVES	
Describe your career objectives below:	

HR planners and organization leaders will have to think about HR planning in new ways. They must make the transition from a strictly quantitative approach to one that incorporates qualitative measures of talent.

Form 3: Worker Competency Inventory Questionnaire

Employee's name	
Employee's work location	
Current position	
Current job title	
Telephone number	
E-mail address	

PART I: BASIC SKILLS COMPETENCIES

Competency	Strength Rating	Context Indicator	Duration
1. Reading comprehension			
2. Reading speed			
3. Reading accuracy			
4. Sentence composition			
5. Operation of a six-function calculator			
6. Mathematical analysis (three-step situations)			

Deciding on Competency-Based or Traditional HR Planning

Before the leaders of an organization commit to competency-based HR planning, they must weigh a number of issues, but they do not have to make an all-or-nothing decision. They may decide to use a competency-based approach to HR planning in some parts or at some levels of the organization, while they may continue to use a traditional approach in other parts of the organization.

Form 3: Worker Competency Inventory Questionnaire (continued)

PART II: OTHER COMPETENCIES OF EMPLOYEE

Competency	Strength Rating	Context Indicator	Duration
1.			
2.			
3.			
4.			
5.			
6.			

PART III: CERTIFICATIONS HELD

Certifying body	
Date granted	
Expiration date	
State	
County	
City	

PART IV: LICENSES HELD

Licensing body	
Date granted	
Expiration date	
State	
County	
City	

Form 3: Worker Competency Inventory Questionnaire (continued)

PART V: PERSONAL FUNCTIONING COMPETENCIES

Competency	Strength Rating	Context Indicator	Duration
1. Flexibility			
2. Team leadership			
3. Work group leadership			
4. Team membership			
5. Motivation to achieve			
6. Interpersonal functioning			

PART VI: TECHNICAL COMPETENCIES

Competency	Strength Rating	Context Indicator	Duration
1. Laboratory technique in microbiology			
2. Laboratory safety awareness			
3. Laboratory safety knowledge			
4. Laboratory safety practice			
5. Electrical system design			
6. Electrical system troubleshooting			

Form 3: Worker Competency Inventory Questionnaire (continued)

LIST THE OUTPUTS OR RESULTS THAT YOU PRODUCE
1.
2.
3.
4.
5.
LIST 10 OR FEWER WORK TASKS YOU COMPLETE TO PRODUCE OUTPUTS OR RESULTS
1.
2.
3.
4.
5.
6.
7.
8.
9.
10.

Competency-based HR planning is advisable when the organization's leaders are willing to experiment with innovative or new methods. This may be entirely appropriate when qualitative approaches would be particularly helpful in meeting the need for talent. For instance, in a research and development department, individual talents may be far more important than head count. In such a situation, the potential payoffs of competency-based HR planning may outweigh the sizable costs of installing it.

An organization that is competing in a rapidly changing environment may have the most need for competency-based HR planning. A high-tech firm such as Microsoft or Intel is highly dependent on first-rate talent that can be found and used quickly and appropriately. Qualitative responses to competitive challenges must be mobilized quickly to head off disaster. Indeed, a competency-based HR planning approach may be more appropriate than a traditional approach that focuses on head count and relies on superficial approximations of talent or other indicators of accomplishment that are not clearly linked to the past or potential work results of individuals.

Competency-based HR planning may be more appropriate in an organization with a large population of professional, technical, or managerial employees. In those work categories, the quantity of the workforce is far less important than the quality of its available talent. Qualitative differences in talents such as interpersonal skill, emotional intelligence, and other, less tangible associations with creative ability may be key to success.

In organizations or departments that must assemble special teams to work on ill-defined and extremely difficult problems, a competency-based HR planning approach may be far more suitable to long-term results. For instance, in a high-end consulting firm, success may depend on the organization's ability to field a dream team of consultants on short notice to meet a unique challenge. Locating a certain number of consultants is less important than finding the most effective team of consultants who can work together to help the client solve a problem.

Organizations that rely on matrix management may benefit from a competency-based HR planning approach. Matrix management encourages cross-functional sharing and is somewhat complex in nature. In effect, leadership is diffuse. One manager may be responsible for a project, while another is responsible for daily supervision. Selecting and maintaining the right mix of leadership talent is essential to nurturing future talent.

A competency-based approach may also be appropriate for organizations that rely heavily on abstract competencies, such as interpersonal skill or achievement motivation. In a sales organization, for example, work results may hinge on a salesperson's ability to consult with clients and achieve complex solutions to difficult problems. Making the sale may require substantial industry knowledge. In that case, a competency-based HR planning approach would be preferable to a traditional approach.

But not all organizations are appropriate environments for competency-based HR planning. The success of a competency-based approach requires leaders who are willing to add a qualitative aspect to their quantitative mind-sets and are open to rethinking what they mean by "performance," especially when the work to be accomplished is strategic to the organization's success. Decision makers also need to adopt an understanding of competencies. Those who believe that competencies pertain only to knowledge components would not be adequate advocates for a competency-based HR planning system.

Creating, implementing, and maintaining a competency-based HR planning system each requires resources, and leaders must be willing to make the necessary sustained commitment. Of course, leaders in some organizations may prefer to use a competency-based HR planning approach selectively. In departments that perform more routine or repetitive work that is not of strategic importance, a traditional approach may continue to be used. The circumstances in each organization will usually provide clues to how or if competency-based HR planning should be used.

A Model for Competency-Based HR Planning

What model might be helpful in guiding competency-based HR planning? This section addresses that question. Consult the model in Figure 3; then read about each step in the following subsections.

Implementing the Model

The model shown in Figure 3 should generally lend itself to step-by-step implementation. There is one exception: If an organization's decision makers do not use a formal approach to HR planning, they may need a deeper understanding of the processes involved in implementing each step. Experienced HR planners will already know most of the following information. However, they may need to be briefed on the need to shift from a purely quantitative to the combined quantitative and qualitative approach utilized in competency-based HR planning.

Figure 3: **Implementing Competency-Based HR Planning**

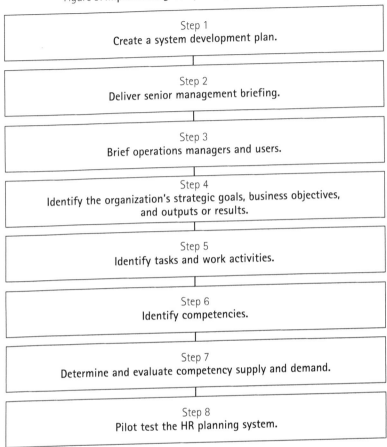

Step 1
Create a system development plan.

Step 2
Deliver senior management briefing.

Step 3
Brief operations managers and users.

Step 4
Identify the organization's strategic goals, business objectives, and outputs or results.

Step 5
Identify tasks and work activities.

Step 6
Identify competencies.

Step 7
Determine and evaluate competency supply and demand.

Step 8
Pilot test the HR planning system.

Step 1: Create a system development plan

A plan is necessary for transforming a traditional HR planning system to a competency-based approach. A well-thought-out system development plan is an essential starting point.

Sometimes practitioners do not recognize the need to put a macrolevel plan in place before briefing the organization's leaders to gain support for the transformation. In other words, there must be a plan in order to plan. Senior leaders need to know the work, time, and resources they must commit in order to achieve the project's objectives. The remaining steps in this model provide the framework for the macrolevel plan, and the plan represents the major content for the senior leadership briefing session. As soon as leaders understand and endorse the approach, HR planners can proceed to later steps of the model.

As with any well-conceived project, the objectives must be clearly stated and effectively communicated from inception. HR planners may begin to establish the project objectives by answering questions such as the following:

- Will the system accommodate HR planning for all work units in the organization or for only certain ones (for example, finance, engineering, research, distribution)?

- What will be the early, intermediate, and long-term outputs and benefits of creating and maintaining a competency-based HR planning system?

- Is the purpose of the new HR planning system to ensure adequate human resources only for specific projects, development teams, and so forth, or will it address organization-wide competency needs?

- What HR planning life cycle will the new or reinvented system accommodate?

- How much emphasis will the system place on head count, and how much on competencies?

Other system design issues and their subsequent objectives should also be raised at the outset of project planning. For instance, will decision makers also want to establish a competency inventory system as part of the project?

The project manager must also accurately assess the organization's environment and develop an estimate of the organization's ability to create, implement, and maintain the system. Answers to questions such as the following may be useful:

- Do senior and other key leaders have a clear conception of the organization's short- and long-term strategic goals or business objectives? Can they name the measurable outputs or results that lead to the organization's success? Do members of the leadership team agree on these items? If not, can they reach agreement on these issues, which affect the direction of the HR planning system?

- Are workers' outputs or results clearly identified through a formal job analysis process? Have worker competencies been identified for key organizational results areas? Is performance management based on competencies? What other roles do competencies play in the organization? If work tasks and competencies are not now available or understood by key leaders, is the transition possible, and how long will it take?

- Are the necessary sustainable human capabilities available— internally or externally—to ensure the creation, implementation, and maintenance of the system?

- Does the organization have the management information resources needed to support a competency-based HR planning system? Planning to meet the new system's information management needs must be a high priority at the earliest stages of development. If the organization's management information staff cannot provide the needed support, use of other resources (for example, software or contractors) must be assured.

- Is a correct mix of human capabilities available to the project manager for as long as is necessary to ensure the system's long-term viability?

- Will resources be available to complete the collection and analyses that produce the needed system inputs, such as data on work tasks, competencies, outputs, or results?

- What is the probability that the persons assigned to work on the project can show immediate results that are important to the organization's senior leaders?

A project plan should be straightforward and easily understood. You might want to consider using the following guidelines for preparing the microlevel project plan:

- Begin with identifying the project tasks, which are the actions that must be taken in order to achieve the project objectives. In the first draft plan, which becomes the foundation for the leadership briefing session, these actions can be broadly stated. Later, they must be made sufficiently detailed and measurable to help guide project operations.

- Specify the resources required to complete each project task.

- Clarify the specific output or result expected from each project action.

- Source assistance from other organizations or persons as needed for successful completion of tasks.

- Set a targeted completion date for each action step.

Both macrolevel and microlevel system plans are essential for formulating and implementing a competency-based HR planning approach. This investment is well worth the cost involved.

Step 2: Deliver senior management briefing

Although each organizational setting is unique, the project sponsor might find it necessary to include the following key objectives in a senior management briefing session on competency-based HR planning. If the organization has an established HR planning system, the briefing should emphasize the benefits of reinventing the existing system. If the organization has no formalized HR planning, the briefing should begin with an explanation of what it is, how organizations are using it, and the benefits those organizations derive from it. From there, it will be possible to compare and contrast the traditional HR planning approach to a competency-based approach.

The following list of topics can help to guide a senior management briefing:

- What is HR planning, and how can it benefit the organization?

- How is HR planning carried out?

- What resources are needed to establish and maintain an HR planning system?

- Why are planning systems based on head count no longer adequate to ensure many organizations the talent they need for success?

- How are the terms *job/work competence* and *competency* defined operationally for employees and the organization?

- What is competency-based HR planning, and how does it differ from traditional HR planning?

- What are the benefits to the organization of using competency-based HR planning?

- What general project plan will help the organization develop, implement, and maintain a competency-based HR planning system?

- What are the costs involved in implementing this plan? Do the costs outweigh the benefits of having the system in place and successfully running?

- What applications within the organization immediately come to mind as initial outputs of the competency-based HR planning system described earlier? What strategic impact will these results have on the organization?

- Do decision makers have any questions or comments about changing to a competency-based HR planning approach?

- Are the organization's leaders willing to support a pilot test of a competency-based system at this time? (Note: The briefing facilitator should insist that senior leaders give the project manager a "go" or "no go" decision at this stage.)

Next steps in the briefing might include the following:

- Summarize the briefing content and leaders' agreements up to this point. On an easel chart page, write the key points and agreements, the specific actions each party will take, and the resources that will be assigned to achieve the project objectives.

- Establish a specific target completion date for each project stage or deliverable.

- Establish guidelines for cross-communication among project participants.

- Set a date for reviewing project progress with the leaders or management group.

It is most important that the project manager establish open communication with the organization's leaders and other key stakeholders who are involved with the project. Involvement encourages commitment, which is necessary for project success. Thank the participants for their attention, time, and support.

Step 3: Brief operations managers and users

The objective of this step is to ensure that those who will be most affected by the new HR planning system—the users or customers of the

HR planning system—are actively engaged in planning it. Human resource management systems must always be customer focused, and customers of the HR planning system must be involved in planning and implementing it.

We suggest that this briefing, which covers many of the same issues presented to senior managers, take place shortly after their briefing, if organizational circumstances permit. The major reason for this is that leadership decisions regarding the project will determine the information presented to managers and other users.

We suggest that this briefing session address issues such as the following:

- What is HR planning, and how can it benefit the organization?
- How is HR planning carried out?
- Why are HR planning systems based on head count no longer sufficient to ensure certain organizations the talent they need for success?
- How are the terms *job/work competence* and *competency* defined?
- What is competency-based HR planning, and how does it differ from traditional HR planning?
- What are the benefits to the organization and to users when a competency-based HR planning approach is used?
- What general project plan will help the organization develop, implement, and maintain a competency-based HR planning system? This plan should contain an overview of the key project steps, with special emphasis on the need to complete work analysis if that information is not yet available. It is essential that system users understand that statements of the outputs or results, work tasks, and the required competencies are prerequisites to competency-based HR planning. Their support in securing these components is critical to project success.
- What resources are needed for implementing the plan? What resources may be needed from participants to create, implement, and maintain the system?
- What applications within the organization immediately come to mind as initial outputs of the competency-based HR planning system described earlier? What strategic impact will these results have on the organization?

- What questions or comments do the participants have about what they heard about the project plan?
- Are participants willing to support a pilot test of a competency-based HR system in their work units as senior leaders have determined? (Note: At this time, the briefing facilitator should communicate the decisions of senior managers regarding their participation if he or she has not already done so.)

Next steps for this briefing might include the following:

- Summarize the briefing content and participants' agreements up to this point. On an easel chart page, write the key points and agreements, the specific actions each party will take, and the resources that will be assigned to achieve the project objectives.
- Establish a specific target completion date for each project stage or deliverable, per the preferences of senior leaders.
- Establish guidelines for cross-communication among the participants and with the project manager, per agreements with senior leaders.
- Set a date for reviewing project progress with the participants and confirm other dates or commitments as appropriate.
- Be sure to thank the participants for their attention, time, and support.

Step 4: Identify the organization's strategic goals, business objectives, and outputs or results

Many people equate HR planning to the related process of organizational strategic planning. Consequently, it is easy to make the case that HR planning must be done with an awareness of where the organization is today and where it hopes to be in the future. Setting business objectives in today's global business environment is like looking into a crystal ball and then throwing the dice. Predictions are often unreliable and may be greatly influenced by chance events. That points to the need for flexible HR planning that can readily accommodate change.

The organization's strategic objectives and desired results are the foundation of HR planning. Analysis of the organization's results determines the results workers should produce for internal and external customers. How specifically should those results be expressed? That depends on several factors. The size of the organization is one consideration. Another is the number of results provided to external and internal customers. The practitioner must carefully manage the degree of grading in the lists of results so that they will be useful in later stages of the project.

These lists should give HR planners (and project managers) a deeper understanding of the resources necessary to achieve project results. HR planners may wish to bear in mind that all workers in an organization are "strategic" relative to their contributions to the organization's strategic success. If the contribution is assessed as inadequate, managers should seriously consider whether the person should complete the assigned work.

In summary, every organization exists for the purpose of producing outputs or results that are needed (or perceived as needed) by its customers. The organization's strategic objectives drive the results it will produce and deliver to its customers and determine the timetable for delivery. The organization's human resources produce these results, either directly or indirectly, so in order to plan the appropriate HR competency mix, HR planners and other HR leaders must start by ascertaining the organization's current situation or competitive position and the results its leaders hope to achieve in the future. Otherwise, the HR planning system will have no justifiable foundation on which to base actions such as recruitment, selection, training, and staff assignment.

The organization's results are interpreted to clarify the results workers must produce to ensure organizational success. In some cases, these results might be the same as those desired from the organization; in others, they will be only indirectly related. The information identified and organized in this step of the model provides the input for the next step: identifying the work activities that produce the necessary results.

Step 5: Identify tasks and work activities
In this step, we attempt to understand the work completed by the organization's workers by identifying the tasks they complete to achieve results that meet the time and quality requirements they are given. Analysts often organize tasks into a hierarchy of macrolevel and microlevel tasks. In a similar manner, meaningful collections of tasks are clustered to form work activities.

Figure 4 illustrates the dynamic relationships that exist among a desired organizational result, a work activity, a macrolevel task, a micro-level task, worker competencies, and the outputs or results expected of the worker. It also underscores the importance of performing a thorough work analysis *before* attempting to identify the competencies necessary for achieving the desired performance and thus the required work results.

A key point warrants emphasis here. The definitions of *macrolevel* and *microlevel* and the detail required for an effective work analysis depend on the answers to several questions. Why is the work analysis being done? How will the results be used? What results will be most useful for the purposes at hand? What are the preferences of the HR planner or work analyst? What is the exact nature of the work to be analyzed, and to what level of detail will it be analyzed? Consequently, it is difficult to provide specific advice for this step of the HR planning system process.[2]

The "Develop A CurriculUM" (DACUM) method is one excellent approach to the identification of current work activities and tasks (Norton, 1997). Created by the vocational education specialists at Ohio State University, DACUM provides rapid, accurate analysis of work completed for a given job by using a disciplined, focus group approach with job experts. The process has been improved over the years by its founders and committed users. The method's two key advantages are that (1) it provides rich results when a limited amount of time is available for collecting information and (2) it has a form of built-in endorsement from the organization's senior leaders, since the focus group includes job experts and managers. These two factors make DACUM a highly appealing method for completing work analyses.[3]

In summary, the identification both of organizational and worker results and of the tasks and work activities workers perform must be focused on helping planners to design a user-friendly HR planning system that is easy to maintain as the work changes. That often requires system planners, analysts, and their clients to revisit their methods of collecting data for the system and the amount of detail they include. Collecting all details inevitably leads to disappointment. It is important to experiment to determine the level that is appropriate for users and to build the system to meet their needs.

Figure 4: **Dynamic Relationships**

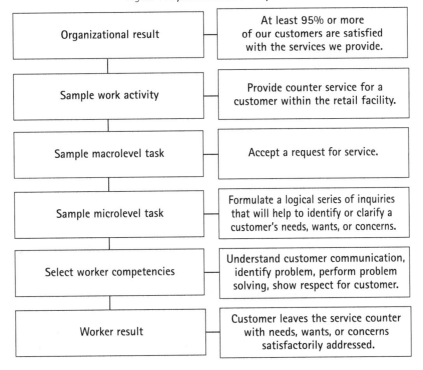

Organizational result	At least 95% or more of our customers are satisfied with the services we provide.
Sample work activity	Provide counter service for a customer within the retail facility.
Sample macrolevel task	Accept a request for service.
Sample microlevel task	Formulate a logical series of inquiries that will help to identify or clarify a customer's needs, wants, or concerns.
Select worker competencies	Understand customer communication, identify problem, perform problem solving, show respect for customer.
Worker result	Customer leaves the service counter with needs, wants, or concerns satisfactorily addressed.

Step 6: Identify competencies

Although we discussed competency identification in chapter 2, we believe it is essential to review the meaning of competent job (or work) performance and the definition of the word *competency.*

What constitutes competent performance? It is performance that meets or exceeds a job's requirements and produces outputs at the level of quality expected within the constraints of internal and external organizational environments. This definition requires users to adopt broad parameters when judging whether an individual is competent. Note that competent performance, although centered on worker attributes, is influenced both by the expectations of other people about the quality of the work and by the individual's willingness to address the constraints imposed by organizational context. Small wonder that leaders, managers, and employees alike have struggled with the notion of competence and competent performance for many years. This definition is not perfect, but it is important that an organization's leaders consider their concepts of competent performance when they decide to establish competency-based HR planning.

How do we define the word *competency?* Perhaps the best definition is the classic one. A competency is an underlying characteristic (motive, trait, skill, aspect of self-image, social role, body of knowledge) that an employee uses and that results in effective or superior performance (Boyatzis, 1982; Klemp, 1980).

A worker characteristic is a competency only if its use can be shown to contribute directly to successful work performance. Many perceptions of certain human characteristics as essential to successful work performance do not stand up to rigorous competency identification methods. That is one reason why an open-ended, or traditional, focus group approach is usually unsatisfactory for competency identification purposes. If an organization adopts a competency-based foundation for its HR planning system, decision makers must be prepared to provide highly valid and reliable lists of the required competencies for the duration of planning. We should note here that competency lists for all levels of the organization should include abstract (for example, patience, perseverance, customer awareness) as well as concrete competencies, since work of any kind requires the effective application of both.[4]

Successful competency identification relies on the following information:

- A thorough understanding of the organization's strategic business objectives

- The current and future work outputs or results to be achieved by the organization

- The outputs or results expected of the worker group under investigation, and how those outputs or results support the achievement of organizational objectives

- The major work tasks that must be performed in order to achieve the required outputs or results

This information must be available for use before competency identification begins. Recall that these components are the outcomes of

Step 4 of the model shown in Figure 2. The components must be investigated in this order if valid and reliable competency identification results are to be obtained.

After competency identification is completed, managers of the workers under investigation and appropriate organizational leaders must endorse the competency lists and their definitions. A general rule to follow is, the more strategic the work, the higher the level of endorsement must be.

Two other questions deserve the attention of those who are considering competency-based HR planning. Is awareness of the competencies that distinguish fully successful from exemplary performance of value to the organization? And if so, for which types of work should differentiating competencies be identified? By knowing the competencies that distinguish an exemplary performer from a fully successful one, it is possible to help all workers who do the same job achieve beyond the fully successful level. Deciding to identify the competencies of exemplary performers will greatly affect the competency identification methods the organization will eventually use (see Dubois & Rothwell, 2000). Although the decision to identify exemplary worker competencies expands the scope of the competency identification initiative, doing so can help the organization direct HR requirements toward achieving exemplary performance. The importance the organization's leaders place on having this capability directly affects how much they are willing to invest in getting those results. HR planners should be keenly aware of this option.

To summarize, competency identification must be an outgrowth of the organization's earlier work to identify its desired strategic results, the relationship of those results to business success, and the connection between worker results and organizational success. After these facts are known, work analyses must identify and verify the tasks workers perform and pinpoint the results expected of them, at a given level of quality, within the constraints of the organization. The information gained in Steps 6 and 7 completes the foundation for competency identification and verification.

Step 7: Determine and evaluate competency supply and demand
At this point in the model, valid and reliable work analysis data should be available. That information should include an estimate of the competen-

cies required for organizational work. It is now time to determine and evaluate the competency pool (or competency supply) among the organization's workers. It is also time to forecast demand for competencies based on current and projected organizational needs. Approaches to completing this step of the model vary according to the scope of the competency-based HR planning system. Certainly a competency-based system for an organization requires more work than does a limited system for only one department or job category. This discussion of supply and demand therefore is somewhat general, so that it may apply to many different situations in which competency-based HR planning might be used.

First, we will examine the supply side of the equation. *Supply* in this context means the availability of worker competencies that are tied to organizational success. After an organization's strategic objectives have been clarified and the desired results are clear, the competencies required to achieve those outputs can be assessed. In its broadest sense, the following question remains: What is the availability of strategic competencies within the current employee competency pool?

Availability is determined by completing a competency assessment process (CAP). A CAP determines which employees, in what performance context, have which competencies of strategic importance, with what amount of performance experience, and to what level of performance strength. Several CAPs are used in organizations today. The HR planner must decide which type of CAP would best serve the competency data needs of the organization and help to establish a competency-based HR planning system. Considerable literature on many methods of competency assessment is readily available.[5] If this is a new practice area for you, we suggest that you consult one or more references for specific guidance on using competency assessment.

We will provide a brief overview of the following common competency assessment methods: self-assessment, superior or "boss" assessment, peer and work expert assessment, customer or client assessment, certification or licensing assessment, and assessment centers.

Self-assessment is one approach to obtaining competency assessment information from employees, but of all the CAPs, it produces the least valid and reliable results. The major reason is that individuals often have inflated perceptions of their competencies. (In some cases, the reverse is true, and workers' perceptions of their abilities are lower than is accurate.) Readers experienced in the use of multirater competency assessment systems in organizations will be among the first to support this assertion. Although individuals are usually able to provide accurate assessments of their competency strengths in the proper rating direction (that is, whether they do or do not have the competency), they are rarely realistic in assessing how strongly they rate on a competency. Individuals sometimes erect protective walls around their egos, and that usually explains why their self-perceptions of competence differ from the ratings of others. Motivation, insight, consistency, and lack of understanding are some of the areas of concern with self-assessment (Cooper, 2000). Competency self-assessment has a place as long as it is properly employed. It is especially useful for obtaining initial assessment screenings with employees to determine the potential competency strengths of an employee group. After an initial competency pool is identified, additional assessment methods can be used to refine estimates of the competency strengths of those in the pool.

Other CAPs rely on external observers, who assess competencies in the context of the corporate culture or performance setting. It is common practice to use competency assessments made by employees' supervisors. These ratings are usually one component of an organization's employee performance management and appraisal system. Their reliability is based on several unspoken assumptions about supervisors: that they are qualified to make the assessments, that they will not be biased, that their contact with employees is frequent enough and of sufficient quality to enable accurate assessments, and that they are "work performance experts" who know how the competency should be applied and can thus provide valid assessments. Even though any one of these assumptions may be flawed, depending on a supervisor's judgment is a very popular approach. These assessments are often used to determine work assignments, areas for future development, and other work activities that affect the relationship between employee and employer. Therefore, it is advisable to remember the possible limitations of supervisor-based CAPs when the assessments are interpreted and used.

A CAP that relies on the judgment of expert work performers is usually valid for those assessed. In fact, many organizations depend heavily on expert judgment to identify the most critical competencies needed to perform the work. Generally speaking, the use of work experts to identify and assess competency is highly regarded by organization leaders.

The popularity of peer assessments has been growing in recent years, and with good reason. Research supports the view that peer assessments are perhaps the most valid and reliable means by which to assess individual competence (Lewin & Zwany, 1976a, 1976b; Kane & Lawler, 1978). Of course, the word *peer* means an individual who performs work identical or nearly identical to that of the person assessed. Many organizations administer peer review or peer assessment systems so that they may gain a view of an employee's performance other than the one offered by the supervisor, team facilitator, or leader.

Another CAP uses a worker's customers as a source of competency assessment. Although these data do provide insight into worker performance from those who count, the validity and reliability of the information could be limited by the extent of the contact between worker and customer. Customer opinions are also easily influenced by one failure. A customer can forget the employee's years of high performance and become fixated on one incidence of failure. For that reason, when they serve as the sole rationale, customer ratings or reviews of an employee's performance must be considered thoughtfully and verified with great care before any corrective action is taken.

Professional associations establish certification programs that assess and verify the competencies of practitioners. The objective of the programs is usually to build credibility for the profession. State and local government licensing agencies often require certification for those who apply to practice in their jurisdictions. In addition to written competency examinations, certification may also necessitate supervised professional practice. It is common, for example, to ask those requesting certification to provide letters of endorsement from professional colleagues, who often must be certified, or from employers or schools that provided training. Competency examination questions generally are developed and endorsed by persons recognized as experts in the subject area covered by the examination. Accordingly, this type of CAP is based on a peer assessment process.

Multirater competency assessment is an increasingly popular approach in organizations. Many variations are possible, depending on organizational setting, resources available, and other factors.

One such assessment occurs at the airline operations for United Parcel Service, headquartered in Louisville, Kentucky. Every six months, between 1,200 and 1,300 management employees participate in an automated 360-degree feedback process. Prior to participating in the evaluation process, participants receive training that describes the purpose and methods of the survey tool. Additional training on giving and receiving feedback is also provided. The Quality Performance Review, as it is called, measures key skills such as "customer focus, financial and internal business process knowledge, people skills, business values and leadership." Employees then develop goals based on the feedback provided during these reviews. Informal meetings, called Talk, Listen, Act, are also held to bring together supervisors and individuals directly reporting to them for discussions on work-related issues. ("Traveling Beyond 360-Degree Evaluations," 1999)

Multirater competency assessments provide very powerful feedback, while at the same time, administrative chores such as preparing, distributing, and tabulating the data are fairly easy (Cooper, 2000). In addition, multirater assessments produce comprehensive information, establish job performance requirements and accountability for performance improvement, identify expectations, and integrate 360-degree assessment results with other systems and subsystems. There are disadvantages, however, such as expense, lack of meaning if ratings are derived using criteria such as competencies that are not specific to the culture, and the overwhelming task of analyzing data from a large number of individuals (Rothwell, 2001).[6] Another area of concern is ensuring that the rater is qualified to assess competencies such as insight, consistency, and motivation (Cooper, 2000).

Assessment centers warrant special attention. They are often used to determine the development needs of high-potential candidates for senior leadership positions. They can also provide competency assessment for managers, supervisors, and individual contributors. These results may be used to help individuals improve performance or prepare for new work roles, to assess individual potential, or to determine which employees would be the "best fit" for specific work projects or roles. Recent evidence suggests that assessment centers are making a comeback for just these reasons (Jansen & Jongh, 1998). An assessment center can be an important element in a competency-based HR planning approach.

In the assessment center process, the persons who are being assessed perform work activities in simulated environments or future scenarios under the direct observation of trained assessors. Assessors are usually work experts, managers, or senior managers. If the work has strategic import to the organization, the chief executive officer or chief operating officer should be chosen as the observer. Participants typically are coached by their managers or mentors beforehand. After the experience, they are given both individual and group assessments and feedback on their performance, including action plans tailored to help build their competencies for current or future work. Assessment center results contain much useful information about current or potential performance in relation to the organization's future talent requirements.[7]

Earlier in this chapter we noted the importance of establishing a management information system that provides sufficient storage capability and allows competency pool data to be easily retrieved. This information is collected from employees through a competency inventory, so named to distinguish it from the traditional, and less useful, skill inventory. The purpose of a competency inventory is to enable the organization's decision makers to find talent quickly when it is needed to solve business problems. Its design therefore should be based on user needs and requirements. Time has become a strategic resource of greatest importance, and few organizations can afford the luxury of not knowing what talent is already available.[8] (For a further review on maintaining talent inventories, see Rothwell, 2001).

After a CAP has been completed, the information must be organized and then stored for easy retrieval and analysis. See Figure 5 for one example of how to organize the data. Other forms may be even more effective if they are grounded in the language used by managers and other decision makers.

Note that the table shell in Figure 5 is centered on key competencies targeted by decision makers for the purpose of competency-based HR planning. It notes employees and the context in which they applied the competencies. Their level of experience with the competency, and the strength of the competency, could also be made an element of the data profile. Of course, other or more detailed data useful for HR planning could be included in the inventory. The table shell in the figure is intended as a starting point.

Finally, the competency inventory should be tested against user needs. For example, the project manager could request specific information for users and observe how well the system performs.

Figure 5: **Summary of Competency Inventory Data Useful for HR Planning**

Employee*	Comp. 1	Comp. 2	Comp. 3	Comp. 4	Comp. 5	Comp. 6
A1						
A2						
B1						
B2						
C1						
C2						
D1						
D2						
*Note: The letters in this column identify employees by department.						

Step 8: Pilot test the HR planning system

There is no real substitute for a pilot test of a competency-based HR planning approach. It will either demonstrate the value of the approach or point out the folly of the effort.

Here are some suggestions on pilot testing the new system:

- Pilot tests should put strain on only the most elemental components of the planning system. For example, try completing a plan for a limited (noncomplex) project that affects a single work unit and allow elongated time frames for completing each step of the work.

- Actively involve the HR planning customer in each step in the planning process.

- Listen to customers' recommendations and agree to only those system changes that will not limit the system's applicability to any organization planning project.

- Identify potential difficulties and make plans for roadblocks that could affect system performance and customer satisfaction.

- Keep the organization's leaders informed about the project. Include mention of the benefits of the system and any other information that will encourage their continued support.

- Work to ensure the user-friendliness of the new system.
- Seek guidance from others, including the organization's leaders, when help is needed to resolve system constraints, concerns, or failures.
- Promise only what can be delivered, and deliver what was promised.

Summary

This chapter was devoted to a discussion of HR planning and the design and implementation of a competency-based HR planning system. The chapter opened by defining HR planning. We then explained traditional HR planning and explored approaches to making HR planning competency based. A competency-based approach has advantages and challenges, and we offered guidelines for determining when HR planning should become competency based and when it should be handled traditionally. We presented and explained an eight-step model to guide the formulation and installation of a competency-based HR planning system for an organization.

CHAPTER 5

Competency-Based Employee Recruitment and Selection

Human resource plans are implemented, in part, through the functions of employee recruitment and selection. Taken together, recruitment and selection provide a key way of sourcing talent with the aim of achieving organizational objectives. There are, of course, other methods of sourcing talent—such as the use of temporary workers and consultants—but in this chapter we will focus on recruiting and selecting so-called full-time workers.

This chapter addresses the following key questions on recruiting and selecting people to implement HR plans:

- What are employee recruitment and employee selection?
- How are employee recruitment and selection traditionally carried out?
- How can employee recruitment and selection become competency based?
- What are the advantages and challenges of a competency-based approach to employee recruitment and selection?

- When should employee recruitment and selection be competency based, and when should they be handled traditionally?
- What model can guide competency-based employee recruitment and selection, and how is it implemented?

Employee Recruitment and Selection

Employee recruitment and employee selection are two sides of the same coin. *Recruitment* is the process of attracting as many qualified applicants as possible for existing vacancies and anticipated openings. It is a talent search, a pursuit of the best group of applicants for an available position. *Selection* reduces the list of applicants to those who are most qualified to achieve the desired outputs or results. During the process, HR practitioners try to predict which applicant will be most successful and will best fit the job and the corporate culture.

Recruitment and selection are important issues in today's workplace. A study of human resource trends conducted by the Society for Human Resource Management indicated that respondents considered finding and keeping qualified candidates to be the greatest employment challenge (*1997 Survey of Human Resource Trends,* 1997).

Traditional Employee Recruitment and Selection

The traditional starting point for recruitment is a job description and a job specification. The *job description* describes the work activities or job responsibilities of the successful job incumbent. The *job specification* specifies the qualifications an individual should possess in order to carry out the work. Qualifications are usually expressed as the minimum education, experience, and other requirements necessary to do the job. Some employers also use a *job requisition,* which justifies the creation of a new position or the replacement of a departing worker.

The Traditional Recruitment Process

The traditional recruitment process requires HR practitioners to carry out four predictable steps, as shown in Figure 6.

Figure 6: **Traditional Recruitment Process**

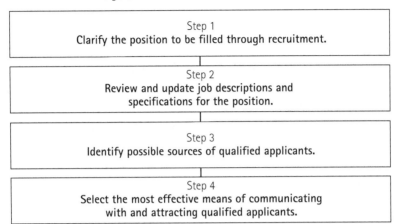

Step 1
Clarify the position to be filled through recruitment.

Step 2
Review and update job descriptions and
specifications for the position.

Step 3
Identify possible sources of qualified applicants.

Step 4
Select the most effective means of communicating
with and attracting qualified applicants.

Step 1: Clarify the position to be filled through recruitment

Employers act according to different philosophies of recruitment. One philosophy suggests recruiting continuously—that is, without regard to the number of vacant positions. For instance, an engineering firm may recruit engineers all the time so that an appropriate applicant pool is available whenever an opening occurs.

According to another philosophy, recruitment should be carried out selectively and only as necessary to fill openings as they occur. For instance, a firm may identify three management trainees as due for promotion, reassignment, or turnover. Recruitment at this firm is then targeted to fill the three openings.

Of course, it is possible for an employer to act in accord with both philosophies, recruiting continuously for some positions and recruiting for others only when openings occur. In either case, HR planning may forecast the number and kind of persons who will be needed.

Step 2: Review and update job descriptions and specifications for the position

Job descriptions, after all, clarify the tasks successful applicants will perform on the job. Job specifications enumerate the required qualifications. Without current job descriptions and specifications, HR practitioners cannot screen applicants by comparing individual qualifications to work requirements.

Step 3: Identify possible sources of qualified applicants
Recruitment is perhaps most often associated with this step. In the broadest sense, of course, applicants may come from inside or outside the organization.

There are a number of advantages associated with recruiting from within. Internal recruitment maximizes the return on the organization's investment in its employees.[1] By seeking internal applicants, management gains increased awareness of individuals who are interested in furthering their careers and reduces time spent on orientation and training for persons with whom it is already familiar (Grensing-Pophal, 2000). Applicants may be found internally through job posting and bidding and by supervisory nominations.

Internal recruitment efforts very often result in promotions. Promotion signifies reward for past performance and encourages employees in their efforts (Sherman, Bohlander, & Snell, 1998). It also sends a positive signal to employees in suggesting that their own efforts may be similarly rewarded.

Yet despite the many advantages to hiring from within, there are also disadvantages. Grensing-Pophal (2000) noted that the practice limits the potential number of qualified candidates, decreases opportunities to gain new ideas and concepts, and creates additional open positions.

Methods of external recruitment include newspaper, radio, and television advertisements; help-wanted signs; database searches of previous candidates; public and private employment agencies and search firms; educational institutions; employee referrals; advertisements with professional associations and labor unions; temporary help agencies; and Web site advertisements.

Organizations vary greatly in their philosophy and practice of internal and external hiring. Some companies are committed to providing development initiatives for their own employees and encourage promotions but are somewhat reluctant to conduct external hiring (Michaels, Handfield-Jones, & Axelrod, 2001). Other companies prefer external hiring, particularly for some senior-level positions, because, among other reasons, "regularly bringing new people in is a good way to constantly calibrate—and even raise—the company's standards for talent" (Michaels et al., 2001, p. 72).

Most employers try to balance the cost of recruitment against their likely success at finding the best talent. The SHRM survey of 2000 indicated cost-per-hire results from various sources as ranging from $99 for job fairs to $30,655 for an executive search (Pfau & Kay, 2002).[2]

Step 4: Select the most effective means of communicating with and attracting qualified applicants

This step usually involves marketing the organization to prospective applicants. After all, people often self-select themselves, which means they choose to apply based on the perception that an organization's image matches their own self-image. HR practitioners are familiar with methods of communicating with possible applicants. These include open houses, campus visits, presentations to groups of possible targeted job applicants, internships, and school-to-work programs. In other words, the organization must find a way to build awareness that it is a good place to work.

Specialized approaches to recruitment include a variety of new Web-based efforts aimed at attracting applicants from a broad range of geographical locations. The Paine Webber Group estimated that businesses will spend more than $8 billion for on-line recruiting by 2005 (Rubin, 2002).

In recent years, considerable attention has been paid to recruiting special groups, such as protected-class employees represented by women, minorities, the disabled, and others whose inclusion helps to achieve a diverse and thereby more creative workforce. In providing equal employment opportunities, many organizations create a formal program that includes the recruitment of protected classes as an integral part.

The Traditional Selection Process

The traditional selection process begins where recruitment ends. The selection process requires HR practitioners to carry out 10 predictable steps, which are shown in Figure 7.

Step 1: Clarify the selection process

It is important to clarify how the selection process will be carried out. For example, will the applicant have to meet subjective or objective criteria—

Figure 7: Traditional Selection Process

Step 1 Clarify the selection process.
Step 2 Clarify the selection methods.
Step 3 Shorten the list of potential candidates by comparing the applicants to the selection criteria.
Step 4 Establish a list of finalists for the targeted jobs.
Step 5 Conduct a detailed examination of the finalists to identify the best candidates for the targeted job.
Step 6 Make the selection.
Step 7 Negotiate a competitive compensation and benefits package with the successful candidate.
Step 8 Extend an offer to the successful candidate.
Step 9 Confirm that all requirements are met.
Step 10 Confirm that the selection decision was correct.

or some combination of the two? Will evaluation be performed by multiple, independent reviewers—or by one? In short, on what basis will a selection decision be made, and who will make it?

Step 2: Clarify the selection methods

It helps to get clear what the organization wants to find. There are many tools and approaches available for pinpointing the most appropriate applicant in a group. Methods include application forms, weighted application blanks (WABs), reference checks, honesty tests, psychological tests, manual dexterity tests, assessment centers, graphology, medical examinations, drug tests, and planned (structured) or unplanned (unstructured) job interviews. HR practitioners must choose the appropriate methods for identifying the most qualified individual.

Step 3: Shorten the list of potential candidates by comparing the applicants to the selection criteria

Develop a list of probable candidates by comparing applicants to the selection criteria. This may require compiling test scores and interview results, or a combination of methods.

Step 4: Establish a list of finalists for the target jobs

After individuals have been screened by one or more selection methods, only a few well-qualified people should remain. One candidate usually emerges as the preferred choice. The names of other candidates may be retained, however, in the event that negotiations with the preferred candidate are unsuccessful.

Step 5: Conduct a more detailed examination of the finalists to identify the best candidates for the targeted job

At this point, decision makers may insist on additional interviews or further evidence of an individual's ability to perform the job successfully.

Step 6: Make the selection

Decision makers in the organization should now be in agreement on which individual they believe is best equipped to do the job. Some organizations may check a candidate's references before finalizing the decision.

Step 7: Negotiate a competitive compensation and benefits package with the successful candidate

The goal at this stage is to match the candidate's expectations with the employer's ability to pay. This step is likely to be completed successfully when applicants have already been informed of the pay range and associated benefits.

Step 8: Extend an offer to the successful candidate
A formal offer may involve requesting the candidate's signature on a letter in which he or she agrees to the terms of employment. Less formal offers are extended orally. Written employment contracts are common at certain executive levels in some professions (and in other nations) but are not generally used in the United States.

Step 9: Confirm that all requirements are met
Final requirements may include tests such as drug screening or evidence of educational credentials.

Step 10: Confirm that the selection decision was correct
This step may require a probationary period. If the individual meets the organization's performance requirements during this preliminary period, he or she becomes a permanent employee. If not, the organization may terminate the individual in a manner consistent with legal requirements and any collective bargaining agreements previously negotiated by the employer.

Making Employee Recruitment and Selection Competency Based

In considering a transition from traditional to competency-based recruitment and selection, one question is uppermost: How can a competency-based approach improve the organization's ability to predict successful job performance from prospective applicants?

The answer to this question is simple, but it does require some explanation. The success of a competency-based approach depends on whether or not the organization has clarified work performance requirements and kept them up-to-date. If, for instance, the organization's managers have not clarified the desired work outcomes, then trying to match applicants to those ill-defined goals will not be easy.

Competency-Based Recruitment

The traditional recruitment process must be reinvented if it is to become competency based.

Competency-based recruitment begins when the organization's leaders identify the key work roles, positions, or other work designations in need of recruitment efforts. This involves setting priorities. Decision makers must also decide on the time span over which the recruitment process will take place.

A competency-based approach to recruitment and selection places more demands on an organization, compared to the effort required for a traditional approach. But what if sufficient resources are not available to adopt a competency-based system for the entire organization? In such a case, the organization should invest its available resources in a competency-based approach to recruiting and selecting for those jobs or positions that are most critical to the organization's success. After key positions have been filled, leaders can evaluate the costs and benefits of extending the use of these methods to other areas.

After the organization's leaders have identified their recruitment needs, they must confirm the accuracy of the descriptions and specifications for the positions to be filled. The information can be gained through moderate to extensive job analyses and should meet the following requirements:

- Work outputs, activities, and tasks as well as job competencies and the behavioral indicators by which those competencies can be measured are clearly stated and aligned, and the managers who are seeking applicants agree on them.

- The competencies necessary for successful performance of the work are valid for the purposes stated.

- Key competencies that are the greatest predictors of job success have been identified and validated by the managers who are seeking applicants.

With a competency-based approach to recruitment, the third step of the traditional recruitment process must be reframed. The task of finding the needed competencies is made easier when the organization has conducted an assessment of existing staff competencies and can access that information through a competency inventory. It is also helpful to identify past sources of exemplary performers. Analysis may reveal that some sources of talent yield the best applicants more often than do others.

In the final step of the recruitment process, the organization actively seeks applicants. It is particularly important that decision makers identify and communicate those competencies that are not developed with training and must be sourced through recruitment and selection. For example, most people would agree that it is difficult, if not impossible, to train new employees to persevere. Consequently, locating this competency may require special attention during recruitment and selection.

Sea-Land, a large U.S.-based member of the global shipping industry, is an example of a company that uses a number of different approaches in its recruitment practices, including, increasingly, Internet technology (Little, 1998). Sea-Land also utilizes various recruitment strategies that include use of both retained and contingency firms specializing in recruitment, temporary and full-time staffing, and contract recruiters and personnel. It has established good relationships with nine core colleges and places strong emphasis on competency-based selection.

Competency–Based Selection

Traditional employee selection methods must also be reinvented if they are to become competency based. The following discussion refers to the 10 steps of the traditional employee selection process shown in Figure 7.

The goal of Step 1 in traditional employee selection is to plan the selection process. Planning is equally essential, if not more so, for the competency-based selection process. The goal of both is, of course, to make the best match between the person and the work.

With the competency-based approach, the criteria for selection are objectively stated. The process is systematic and disciplined. Perhaps the most desirable method of application is multiple interviews conducted by trained professionals, either individually or in teams. The goal of the interviews is to determine whether individuals possess the competencies necessary to achieve exemplary work results. This may be done by requesting work samples from experienced applicants or examining work histories for the behavioral anchors associated with the desired competencies. Consequently, selections are based on data rather than opinions. HR practitioners frequently comment that competency-based selection is probably one of the fairest and therefore most defensible approaches their organizations have used.

Next, HR practitioners clarify the selection methods to be used in reaching a decision. Regardless of the work to be performed, the selection methods chosen should provide as much advance information as possible about those competencies that are the most critical for exemplary performance of the work. A competency assessment report from a former supervisor would offer this kind of valuable insight, for example.

Selection methods generally fall into two categories. One category has to do with assessing the individual's ability to perform the work. Methods in this category are competency based. One example might be job applications that seek information about individual competencies instead of work history or credentials that may not be directly related to proven performance. Another example is preparation of structured interview guides to solicit information about competencies linked to successful or exemplary performance and the behavioral indicators associated with them. Methods in the second category address the individual's fitness to perform and take into consideration additional requirements, such as drug tests and medical examinations, that are peripheral to an applicant's ability to perform.

In Step 3, HR practitioners shorten the list of applicants; when using the competency-based approach, they work with managers to compare evidence of competencies with competency-based selection criteria. HR practitioners should focus their attention on the applicants' competencies as discovered and documented to the minimally acceptable, fully successful, or exemplary competency requirements for the department, occupation, work role, or job category. Individual competencies are therefore the primary criteria for narrowing the field of applicants.

Finalists are chosen in the next step. What is the difference between a traditional approach and a competency-based approach at this stage of the selection process? The traditional approach relies on a considerable number of assumptions about a candidate's qualifications, based on superficial evidence of ability, such as academic degrees or work and salary history. In a competency-based approach, the guesswork is largely eliminated. The goal of competency-based selection is to go beyond the superficial to discover real evidence of ability to perform, based on interview questions that explore actual experience or work samples that verify an applicant's ability to create outputs much like those required for the position. Persons with little experience may be tested for the ability to create the work products necessary for job success.

Steps 5 and 6 of the traditional selection process shown in Figure 7 cover interviews and final selection. Competency-based selection relies on carefully planned behavioral event interviews. Much attention is focused on the interview questions, how they are asked, the setting, and the approach used to assess results. We provide a detailed discussion of these points in a later section of this chapter.

———————————

An example of competency-based interviewing using a behavioral event interview can be seen at the Veterans Affairs Medical Center (VAMC) in Gainesville, Florida. Competency-based interviewing has been used at the Gainesville facility for more than ten years since a train-the-trainer program was introduced by the Veterans Affairs Nursing Service. In developing an interview tool for a staff nurse position, key criteria for a nurse to succeed are identified by a nurse manager and experienced unit staff. Expectations for the job are developed along with a job description. Questions are then prioritized, and the method of interviewing is determined. VAMC has found that an important consideration for the interviews is matching the number of questions to the amount of time for the interview. Applicants are prescreened, and a determination is made as to whether eligibility requirements are met. The nurse manager then decides who will conduct the interview.

Panels are often preferable in competency-based interviews; however, an individual can also conduct the interview. At VAMC, a panel of two or three members, including the first-line manager, experienced staff members, and an additional head nurse, is often used. Sometimes an applicant is interested in more than one position, and then other appropriate nurse managers are included on the panel.

Before the interview is conducted, representatives of VAMC welcome the applicant and introductions are made. An overview of the interview is then described to the applicant. VAMC notes that it is beneficial to indicate to the applicant that the interview will provide the opportunity to share work experiences as well as the demonstration of both skills and capabilities. The applicant is also informed that there will be notes taken during the interview. While the interview is taking place, interviewers rate both verbal and non-

verbal responses to questions and scenarios that afford the opportunity for both objectivity and consistency. It also serves as a reminder following the interview.

Ratings at VAMC are (+) positive, (0) neutral, or (−) negative. Ratings are done independently without any discussion. Final scores are calculated by figuring the percentage of each rating based on the possible number. Finally, it is determined which applicant is the best match for the job. At VAMC, guidelines on acceptable scores are not available, but decisions are made by those conducting the interview. In arriving at a decision, competencies are considered as are the learning needs and the willingness of staff and the organization to support training. At VAMC, much credit is given for the success of a competency-based interview to the planning of the interview process itself. (Blazey & MacLeod, 1996)

Step 7 involves the negotiation of a compensation and benefits package with the successful candidate. This step is essentially the same for both approaches. It is worth noting, however, that in competency-based selection, the organization's representative is negotiating primarily to purchase the candidate's talent, or competency, pool rather than to simply "fill the slot." Thus, competency issues dramatically underlie the negotiations, even if they are not explicit. It is important for HR practitioners to understand this as a philosophical point.

Steps 8 and 9 of the traditional selection process are basically unchanged with a competency-based approach. The purpose of Step 9, however, is slightly different. Verification applies to the successful candidate's competency in a technical or professional area—for example, medicine, engineering, plumbing, boiler maintenance, or psychotherapy—and may require evidence such as licenses or employer references to support an applicant's claim of experience or credentials.

The last step is to validate the selection decision. In a competency-based process, HR practitioners work with the new employees' managers to determine how well performance matches up to expectations and work requirements.

A key consideration is the demonstration of competencies within the employer's unique corporate culture.

A competency-based, multirater feedback process is just one of many possible methods. Or employees and their immediate supervisors might participate in a two-part probationary performance management process in which both parties provide competency and results ratings.

In summary, there are significant differences between traditional and competency-based employee recruitment and selection processes. Consequently, making a transition to a competency-based approach requires considerable time, money, and effort on the part of the organization and its HR staff. The benefits, however, may exceed the costs, particularly if the competency-based approach increases the percentage of exemplary performers within the organization.

The Advantages and Challenges of Competency-Based Employee Recruitment and Selection

There are several key advantages to competency-based employee recruitment and selection.

First, competency-based recruitment and selection are results oriented. They make it easier to concentrate on the results expected of a successful or exemplary performer. They focus less attention on approximations of competence—such as educational level or years of experience—that have little connection to verifiable results.

Second, competency-based recruitment plays an important role in attracting individuals who possess characteristics that might be difficult, if not impossible, to acquire by training or development efforts. A competency-based approach encourages managers and other decision makers to clarify the verifiable, measurable results they expect from successful performers before a selection decision is made. That makes selection methods more effective, which reduces turnover, since the persons who are hired are more likely to do well in jobs or work roles that are matched to their existing or potential competencies (Wood & Payne, 1998). Competency-based selection also provides some insight into whether or not a new hire will be a good fit with the organization's culture (Guinn, 1998). In addition, competency-based practices can be very effective in hiring for virtual or flextime positions (Vincola & Mobley, 1999).

Third, a competency-based recruitment and selection process provides applicants with opportunities to outline, explain, and demonstrate their qualifications in competency-based terms. People will not be confronted during the selection process with questions that have little or no bearing on their ability to produce desired work results.

Fourth, since competencies are readily transferable across work situations, competency-based selection may help the organization to function effectively even during times of rapid or unanticipated change. Of course, there are limitations. For example, the demonstration of a competency is often grounded in a unique segment of the corporate culture and might not be amenable to transfer.

Fifth, competency-based recruitment and selection processes give HR practitioners an opportunity to plan for developing competencies for new hires and for experienced workers who must be reassigned.

Sixth, competency-based hiring methods do not discriminate. They encourage managers to clarify the desired work results and to find individuals who can achieve those results regardless of age, race, gender, sexual orientation, ethnic background, religion, or other considerations that have little or no bearing on their ability to perform.

Seventh, competency-based selection methods can underscore the competencies of candidates during succession planning initiatives. That makes it easier to identify backups for key positions.[3]

And eighth, competency-based hiring processes can reduce traditional training times by ensuring the selection of applicants who can perform. It also helps to raise the bar on performance, especially in organizations that seek potential exemplary performers.

There are no panaceas, however. Competency-based recruitment and selection present some challenges.

Competency-based processes require a disciplined and regulated approach to job and work analyses. HR practitioners must verify and validate the outcomes of the analyses and ensure their accuracy. Competency identification and modeling also demand commitment of time and other resources. Many organizations are unwilling or unable to invest in these activities.

Competency-based approaches are not appropriate for recruiting and selecting unskilled or semiskilled workers. Individual discretion, a key issue in competencies, is not a major factor in these jobs as it is in professional and managerial positions.

Using competency-based job information in recruitment could dramatically increase the cost of advertising, since extensive information on the job and candidate requirements must be published.

Competency-based selection requires the investment of substantial numbers of hours by managers and others involved in group interviewing and assessments. Managers in particular are often difficult to schedule for these activities, especially when an organization has downsized.

Deciding on Competency-Based or Traditional Employee Recruitment and Selection

Employee recruitment and selection should be handled traditionally under the following conditions:

- Decision makers are unwilling to make the substantial investments in time, money, and effort that are necessary for researching and validating competencies for any of the organization's jobs.

- The organization's resources are limited and cannot be committed to establishing a competency-based approach.

- The organization's need is for unskilled or semiskilled workers with whom a competency-based approach is not that useful.

- Candidates' competencies have already been documented or verified through a comprehensive and systematic process, as is the case with medical doctors, and only minimal additional competency assessment must be completed in order to select a capable job candidate.

- Recruitment and selection activities must be completed within a very limited period of time.

A competency-based approach to employee recruitment and selection is probably most appropriate in the following situations:

- The selected workers must complete work of strategic importance to the organization.

- The organization needs to fill leadership and management positions.

- Decision makers will commit the resources needed to carry out the competency-based recruitment and selection processes.

- It is necessary to fill "high stakes" jobs or specialized work roles for individual contributors or team members in an intensely demanding work environment.

There have been many research studies on competency-based recruitment and selection.

In a study conducted by the American Compensation Association published in 1996, researchers found that 88% of respondents use competency-based interviews, which is the most frequently cited competency-based technique. The study also surveyed respondents on their decision-making practices in the five major staffing categories: hiring and selection, job placement, promotions, succession planning, and terminations. Results in these areas were as follows: for job placement, 70% used competency-based interviews and 59% used supervisor assessments; for promotions, 68% used supervisor assessments and 49% used competency-based interviews; for succession planning, 54% used supervisor assessments and 32% used multirater assessments; for termination, 42% used supervisor assessments. Managers have received training in conducting behavioral interviews, as indicated by 6 out of 10 respondents, and 57% provide competency criteria to recruiters and placement firms. The majority of respondents, however, do not believe that candidates should be rejected because of poor alignment of competencies, and only 38% reject candidates based on competency assessment as long as they meet or exceed all other job or role criteria. Only one respondent faced a legal challenge in any of the five major staffing categories ("The Role of Competencies in an Integrated HR Strategy," 1996).

The findings of another study indicated that 75% of respondent organizations use job and role competencies in selection and promotion (Cook & Bernthal, 1998).

In a study of nonprofit organizations, 29 respondents suggested competency-based selection as a way of creating a higher quality applicant pool. Recommendations based on the study included wider dissemination of information about job openings and hiring practices based on measurable competencies linked to requirements for the job rather than on colleague referrals (Knowlton, 2001).

Results from a 1999 survey of more than a thousand North American companies indicated that lower turnover rates are experienced by 36% of those respondents that use competency-based selection and hiring practices. The survey also indicated that 43% of respondents using competency-based selection experience higher levels of productivity (O'Daniell, 1999).

Findings in a survey conducted in by Schoonover, Schoonover, Nemerov, and Ehly (2000) indicated that 53% of respondents consider hiring as the area in which the application of competencies is "very effective" or "effective," and 38% find competency-based job descriptions "very effective" or "effective."

A Model for Competency–Based Employee Recruitment and Selection

How does an organization go about implementing a competency-based recruitment and selection system? The main difference between the traditional and the competency-based approach is largely one of emphasis. The competency-driven system naturally is weighted toward competencies that can be documented, discussed during formal interviews, and demonstrated on the job.

The model portrayed in Figure 8 can be applied to implementing competency-based recruitment and selection for an entire organization or for only select portions of it. In an ideal world, we would be able to implement the model organization wide, but finite resources often dictate more limited use.

Implementing the Model

Steps 1 through 4 describe competency-based recruitment. Competency-based selection is explained in Steps 5 through 11.

Step 1: Identify HR and job recruitment needs
Every recruitment action should be an outcome of a larger, competency-based HR planning process. Therefore, the first step of this model requires the organization's leaders to return to their HR system plans and account for their recruitment need in strategic terms. As a result of this inquiry, they should be able to answer the following kinds of ques-

Figure 8: **Competency-Based Employee Recruitment and Selection**

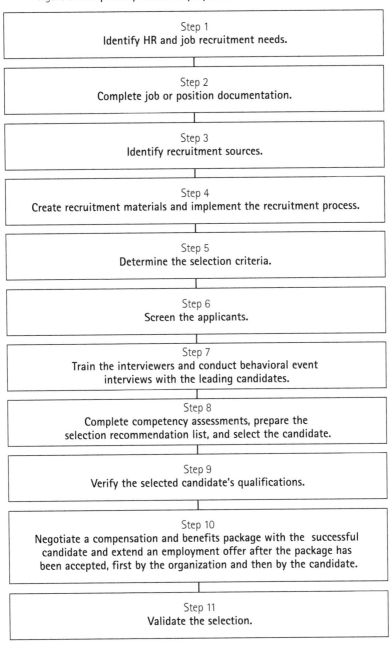

Step 1
Identify HR and job recruitment needs.

Step 2
Complete job or position documentation.

Step 3
Identify recruitment sources.

Step 4
Create recruitment materials and implement the recruitment process.

Step 5
Determine the selection criteria.

Step 6
Screen the applicants.

Step 7
Train the interviewers and conduct behavioral event interviews with the leading candidates.

Step 8
Complete competency assessments, prepare the selection recommendation list, and select the candidate.

Step 9
Verify the selected candidate's qualifications.

Step 10
Negotiate a compensation and benefits package with the successful candidate and extend an employment offer after the package has been accepted, first by the organization and then by the candidate.

Step 11
Validate the selection.

tions. What outputs or results will the recruited employee produce? How will those outputs or results contribute to the strategic success of the organization? Could the organization continue to meet its strategic business objectives without filling this job? When is the best time to implement this job? Demonstration of what key competencies will enable the successful candidate to produce the expected outputs or results? What are the best sources of those competencies?

After decision makers have determined that embarking on the recruitment process will serve the best interests of the organization, the HR practitioner can proceed to the next stage of the recruitment effort.

Step 2: Complete job or position documentation

With recruitment activities commencing, the HR department begins documenting the job and work to be completed in the forms of a job description and a job specification. In doing so, HR practitioners must keep in mind that competency-based job or position documentation must embody the premise that competencies are the foundation for all performance.

If job information has not yet been assembled, the HR practitioner must complete the work, since the analyzed data will be part of the job documentation. The following job analysis information must be re-searched:

- Work outputs or results
- Work activities
- Work tasks
- Competencies and associated behavioral indicators
- Competency model

In addition, the functional manager for the job must identify any of the following that are appropriate:

- Educational requirements or qualifications
- Work samples of successful outputs
- Experience with the same or related work, including possibly the length of time spent performing the work
- License or certification requirements from government, academic, professional, or other organizations

- Other requirements related to the employee's ability and capability to complete the work

Step 3: Identify recruitment sources

At this stage of the process, the HR practitioner, usually with suggestions from the functional manager for the position, who is responsible for the work to be performed, will identify sources for recruiting high-potential candidates. In a competency-based environment, the recruitment process requires a focus on competency sources or pools of recognized effectiveness in the area of the recruitment. The HR specialist must work with the manager and others in the functional area to identify traditional and nontraditional sources of talent so that information on the position can be made available to them. It may be worth analyzing sources of exemplary performers and targeting recruitment to historical sources for the best talent.

Step 4: Create recruitment materials and implement the recruitment process

The major objective in this step is to encourage only the most highly qualified candidates (i.e., exemplary performers) to express their interest in the job. Remember: Competencies and their availability in the applicant pool drive this type of recruitment effort!

The content of recruitment materials is a critical element at this stage of the process. It should communicate the values, vision, core competencies, and industry status of the organization with the intent of encouraging exemplary applicants to want to work for the organization and thereby share its vision, values, and intentions. The expected work outputs or results and general requirements and conditions of the job should also be made very clear in recruitment materials. In addition, the minimum and preferred educational, age, and other requirements (for example, certifications) must be mentioned in recruitment materials. The competencies needed for successful performance must be described in plain language that can be understood by any person who can read at the intermediate-school level.

Written applications should give specific information on what the HR department needs from applicants in order to determine their viability as job candidates. An organization that is serious about hiring for competencies should be able to screen applicants on competency requirements with a high degree of reliability using documentation the applicants provide. This can be done in a straightforward manner by instructing applicants to list each competency followed by a two- or three-sentence description of its use in the same or a similar performance context and how much time they spent using it. They should also be directed to specifically document their competencies with education, training, or long-term learning experiences. Although the application received from a candidate in a competency-based recruitment process might be considerably lengthier than a traditional application, it enables more effective screening for the position.

Step 5: Determine the selection criteria
As they begin the selection part of the hiring process, HR practitioners and their customers must determine the criteria to be used. They must agree on the correct mixture of information, out of the volume of data received from applicants, and weight each item so as to accurately assess the candidates' competency strengths and predict their likelihood of success on the job.

What information should be used to establish the selection criteria? Organizations use the following items to collect information from job candidates:

- Job application form specifically designed to collect detailed competency information as well as traditional information
- Reference statement from former organizational leaders and competency assessments completed by persons with in-depth knowledge
- Statements of work, academic, and life accomplishments
- Test data and their analyses with the use of instruments such as the *Sixteen Personality Factor™ Questionnaire* (16PF®) assessment, *California Psychological Inventory™* (CPI™) assessment, *Edwards Personal Preference Schedule* (EPPS), Holland Types, *Jackson Vocational Interest Survey* (JVIS), *Kuder Preference Record,* and *Strong Interest Inventory®* assessment.
- Work sample assessments
- Simulation interviews
- Documented work and life experience factors

- Certificates
- Licenses
- Ratings from peers, immediate supervisors, or direct reports, including competency assessment data from a multirater competency assessment process
- Assessment center data, if available

Since every selection situation has its own unique set of competency requirements, it would not be appropriate for us to suggest a formula or weighting method for general application. Decision makers must specify the required versus the preferred competencies before reviewing candidates' qualifications. Next, a qualified HR practitioner or other qualified professional should construct a one-to-one or one-to-several correspondence between the job competency requirements and the qualifications data submitted by the candidate as documentation for each of the competencies.

Step 6: Screen the applicants

Typically, the number of responses an employer receives for an advertised position far exceeds the number of job openings. Consequently, only the most promising among the pool of candidates will be selected for a formal interview or otherwise continue to participate in the selection process.

Although screening will never be an entirely scientific procedure, it certainly must be systematically completed. The process must give equal weight to all candidates when competency profiles are assessed and the first pool of finalists is chosen. The HR professional must have a clear understanding of the minimum requirements for competency, experience, education, and other credentials and apply them equitably to each profile. When there is doubt regarding a candidate's qualifications, the organization should err on the side of having too many candidates and include the person in question in the pool.

A two-level screening process may be completed for candidates whose qualifications are still unclear. Sometimes a simple telephone call to the candidate will clarify the situation so that a decision can be made.

When the paper screening is complete, the functional manager will review the list of the most qualified candidates. The HR representative might want to review some of the findings from the screening process in order to obtain guidance on the customer's preferences for formal interviews or other interventions.

Formal interviews with the leading candidates make up the next stage in the screening process. With a competency-based interviewing process, we suggest that only the top five candidates be included in the first interview pool. Ideally, competency-based interviews should be completed by an interview panel, and competency assessments by the panel should follow completion of the interviews. Each candidate, all members of the panel, and possibly a recorder must participate in both the interviews and the assessment sessions. This presents quite a challenge in today's business world, in which staff resources are stretched so thin. If the process is to be completed virtually, the logistics become even more labor-intensive. After the interviews and assessment sessions, the panel must meet and reach agreement on the competency assessments for each person interviewed. This requires more logistics. We don't want to discourage you from using these processes. It can be done if they are well planned.

Step 7: Train the interviewers and conduct behavioral event interviews with the leading candidates

What is wrong with traditional job interviewing questions and techniques? The answer to this question could consume many pages in this book, but we will keep our answer brief.

First, traditional interview questions such as "Tell me about yourself" tend to provide little or no information about the candidate's qualifications for the job. You might learn that this person really enjoys cooking French food, but what does that have to do with the competencies that are required to successfully teach Greek archaeology in a secondary school in Yugoslavia? The connection is not an obvious one.

Second, traditional job interviews are not conducted systematically. This leads frustrated candidates to charge that they did not have an adequate opportunity to outline their qualifications for the position, that inappropriate discussion items were raised, or that deliberate or systematic bias was introduced, thus compromising their candidacy.

When a systematic, planned, and disciplined competency-based interview process has been used, all of these criticisms vanish. The interview process focuses only on the work to be performed by the successful applicant, the relationship of his or her experience to that work, and the competencies presented by the candidate to be used in producing the expected outputs or results. The process alone is sound, but it is made even more so because interviewers are trained, were certified by their trainers, and have practiced the use of the behavioral event interview technique for selection purposes.[4]

L'Oreal, an international cosmetics firm, uses behavioral event interviews in its competency-based selection practices for hiring salespeople, according to the Consortium for Research on Emotional Intelligence in Organizations. The behavioral event interview used by L'Oreal was developed by its consultant, with the goal of identifying key competencies in successful sales. Those selected through the behavioral interview method achieved $91,370 more in sales annually than did those selected by the previously used method (*Competency-Based Selection*, 2002).

Since the details for training interviewers and using behavioral event interviews for selection purposes are quite extensive and have been explained elsewhere, we will not duplicate that information here. Instead, we suggest that you review portions of *Competence at Work* that focus on interviewing (Spencer & Spencer, 1993, pp. 114–155).

Before we proceed to the next step of our model, we offer the following suggestion. Because behavioral event interviews typically require at least 1 to 2 hours for each candidate, we recommend that the HR customer (the functional manager, for example) identify for interview panel members the strategic competencies that must be present for exemplary performance of the work. These strategic competencies should be the ones explored during the interview process. With a concise list, the panel might be able to concentrate on key competencies and interview a larger number of candidates. Under all circumstances, we strongly recommend identifying key items for all interviews.

Step 8: Complete competency assessments, prepare the selection recommendation list, and select the candidate

After the interview panel has completed its competency assessments and selection recommendations, a selection can be made.

Typically, although not always, the interview panel sends a report on the candidates' competency ratings to the decision maker. Panel members usually complete further analyses of the competency strengths of the candidates relative to work demands, and they will often call special situations to the attention of leaders in charge of selection. The report must be objective, fair, and free of bias. The panel must never attempt to subvert or undermine the selecting manager's authority to recommend or make a decision. More often than not, a decision maker who was not a member of the interview panel will want to interview at least the leading candidate for the position and come to his or her own conclusions on the candidate's qualifications and fit in the work environment. The manager might decide to interview additional candidates or even all the candidates who were interviewed by the panel. This is his or her right and it must be honored. HR practitioners might need to provide guidance on the details of a competency-based approach to recruitment and selection, and they should speak frankly about the professional aspects of the processes and the outcomes to date.

In some situations, selection decisions must be supported by higher management. Interview panel data on competency strengths can be highly useful for making a final decision.

Step 9: Verify the selected candidate's qualifications

Before an employment offer is made, it is essential to verify the preferred candidate's qualifications as they were presented in the application materials and during the interview process. Organizations of all types and sizes must complete thorough due diligence investigations in human resource matters.

In some circumstances, an organization could put the lives or well-being of others at risk by hiring an unqualified person. For example, a medical doctor without a verified M.D. degree or a license to practice medicine in the proper jurisdiction could cause injury and possibly death to patients. The same cautions apply to other areas of expertise, such as, for example, building engineering staff. Having less than a fully skilled and licensed boiler engineer in charge of an office tower heating system would be irresponsible. Never neglect due diligence responsibilities, especially when making a selection decision.

Step 10: Negotiate a compensation and benefits package with the successful candidate and extend an employment offer after the package has been accepted, first by the organization and then by the candidate

This step proceeds as it typically would in a traditional hiring situation, but one suggestion seems appropriate for a competency-based environment. Representatives of the organization who handle this step of the process must remember that the organization is negotiating to purchase a highly valuable commodity: human competence. This means that the process and the candidate must be treated with a high degree of respect and consideration. It is important also for the representatives to remember that many person-hours have been invested in the competency investigations and the dividends on this investment must be captured through a successful and reasonable outcome to the negotiations.

Step 11: Validate the selection

Now that the employee is on the job, one final question remains: Was this a valid selection? If the use of a competency-based recruitment and selection process resulted in an organizationally useful selection, then we are satisfied that the approach is working. In this step, we are not presenting a method of determining whether the best selection was made, nor are we attempting to determine the future use of the process based solely on the outcomes of one selection. Research needed to answer those questions must be more rigorously designed and controlled.

The most direct method of validating the selection is to examine the new employee's performance at key points during his or her employment history. Always keep in mind when reviewing performance that persons are employed by organizations to produce outputs or results that are valued by the organization, its customers or clients, or both. The new employee must have been on the job and had sufficient time to begin producing the expected outputs or results. This consideration affects the timing and circumstances of data collection.

In our experience, an individual must be on the job and fully immersed in the work culture and external environment of the organization for 12 to 18 months before useful data can be collected. Except for low-skilled or unskilled jobs, a 6-month probationary period is not sufficient to allow the employee to become fully integrated with and productive in an organization.

Others might disagree with this position. They might argue that their organizations have highly structured and competency-based performance management systems in place that support new-hire performance at every step during the first 6 months of employment and that reliable and valid conclusions can indeed be drawn after only 6 months on the job. We accept that possibility. However, our experience with a wide variety of organizations indicates that our caution is reasonable. Allow time and provide performance support before making decisions on performance.

What kind of data should an investigator collect and analyze in order to validate a selection decision? Answering the following questions should provide much of the needed insight:

- What measurable outputs or results did the employee produce, and at what level of quality? Were they produced in a timely or agreed-upon manner? Was the customer or client satisfied with the outputs or results?

- What were the outcomes of a competency assessment (with data provided by, at a minimum, the new-hire's immediate manager) for the competencies that were used to make the selection decision? How do the results of the on-the-job assessment compare with those of the pre-hire interview panel members?

- What are the new-hire's thoughts, feelings, and actions relative to his or her work performance, the organization, its customers, and his or her fit with those entities?

In an ideal world, the answers to these three classes of questions would reveal a consistently high fit between the employee and the organization. When that does not occur, as may be the case, then the following additional questions might be helpful:

- Did we hire a competent person (as defined by the selection criteria) but then place performance roadblocks in the way that impeded the new hire's producing the expected outputs or results in a timely manner and at the expected level of quality?

- Did we provide adequate performance support for this new employee?

- Have there been changes in the organization or its clients or customers since the selection decision was made, and, if so, has the situation affected the employee's performance in an adverse manner?

- In what ways do the organizational and work unit cultures affect the employee's thoughts, feelings, and actions? What are the dimensions of these impacts? If there is a mismatch, how could it have been averted or possibly detected during the interview processes?

These questions may be sufficient, depending on the work situation. A one-time assessment is probably not entirely enough to determine the validity of the selection decision, but at the least, an initial investigation should be made.

Summary

This chapter examined competency-based recruitment and selection, two closely aligned processes. A competency-based approach differs more in focus than in content from its traditional counterpart and demands more resources from the organization. For a competency-based approach, HR practitioners establish competency models by job category, department, work role, or occupation and attempt to match individual competencies to those models. In contrast, the traditional approach relies on implicit links between the work as defined in job descriptions and the qualifications of an applicant to carry it out. Competency-based recruitment and selection are not always appropriate for all positions and present challenges as well as offer significant advantages.[5]

CHAPTER 6

Competency-Based
Employee Training

Through employee training, individuals learn to adjust to the corporate culture of an organization and become or remain productive under changing conditions. This chapter compares traditional and competency-based views of employee training. As we explore those processes, we will address the following questions:

- What is employee training?
- How is training traditionally carried out?
- How can training become competency based?
- What are the advantages and challenges of a competency-based approach to employee training?
- When should employee training be competency based, and when should it be handled traditionally?
- What model can guide competency-based training, and how is it implemented?

Employee Training

Rothwell and Sredl (2000) describe training as "a short-term learning intervention. It is intended to build on individual knowledge, skills, and attitudes to meet present or future work requirements" (p. 9). Training should have an immediate and highly specific impact on work performance and should be grounded on the organization's requirements and unique corporate culture. It differs in this respect from education and employee development, which prepare the individual for life and work.

There are various types of training. Remedial training helps people meet the basic screening or entry-level requirements for a job. Orientation training helps to socialize individuals into a corporate culture. Qualifying training assists individuals with meeting basic performance expectations and thus increases their productivity. Second-chance training is provided to those who may be transferred or terminated because they are not meeting organizational work standards. Cross training is for people who are trying to master new jobs or job skills. Retraining provides upgrading to keep skills current as technological or organizational conditions change. Outplacement training prepares individuals for departure from an organization in the wake of retirement, or organizational staffing changes.[1]

Research suggests increased spending on training. In 1998, the amount spent on corporate training was $62.5 billion ("Industry Report," 1999). The American Society for Training and Development (ASTD) annual review reported that overall expenditures for training increased from $677 per employee in 1999 to $704 in 2000. The same study noted that training costs climbed from 1.8% of annual payroll in 1999 to 2.0% in 2000 (Van Buren & Erskine, 2002).

Van Buren and Erskine (2002) reported the results of the Future Search conference, held in June 2001 in conjunction with the ASTD International Conference and Exposition. The Academy for Human Resource Development and ASTD's Research-to-Practice National Committee were cosponsors. During the conference, "Shaping the Future: Leading Workplace Learning and Performance in the New Millennium," more than 60 specially selected individuals discussed their perspectives on the future of the field and predicted the trends that they believed would affect workplace learning and performance. The top ten trends, in order of importance, centered on money, diversity, time, work, world, meaning, change, knowledge, technology, and careers (Van Buren & Erskine, 2002).

Traditional Training

Training may be unplanned or planned. In unplanned training, individuals are asked to shadow experienced performers. That may involve "sitting by Nellie" or "following Joe around the plant." It is rarely effective, since people cannot learn how to perform by merely watching others.

If training is planned, then it should follow an approach based on the instructional systems design (ISD) model. The ISD model is a systematic approach to training. Although many models depicting ISD have been published, they have several important features in common.

The ISD model begins by analyzing the performance problem, with the goal of determining its underlying cause. Is the reason for the problem a lack of individual knowledge, skill, or appropriate attitude, or is there some other cause? If the problem is not rooted in the performance of an individual, it must be addressed through management action, not through training.

The second step of the ISD model is to examine organizational requirements, job or work requirements, and individual requirements. The following key questions may be included in this step:

- What are the working conditions in which individuals are expected to apply what they have learned in training, and how will those conditions affect that application?

- What are the job or work requirements, and how clearly do individuals understand the results expected from them?

- Who is being trained, and what can we reasonably assume that they already know about the topic on which they are being trained?

The answers to these questions and consideration of related conditions should clarify both the training context and the context in which learning is applied. In this step, HR practitioners seek to clarify the context in which training occurs and is subsequently applied.

In the third step of the ISD model, the HR practitioner conducts a thorough training needs assessment (TNA). A TNA identifies what workers must know, do, or feel if they are to perform work that meets organizational expectations. It then compares those performance requirements to what the individuals actually know, do, or feel as they work. The purpose of a TNA is to pinpoint knowledge, skill, or attitude deficiencies that can be addressed through training.

Writing instructional objectives is the fourth step of the ISD model. An instructional objective states successful results of training and thereby how to meet a training need. Attaining the objective rectifies the deficiency. In a sense, then, an instructional objective expresses what a person can do when training is completed.

In the fifth step of the ISD model, decision makers determine whether to prepare or purchase the training content needed to achieve the instructional objective. In some cases, they may feel the need to tailor the training content to the corporate culture, in which case it must usually be designed in-house.

The sixth step in applying the ISD model is to decide on the means of delivering the training. There are, of course, many methods, such as classroom-based training, e-learning, on-the-job training, and video- or audio-based instruction. The chosen approach must strike a balance between cost and instructional effectiveness.

A process that utilizes technology to deliver learning is called a *learning technology*. Learning technologies are frequently divided by method into two types: the presentation method and the distribution method (Van Buren & Erskine, 2002). A *presentation method* presents instruction to learners, as occurs in computer-based training, for example. A *distribution method* sends training to users, such as by providing courses to company suppliers on CD-ROMs.

Electronically driven training is sometimes called *e-learning*. The term is applied to a variety of applications and processes that include Web-based and computer-based learning, virtual classrooms, digital collaboration, and the use of the Internet, intranets, extranets, audiotape, videotape, satellite broadcast, interactive TV, and CD-ROM (Kaplan-Leiserson, n.d.). Research results suggest that the e-learning market for the United States will grow to reach an estimated $23 billion worldwide in 2004 (Goodridge, 2001). *Blended learning,* which is gaining popularity, combines several presentation methods (Kaplan-Leiserson, n.d.).[2]

Conducting a formative evaluation is the seventh step in applying the ISD model. It pilot tests the training before it is delivered on a widespread basis.

The eighth step of the ISD model is the implementation phase, when the training is delivered to targeted participants.

The ninth step in applying the ISD model is a summative evaluation. This final assessment is designed to evaluate issues such as the participants' reactions to the training, the effectiveness of the training process and its content, and the impact to the organization's bottom line.

The ISD model has proved effective in improving job performance. Unfortunately, this well-known approach tends to place much responsibility for all phases of training on trainers, which may weaken a sense of ownership among learners and their organizational superiors.[3]

Making Training Competency Based

Organizations today are finding competencies to be of great value in their training practices. Greengard (2001) offers a discussion on some of these practices. For example, Ford Financial uses a skill- and competency-based learning program that affords employees an opportunity to view information such as the skills and competencies needed for positions. General Electric uses a formal competency analysis program, based on 45 different behaviors, to assist in meeting its training needs.

The American Compensation Association (now WorldatWork) surveyed 60 respondents whose organizations either used or were developing competency-based training about practices in their organizations (*Raising the Bar,* 1996). Respondents indicated that methods such as formal classroom training, job expansion or development experiences, formal coaching or mentoring, self-directed study, and job rotation were most frequently successful in building competencies. Respondents noted that their most commonly used approaches to competency-based training and development included unrestricted eligibility for programs, self-selection, application of job, service, grade, or similar criteria, and objective assessment of needs.

Researchers Cook and Bernthal (1998) found in a 1998 study that 75% of 292 participants indicated the extent to which job and role competencies support HR systems was "moderate/great." Only 25% indicated "small/not at all."

Training can become competency based in at least three ways.

1. Reinvent the ISD model.
2. Train to build individual competence relative to a competency model of exemplary performance.
3. Build individual competence in a work team context.

These approaches are not mutually exclusive, but they do represent different emphases.

Reinventing the ISD Model

When the ISD model is reoriented toward building worker competence to achieve exemplary performance rather than matching individual abilities to work requirements, training becomes competency based.

One key point of change centers on the third step in the ISD model, the training needs assessment. A traditional TNA pinpoints performance gaps that can be closed through training, but the focus of the TNA changes with a competency-based approach. Since competency models encompass all the variables that underlie successful job performance—not just knowledge, skill, and attitudes—then performance gaps must be systematically identified in broader terms for competency-based practices. In short, the competency-based approach views training as more than providing knowledge, building skill, or improving attitude.

It may sound easy to move training from its traditional focus on meeting needs to a new focus on building competencies, but that is not really the case. Training people to become successful (or even exemplary) performers dramatically expands the role of training. For instance, that might mean pinpointing and building competencies that go beyond knowledge, skills, and attitude to include motivation levels, personality traits, awareness of bodies of knowledge, or any of those variables that may be developed and which distinguish exemplary from fully successful performers.

The key to transforming traditional training into competency-based training is thus centered on the training needs assessment process and its focus. Instead of limiting attention to work requirements as in the traditional approach, the goal is to discover the differences between exemplary and fully successful performers and trying to narrow those differences. Competency-based training may involve the more challenging activities of changing individual motivation levels and cultivating the development of personality traits. Not all competency deficiencies can be resolved with a high-powered training program, however, no matter how innovative its design or method of delivery. For example, how can an organization train its employees to be more patient? If a particular competency is critical to success in the work, decision makers may prefer to modify the selection criteria for that job.

Other enhancements to the ISD model can also make training competency based. During performance analysis, for example, trainers may adopt a broader goal than to determine whether a problem is due to a lack of individual knowledge, skill, or appropriate attitude or is rooted in some other cause. They may instead reframe the question in the following terms: "Is the problem caused by a lack of individual competence, or by an organizational or environmental factor that cannot be controlled by individuals?" If the reason is a deficiency in competence, training to build competence may resolve the problem, but if an organizational or environmental factor is the cause, management action, not training, is the appropriate response. This broader focus is what CEOs increasingly expect (Rothwell, Lindholm, & Wallick, 2003).

Training to Build Individual Competence

Another approach, the strategic systems model (SSM), is generally analogous to the ISD model. The SSM is implemented relative to internal as well as external factors that affect organizational and employee performance and is designed to accommodate the participation of persons from both environments. It is particularly useful for practitioners who must develop a curriculum that includes numerous training and other opportunities in systematic and strategic contexts for a diverse population of employees.[4]

In this approach, the responsibility for training—and for competency building—shifts from the organization to the individual. Although the organization remains responsible for clarifying the competencies essential for successful performance in a job category, work role, department, or occupation, individuals are expected to be more responsible for building their own competencies. They do that by being more proactive, assessing their competencies against existing competency models or those they develop on their own by, for example, talking to mentors or exemplary performers or keeping competency journals in which they record their process of building competencies.

Building Individual Competence in a Work Team Context

Most organizations in the United States have experimented with work teams. They present a special challenge, however, since team-based management usually directs attention to group rather than individual performance.

When teams become the focus of attention, it just makes sense to start thinking in terms of team or team member role competency models rather than job, department, work role, or occupational competence. Each individual works within a team, and its members should contribute to the collective ability to meet or exceed customer requirements. With a team competency model, individuals can be assessed against how well they demonstrate the needed competencies. Training can then help to narrow deficiencies in individual performance.

The Advantages and Challenges of Competency-Based Employee Training

Each of the three methods of transforming training from a traditional to a competency-based approach has its own set of advantages and challenges.

Advantages and Challenges of Reinventing the ISD Model

A competency model adds a rich dimension to traditional job analysis results. It portrays worker competencies clearly in terms that are specific to the organization. In short, competency models do more to ground training in the corporate culture.

The ISD model and the analogous SSM bring a systematic approach to training design, development, and delivery. Competency models augment both approaches by portraying how exemplary performers achieve their success. Using competency models as a foundation for training supplies a broader range of alternatives for raising performance levels than does training alone. Competency models provide a holistic approach that acknowledges dimensions to performance other than knowledge, skills, and attitudes.

There are also special challenges involved in reinventing the ISD model to accommodate competencies. Resources and time are required to research each competency model. In addition, competency-based training requires a paradigm shift from instruction for achieving single behavioral objectives to instruction for acquiring and applying the competencies needed for fully successful or exemplary performance. When the number of prospective learners is small or the shelf life of the training will be short, investments in competency-based training may not be cost-effective.

Advantages and Challenges of Training to Build Individual Competence

There are several possible advantages to orienting training toward building individual competence. Competency-based training is highly individualized to meet learner needs. Because the use of competencies focuses on learning objectives and expected performance outcomes, it allows learners to structure their activities and processes in ways that are most meaningful to them. With this approach to training, learners are able to identify and use many learning resources in diverse settings.[5] Training design based on competencies is especially desirable when the targeted performance area is of high strategic value to the organization.

There are, however, challenges to using this approach. Time and money must be available to carry out individualized competency identification and assessment for those targeted to receive training. And even after the organization commits its resources to the effort, some persons do not thrive with learning or processes that demand a high degree of personal involvement. Typically, these persons lack the self-discipline necessary to work in a self-directed way to achieve their own learning outcomes. Others may prefer to blend socialization with the learning process rather than pursue their goals individually, especially when they are building abstract competencies.

Advantages and Challenges of Building Individual Competence in a Work Team Context

A competency-based approach to training consistently communicates a common set of performance expectations to every team member. It focuses all training on meeting the individual needs that support successful and creative team performance. Competency-based training helps to keep team members focused on achieving exemplary performance.

There are special challenges to building individual competence within a work team context. Team-based training sometimes assumes homogenous thinking among team members, which can become groupthink. In short, the nature of teams is often a disincentive to becoming an exemplar because group cohesiveness, not stellar individual performance, is more prized. In a team culture, personal learning and growth take place within the boundaries established for the team and its performance in the organization. That can be experienced as restrictive to both individual or even group performance.

Deciding on Competency-Based or Traditional Employee Training

It is important to know when to use traditional training and when competency-based training is an appropriate choice.

Use traditional training based on the ISD model in the following situations:

- The organization's resources are insufficient for researching and validating a competency model.
- The shelf life of the training is limited or its objectives are short term.
- The targeted training population is small.
- The work does not have a strategic impact on organizational success.

Use competency-based training in the following situations:

- The organization has the resources available to research and validate a quality competency model.
- The work and related training content have a significantly high strategic impact on organizational success.

- Time is available to devote to competency identification, validation, and modeling.

- The training content shelf life is of sufficient length to justify the expense of researching and validating the competency model.

- The training population is large enough to warrant resource expenditure.

- Decision makers consider it appropriate to focus on achieving exemplary rather than fully successful performance when the training is complete.

Models for Competency-Based Training

There are three models for reinventing training around a competency foundation. The models correspond to the approaches to competency-based training we described in the previous sections of this chapter.

1. Reinventing the ISD model

2. Training to build individual competence relative to a competency model of exemplary performance

3. Building individual competence in a work team context

A Model for Competency-Based ISD

The competency-based ISD model reinvents each step of the traditional ISD model around a competency foundation.

The first step in applying the competency-based ISD model is called *performance analysis,* in which trainers analyze the performance problem. Traditional performance analysis is designed to separate problems that can be solved by training from problems that require management action, but performance analysis in the competency-based ISD model is different. The goal of the competency-based process is to determine whether the problem is caused by a lack of individual competence or by a lack of organizational competence.

Individual competence is related to the characteristics needed for an individual to meet or exceed organizational or customer performance requirements. *Organizational competence,* in contrast, refers to the organization's core competencies. In the competency-based ISD model, it is important to align individual performance with organizational or, more important, customer expectations. Some customer needs are predictable, such as for products or services, but there are additional, value-added elements that make some organizations preferable in a customer's eyes. Those elements are tied to the organization's core competence, which amounts to its strategic strengths.

By focusing attention on both individual and organizational competence, trainers move beyond a simple focus on an individual's knowledge, skill, and attitude and begin to consider organizational factors that may create barriers to individual—or exemplary—performance.

As in the traditional ISD model, the competency-based model requires trainers to examine organizational, individual, and work requirements. Instead of focusing on the minimum performance requirements, however, trainers who use the competency-based ISD model must specify the conditions essential for exemplary performance. Key questions to consider in this step may include the following:

- What working conditions are essential for exemplary performance?
- What competencies enable individuals to match the outputs of exemplary performers?
- Who is targeted for training, and how closely do those individuals approach the characteristics of exemplary performers?

The answers to these and related questions clarify the optimal context in which learning will subsequently be applied. The focus is on what it takes to create exemplary, not minimal, results.

In the third step in the model, the training needs assessment, the competency-based model expands the traditional focus of the ISD model to address all the variables that support exemplary performance. (See the section on reinventing the ISD model, on pp. 130–131, for more details.)

The fourth step in applying the competency-based ISD model is to write instructional objectives, specifying the behavioral indicators tied to exemplary work performance that must be demonstrated upon completion of training. Those indicators must be observable and measurable.

In the fifth step trainers must decide whether to prepare or purchase training content to achieve the instructional objectives identified in the previous step.

The sixth step in applying the competency-based ISD model is to select a method of delivering the training. Trainers must consider not only traditional issues such as the relative costs and benefits of different delivery methods but also whether the method is appropriate for the competency and perhaps even how to blend methods to achieve the best results. For instance, if the objective is to build writing skills, audiotape-based instructional delivery may not be the most effective approach.

The seventh step in applying the competency-based ISD model is to conduct a formative evaluation. In competency-based training, the formative evaluation is focused on how well the training builds competence. It is therefore particularly effective when exemplary performers or other work experts participate in reviewing the training and contribute their insights and know-how on achieving enhanced outputs or results.

The eighth step of the model is the implementation phase, when trainers actually offer the training to targeted participants.

A summative evaluation is the ninth step of the competency-based ISD model. Evaluation has long been an important topic in the training field. Increasingly, decision makers want to know what returns they have received on their expensive training investments. If training is competency based, the answer should be apparent, because every step of the process is linked to the results of fully successful or exemplary performance and the competencies required to achieve them.

HR practitioners should consider three key questions in evaluating competency-based training:

1. How well did the training succeed in building the competencies associated with essential results for the work to be performed?

2. How well does the learner's performance compare to the outputs of the organization's exemplary performers?

3. How well does the learner's performance match the organizational and customer requirements essential to maintaining a competitive advantage and optimal customer service?

These questions may be answered by asking learners to produce work products or simulate service delivery and then measuring the results against the objectives established before training was delivered. Another method is to note key discrepancies between a 360-degree competency assessment conducted before and after training for each learner. The goal of any 360-degree assessment should always be to determine how well the learner demonstrates the competencies required for essential work outputs or results on the job.

A Model for Competency-Based Self-Directed Training and Development

A competency-based model for self-directed training and development emphasizes the individual's increased responsibility for his or her own learning.

In the first step of the model, individuals decide to take more responsibility for their own learning and competency development. In the second and third steps, they access existing competency models and compare themselves to those models with input from organizational superiors or work experts. In the fourth step, they create individual development plans (IDPs) to close the gap between their perceived competencies and the competencies required for work success or exemplary performance. The fifth step is to implement the plan by participating in training and other developmental experiences designed to build the competencies specified in the IDPs. In the sixth step, they periodically compare their competency development to the models and consult knowledgeable performers and mentors. In the seventh step, they modify their IDPs as necessary in order to ensure that they are building competence and possibly to do further planning.

The individual learner evaluates the results of this approach in cooperation with mentors, peers, immediate organizational superiors, coworkers, and particularly with exemplary performers. A key concern throughout the process is to determine whether the individual produces at or near the level of an exemplary performer when the objectives of the IDP have been met.

A Model for Competency-Based Work Team Development

This model emphasizes both the group's ability to carry out its collective work and each individual's competence within the team context.

In the first step of the model, team performance is examined against the performance of exemplary teams. Second, HR or other practitioners develop a team competency model that includes specific competencies and behavioral indicators associated with exemplary team performance. In the third step, individual members are assessed against the team competency model using a 360-degree competency assessment or other method such as a performance test. Fourth, trainers compile the ratings of the entire team and use them to guide the training plans for team members. This may also result in a work team development plan for bringing the team's current performance closer to the level of an exemplary team. In the fifth step, team members undergo training and thus implement the plan to build the identified competencies. Sixth, team members periodically compare their team's competency development to the model. Seventh and finally, they modify the development plan to ensure that they are building competence.

HR practitioners evaluate the outcomes from the work team development plan. Did the team achieve performance that rivals exemplary teams? If it did, then the plan has been successful in guiding team development. If not, additional team development may be necessary.

Summary

In this chapter, we compared and contrasted traditional and competency-based views of employee training. We defined employee training and explained its purpose in organizations. The traditional approach to training was described in step-by-step form as it is applied through the ISD model.

Next, the question "How can training become competency based?" was answered. Three approaches were explained: reinventing the traditional ISD model; focusing attention on training to build individual competence; and building individual competence in a work team context. The advantages and challenges of each of these approaches to employee training were delineated and discussed.

This was followed by a discussion about when it is appropriate to use traditional and competency-based training. The chapter concluded by considering three models for competency-based training.[6]

CHAPTER 7

Competency-Based Performance Management

A formal system of performance management, carried out by executives, managers, supervisors, and team leaders, along with other members of the workforce, shapes human performance within an organization and affects the organization's ability to achieve its objectives.

This chapter answers the following questions:

- What is performance management?
- How is performance management traditionally carried out?
- How can performance management become competency based?
- What are the advantages and challenges of a competency-based approach to performance management?
- When should performance management be competency based, and when should it be handled traditionally?
- What model can guide competency-based performance management, and how is it implemented?

Performance Management

The term *performance management* means several things to workers in organizations around the world. For the purpose of providing a context for the information that follows, we are using Cripe's (1997) definition: a systematic process for "improving and sustaining human performance throughout an organization." Performance management acknowledges human competence as a key performance driver (adapted from Cripe, 1997). It is multidisciplinary and uses an integrated approach to competency assessment and development, performance observation and feedback, training, employee development, performance appraisal, and rewards.[1] It is important not to confuse performance management, which involves planning for performance and reviewing results, with *performance evaluation,* which reviews results at the end of a time period.

Traditional Performance Management

Traditionally, performance management systems concentrate on performance planning and evaluation, rewards and discipline, according to the *2000 Performance Management Survey* (2000).

Traditional performance management in organizations includes many HR activities that are intended to improve worker performance. These practices achieve an uncertain level of success, judging from the following common complaints from employees:

- "I dread my annual performance review. It's always the same. First, my supervisor tells me about how wonderfully I did certain things over the past year. And then the mood radically changes, and she tells me about all the things I did *not* do so well over the performance period. I wouldn't mind hearing about these things during my final appraisal if she had told me about them when she noticed them during the performance period. In fact, she knew about some of these issues months before the current performance period began but didn't tell me about them. If she had, I would have done something about them, and they wouldn't have shown up as performance deficiencies at the end of the year. I think it's my supervisor who's 'deficient'!"

- "I don't know what my job is and isn't around here. One day I'm supposed to move mountains and the next day I'm putting out fires. A week later, I'm told to change the course of a river! I'm afraid to see my performance review this year!"

- "I come in at eight o'clock, sometimes later, and I always leave no later than five. My boss doesn't seem to know when I'm here and when I'm not, and he never talks to me about my work or what he expects. When I ask him what he expects from me on a project, he says something like, 'You know what to do.' Sometimes my friends tell me that he asks my colleagues to redo my work. This really annoys me because he never comes to me and explains what I did wrong. My annual performance appraisals are like carbon copies of each other from year to year: 'Overall performance for the year: Satisfactory.' I think it's time to look for another job—or a different boss."

- "In the past 2 years, I achieved dramatically more results than I'm normally expected to achieve. But I didn't receive any recognition from my boss since he doesn't ever measure my accomplishments in a consistent way. Frankly, I don't think he even knows how to measure the quality or quantity of my results. So that means I'm never rewarded for exceptional performance."

- "I'm in a dead-end situation here, even though it does pay a lot of money. The CEO talks with me about the eight divisions I'm responsible for, but he never wants to discuss my need for growth. All we ever talk about are 'the numbers.' I was made vice president because I was a good technician and team player, and I've had to learn about how to fill my executive role while I was on the job. When I ask the CEO for some help or coaching, he's always too busy. Maybe he thinks my needs just aren't his concern."

We hear stories like these again and again from employees at all organizational levels. The problem situations we described could be eliminated or at least ameliorated by the use of a competency-based, systematic approach to managing performance. Yet many organizations have minimal or no performance management practices in place, at least not when a group of researchers last checked in 2000.

Research by the Society for Human Resource Management (SHRM) provides insight into traditional performance management practices and describes the current state of the practice regarding the use of performance management practices in organizations. For the *2000 Performance Management Survey,* SHRM researchers measured current and best practices in performance management and sought to determine respondents' perceptions of the effectiveness of their overall performance management systems and tools. The survey also suggested a profile of performance management in the near future.

Respondents to the SHRM survey provided their perspectives and indicated that the purpose of an organization's performance management system should be focused on objectives related to employees rather than record keeping or other data collection functions. The highest ranked objectives for having a performance management system were providing performance feedback to employees, clarifying organizational expectations of them, and focusing on their development needs.

How satisfied were respondents with their organization's performance management system components? SHRM's research report suggested that respondents were much more satisfied with components of traditional performance management systems rather than with developmental components intended to provide employees with feedback about others' perceptions of their performance and about their needs for development. About one-third of the survey respondents were not satisfied with their organization's performance management system. This lack of satisfaction was again attributed to respondents' concern about the development components of the performance management system in their organization.

Written performance plans are a major ingredient of any successful performance management system. SHRM survey findings showed that 70% of the respondents wrote performance plans for at least 75% of their executives, approximately 66% of their nonexempt employees, and less than 50% of their exempt employees. Executives' performance goals tended to be linked to operating results, but this was true for a much lower percentage of nonexempt and exempt employees. Most respondents' organizations conducted performance evaluations on an annual basis, with development plans used more often than long-term career plans.

Senior management support is essential to the long-term success of any performance management system, whether or not it is competency driven, but the SHRM survey found that executives did not review the performance management system at all at 42% of participating organizations.

From a different perspective, in a survey of 217 companies that was sponsored by the American Compensation Association, 195 of the 217 companies, or about 90%, reported using competency-based performance appraisal data as a guide for developing their employees ("Competencies Drive HR Practices," 1996).

In summary, many organizations take a traditional approach to performance management by using a performance appraisal and disciplinary format. The biggest challenge for HR professionals is in gaining executive support for the use of more comprehensive and systematically delivered performance management practices.

Making Performance Management Competency Based

An organization's choice of performance management practices is influenced by factors such as its size and culture, the geographic distribution of its divisions and their degree of management autonomy, the types of outputs or results its employees are expected to produce, senior management's interest in and commitment to the concept of systematic performance management, the organization's business plans, and the relationship perceived between workers and organizational success. There is no one correct performance management system for all organizations or even for all work units within an organization. The competency-based approach proposed, however, is applicable with some variation to every organization, regardless of the preceding factors. Transitioning from a traditional performance management process (for example, performance appraisal and discipline) to a competency-based performance management system does require some change.

The organization's leaders need to be willing to support change in this area of critical importance to organizational performance. It requires a major change in their thinking about performance management. They must commit resources to the systematic assessment of employees' competencies, plan and make available job-specific training opportunities and coaching, set performance goals and develop work plans, monitor performance, collaborate with employees on a planned schedule regarding their performance, and deliver both good and bad news about performance in an open and supportive manner. They must also create and implement an ongoing communication strategy for keeping all employees informed about the features, processes, and benefits of the competency-based system.

Figure 9 depicts our model for a competency-based approach to performance management. In an organization with no performance management system, it is important to start fresh regarding employees' past performance and with little or no preconceptions about the proposed system. If an organization already has a performance management system, adopting a competency-based approach may require reinventing, which is usually a bit more challenging.

Process reinventions are often challenging because workers can become comfortable with the status quo, regardless of how difficult or dysfunctional existing practices might be. Consequently, HR practitioners who plan to reinvent their existing performance management practices to those that are competency based will need to incorporate change management strategies in order to smooth the transition.

One approach is to ask operating managers to identify their concerns about current performance management practices and use this as a foundation for having them create their own "ideal" system. Next, the facilitator presents the process in Figure 9 and asks participants to compare the details of their ideal system with those included in a competency-based approach. Although we hope the two will match exactly, this is seldom the case. However, the closer the fit between the operating managers' ideal and the model in Figure 9, the easier the transition to a competency-based performance management system will be. This approach gives participants the opportunity to compare the similarities and contrast the differences between the two systems. The differences that are noted are often reflections of such factors as organizational culture, how the organization does business or works with its constituents, the nature of the organization, and other factors. Patience is required in getting operating managers to make this transition since they require, and should be given, time to

Figure 9: **Competency-Based Performance Management**

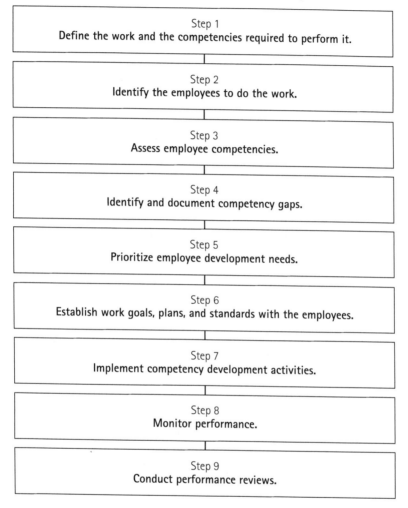

Step 1
Define the work and the competencies required to perform it.

Step 2
Identify the employees to do the work.

Step 3
Assess employee competencies.

Step 4
Identify and document competency gaps.

Step 5
Prioritize employee development needs.

Step 6
Establish work goals, plans, and standards with the employees.

Step 7
Implement competency development activities.

Step 8
Monitor performance.

Step 9
Conduct performance reviews.

process the information that was presented and then revisit the new process at a later time—for example, a week or two later.

A Model for Competency-Based Performance Management

Next, we take a look a competency-based approach to performance management, using the steps shown in Figure 9 to guide the discussion.

Step 1: Define the work and the competencies required to perform it
The first step in competency-based performance management is to define the employees' work by means of effective work analysis. In most cases, this includes naming the specific outputs or results that employees are expected to produce. These outputs or results must align with the organization's strategic goals or objectives, and the relationship must be made very clear to the operating manager and the employee. If the work is not considered strategic—meaning that the outputs or results do not contribute directly and overtly to the organization's success—then there is little justification for completing it, and it should be eliminated from the employee's list of required tasks. After this process of elimination is completed, the work that remains is therefore strategic to the organization's success. Employees who are performing unnecessary tasks can be reassigned to activities that are meaningful both to them and to the organization. Process improvement alone is a significant reason for undertaking work analysis. Also key to our approach to performance management is the identification of the competencies employees must have and use in appropriate ways to produce the expected measurable outputs or results.

Steps 2 and 3: Identify the employees to do the work and
assess employee competencies
Next, employees are identified to perform the work, generally using selection methods. The degree to which they possess and can consistently demonstrate the key competencies required for successful performance is determined through the application of competency assessment methods.

Step 4: Identify and document competency gaps
Competency gaps for which development is needed are identified and documented.

Step 5: Prioritize employee development needs
Priorities for developing employee competencies are determined, and a plan for developing the competencies is prepared.

Step 6: Establish work goals, plans, and standards with the employees
After reviewing the plans, operating managers and employees establish goals, plans, and standards to which both parties agree. Standards set a minimum expectation for measurable results. Goals establish desirable targets.

Step 7: Implement competency development activities

Employees begin training or engaging in other learning activities to acquire or build the competencies identified in Step 1 and work toward accomplishing work goals or objectives.

Step 8: Monitor performance

As employees proceed to accomplish their work goals or objectives over the performance period, operating managers monitor their performance and provide feedback. Work goals and plans are formally reviewed according to schedule and are modified as warranted. To be most effective, these reviews should include discussion of how employees use their competencies to achieve the expected work results as agreed in Step 6. This approach to performance management builds and enhances the organization's competency bench strength—its competency pool. The competency development plan may be modified as necessary.

Step 9: Conduct performance reviews

Competency-based performance management utilizes both interim reviews and performance period reviews. Planned interim reviews enable both employees and managers to address issues that could affect successful performance. This type of review can be an advantage for employees, providing scheduled opportunities to inform managers of roadblocks to performance that could affect their ability to produce the expected outputs or results. Use of interim reviews eliminates surprises for employees and their organizations.

When the performance period ends, managers and employees meet to review employee performance over the entire period and complete a performance appraisal. It is interesting to note that many employees and managers find a high degree of agreement regarding their ratings of employee performance. For example, at a large client organization, there was about 75% agreement between the ratings employees gave themselves in their draft reviews and the ratings assigned to them by their managers.

From a design, development, and implementation point of view, moving to a competency-based approach to a performance management system requires that the HR function focus on achieving the following:

1. Obtain senior management support for, and willingness to commit, the needed resources to design, implement, and maintain the system.

2. Identify the scope of the application (for example, work units, divisions, employees by work roles) and ensure alignment among the organization's strategic objectives and the affected workers' measurable contributions to the organization success.

3. Define the work or roles that will be a part of the competency-based approach to performance management. This includes the completion of detailed work analyses that result in the identification of outputs, work activities, key worker competencies, performance standards, job descriptions, job specifications, and any other information that would contribute to implementation success.

4. Create system administration documents (for example, competency assessment materials, record-keeping forms needed to track performance, employee competency development plan forms, and so on). Most organizations that use an automated human resource information system usually have the capability to automate this process; however, smaller organizations might not have this capability.

5. Create and implement an organization communication strategy to in-form all employees about the system, its benefits, processes, and plans.

6. Design and deliver competency-based training that communicates the competency-based performance management system processes, elements, and instruments as well as how participation will benefit operating managers and their employees. It is suggested that an HR representative and members of the performance management task group draft two competency models for those who will participate in the system: one for the managers and the other for the employees. These models are designed specifically to address the system requirements as needed. Developing these models allows the managers' superiors to manage the performance of their direct reports in the same manner as they are managing the affected employees. The same model of performance management applies. In order for executives to serve as role models for the venture, the same approach could be applied to them. How the organization decides to proceed on these ideas will depend on a number of factors, including the availability of resources.

Competency assessment for the performance managers would add value to the training since it could be highly individualized to their development needs. Performance managers will, depending on their individual background in the area of performance management, generally require extensive training before they use the processes and instruments. The plan for this training should include topics such as understanding human performance, recognizing performance roadblocks and what to do about them, competency assessment, identifying and closing competency gaps, observing and assessing performance, conducting effective performance reviews, coaching, managing and resolving conflict, and other topics dictated by the system elements that are selected. Similarly, affected workers need to be trained to perform their new roles in the competency-based performance management process. They need to understand and accept responsibility, for example, for their competency assessment results, their competency development activities, and their day-to-day performance. They must openly receive performance feedback from their managers and respond to conflicts or disagreements in win-win organizational ways when possible.

7. Perform complete baseline competency assessments for employees relative to the performance requirements for the work they perform. The outcomes of those assessments must be carefully documented and remain in a secure location, along with all other employee performance assessment materials.

8. Complete performance analyses for all work to be included in implementing the competency-based performance management system. Identify performance roadblocks and ensure that managers have identified ways to mitigate those roadblocks to their employees' performance. When surmounting a particular roadblock is actually a result that employees must achieve through performing the work, this must be made very clear to the employee, and the competencies that must be used in appropriate ways should be fully communicated to the employee.

9. Identify performance support opportunities other than formal training that can be made available to employees before implementing the system processes.

10. Establish an individual development planning process for all affected employees.

11. With performance managers, develop a schedule for interim and final (that is, consistent with the close of the performance period) performance reviews. A major issue to address before the system is implemented is whether all employee performance assessments will be completed on the same timetable. It is suggested that organizations consider using the option of staggering the dates for employee performance reviews that mark the close of a performance period unique to the employee.

12. Identify training, performance improvement, and other strategies that employees can use to develop their competencies.

One of the purposes of presenting the preceding items is to communicate the major work that must be completed in order to design and implement the use of a competency-based approach to performance management. The list is not exhaustive of the many actions that must be taken and successfully completed by the HR representative and others before the system can become a reality in the organization. Moving from a traditional to a competency-based performance process is a major undertaking for the organization and its employees. For the HR function, moving to a competency-based performance management system requires a resource commitment from the organization's senior managers. Although this work may be daunting at first, the results achieved are well worth the investments made.[2]

The Advantages and Challenges of Competency-Based Performance Management

The benefits of applying a competency-based approach to performance management can be dramatic. The process encourages frank and non-adversarial communication between employees and their managers. It is not unusual for employees to express their concerns in performing work that is not aligned with their competency strengths or interests. And it is not only the less productive employees but often exemplary performers as well who will express these concerns. It also gives employees the opportunity to convey their interests and satisfaction in performing work that is aligned with their competencies.

In a competency-based approach, employees' work results are aligned with achievement of the organization's strategic objectives, and the contributions of the results are identified in specific, and usually measurable, terms. Work that is identified as nonstrategic and can be eliminated allows available resources to be used in other, more productive ways.

The approach affords the opportunity to identify and develop needed competencies. In turn, competency assessment results provide training needs assessment data that can be used to plan and deliver employees' training in a targeted manner. It also gives employees information that is essential for their life and career development and provides them with opportunities to plan to meet their needs. For some employees, the benefits of a competency-based system are more valuable than immediate financial rewards. In addition, a competency-based approach reduces the chance of legal and other complaints from employees—caused by issues such as performance appraisal disagreements and frustration due to performance roadblocks beyond their control—as it encourages communication to openly discuss these concerns.

Outputs or results expectations and metrics for employees are clarified at the outset of the performance period in a competency-based approach. In addition, the approach is an incentive and retention tool especially for exemplary or high performers as they value the recognition and rewards that such a system could bring to their work situation. They appreciate knowing what is expected of them because they can then create ways to exceed performance expectations.

In summary, a competency-based performance management approach establishes a work environment in which the roles, relationships, and responsibilities of both managers and employees are well defined and clearly stated. This straightforward and mutually understood system builds trust as it ensures accountability and improves performance.

The decision to adopt a competency-based performance management system does present challenges, however. The organization's senior managers must provide strong, long-term support for the project and act as role models for the process. Required resources need to be available over the long term. Managers will face increased workloads as a competency-based approach requires them to provide employees with additional and more effective feedback as well as accept responsibilities for addressing performance obstacles. The tremendous benefits in improved performance will not be realized overnight, and their patience and understanding are critical to successful implementation. There must also be a strong alignment between the organization's strategic direction and the benefits and costs of adopting this system.

The long-term success of a competency-based system depends on the creation, completion, and maintenance of HR records of various types. The organization must have the capability to preserve this information in a secure yet convenient Human Resource Information System (HRIS) that assures long-term availability.

The organization's participating managers must remove, when possible, roadblocks to employees' successful performance. When performance roadblocks cannot be removed, performance managers should inform their employees accordingly. It must be remembered that employees might not be able to surmount some performance roadblocks, no matter how competent they are, because they might lack the control or authority needed to do so. Managers need to accept responsibility to problem solve. And the organization must be willing to commit project resources to communicating the competency-based approach to all employees, even if the system is planned for only a small segment of the organization. Employees are likely to be curious about a system that will affect their performance and work lives.

Managers must be trained on their roles and responsibilities as well as how to use the system to carry them out. Competency-based training should be consistent with the corporate culture, which means that vendor training is not always appropriate for designing and developing an organization's competency-based performance management system. The organization should be prepared to design, develop, and deliver the necessary training for its own competency-based performance management system.

Deciding on Competency–Based or Traditional Performance Management

Launching any performance management system is a major undertaking for most organizations. It requires broad-based endorsement and acceptance. As a client remarked about a 2-year-old competency-based performance management system, "maintaining a competency-based performance management system is like tending a rose garden. It requires constant, loving attention and lots of good fertilizer." HR practitioners and other persons associated with performance management are well-advised to remember this astute remark as they consider how to meet their organization's performance management needs.

When an organization's senior managers endorse the approach, then a major hurdle to meeting the objective has been surmounted. Next, the organization's key managers must understand and accept their responsibilities and take the risk of changed performance. Finally, employees must understand what the system will accomplish and what they must do to help achieve the system objectives. One way to encourage this support is to help them recognize the potential benefits they will realize from making the investment in the process: increased recognition for their contributions, reward opportunities, growth, and opportunities to improve work conditions.

Regardless of what decision is made regarding an organization's performance management system, it's clear that if an organization expects to attract and retain exemplary employees, it must provide performance support and management for its human talent. Using a competency-based performance management approach is one way to provide employment incentives for external job candidates and also improve employee retention.

Despite the benefits to be realized from a competency-based system, if the preceding conditions cannot be met, then the organization should select a more traditional approach to performance management.

A Model for Implementing Competency-Based Performance Management

In earlier sections of this chapter, we presented a systematic process for carrying out competency-based performance management and action steps required to transition to this approach. The model depicted in Figure 10 provides a step-by-step guide to implementing the process in an organizational setting.[3] The steps in the process are flexible, and can be adjusted to fit the blueprint of the system proposed. The following review provides general guidance on completing each step.

Figure 10: **Implementing Competency-Based Performance Management**

Step 1 Determine ownership.
Step 2 Brief senior managers and obtain endorsement to proceed.
Step 3 Form a task group and design a system blueprint and project plan.
Step 4 Brief senior managers on the key elements of the work plan.
Step 5 Create system materials, collateral documents, and training for participating employees and their managers.
Step 6 Pilot test the system and the training with task group members.
Step 7 Implement the competency-based performance management system.
Step 8 Evaluate the implementation.

Step 1: Determine ownership

This first step is essential. Launching a competency-based performance management system can be a challenging experience at the blueprint development stage if certain requirements are not met.

HR practitioners and others involved in developing and installing the system should ask the following questions:

- Who wants this system?
- What prompted the request for the system?
- What does the sponsor expect to accomplish by putting the system in place?

- Will it be a cost-effective investment for the organization?
- What will be the return on investment relative to the organization's strategic objectives?
- Why implement the system in these work areas at this time?
- When must the system be implemented, and why at that time?
- Will it replace current performance management practices?
- How should it be implemented?

These questions must be answered at this early stage since they have financial and management implications.

The long-term success of any competency-based performance management system depends on senior managers understanding, endorsing in principle, and committing considerable resources to the project. In this case, we define "long-term" as at least an 18- to 24-month period following endorsement by senior managers.

Step 2: Brief senior managers and obtain endorsement to proceed

This step presents a major challenge to the HR department and the managers who will operate the competency-based performance management system. Those delivering the briefing must provide definitive and convincing answers to the questions in Step 1, supported by examples specific to the organization. The goals of this briefing are to get secure support from senior managers for implementation of the project and obtain their agreement to act as role models for the competency-based system. If there is little or no commitment at this point, then additional resources need not be devoted to the project.

Step 3: Form a task group and design a system blueprint and project plan

Members of the task group should be selected from these managers and employees who will be directly affected by the competency-based performance management system. Involving stakeholders at the conceptual stage ensures representation of a significant cross section of the organization's employees.

An HR representative should provide technical leadership and also manage the group's activities and contributions to the project. This person must have expert knowledge of the requirements and practices of a competency-based system. He or she will be responsible for providing considerable training, explanations, briefings, speeches, and overall guidance and technical leadership on the competency-based approach to performance management.

The system blueprint should define the target populations and the divisions or work units and key managers, supervisors, or team leaders who will have a major impact on the successful implementation of the system. Answers to the ownership questions listed in Step 1 must be included in the blueprint.

After task group members become knowledgeable about the work to be accomplished, they should develop a detailed project plan for completing the steps outlined in the blueprint. The project work plan should include, at a minimum, the following elements: work tasks, the outputs or results that will be achieved by successfully completing the tasks, the urgency of the tasks, the target date for obtaining the outputs or results, plans for evaluating the implementation, and the persons responsible. The plan, with appropriate explanations, serves as the basis for the next senior management briefing.

Step 4: Brief senior managers on the key elements of the work plan

In addition to presenting the details of the blueprint developed in Step 3, the presenter should respond to any concerns or questions that were raised at the briefing in Step 2. Task group members should allow ample opportunity for senior managers to ask questions and can then offer direct and realistic answers. It is essential not to inflate expectations for the competency-based system.

Step 5: Create system materials, collateral documents, and training for participating employees and their managers

The key elements required for implementing a competency-based performance management system are described in the discussion accompanying Steps 1 through 4. Necessary system materials generally include work analysis results, competency models and assessments, development plans, performance analyses, and project evaluation plans. Requirements may vary according to individual organizational needs. The details of how to create the system elements, documents, databases, and other items have been published elsewhere.

Training for managers and their employees must be competency based and designed to ensure that new managers can complete the forms and implement the other processes of the performance management system. Process maps can be a helpful first step in developing this training.

Step 6: Pilot test the system and the training with task group members

Since task group members were drawn from the targeted application groups, they are appropriate persons to review and critique the system processes and collateral materials. Pilot test delivery of the training with fictitious but realistic employee cases that provide opportunities for group members to make use of performance management processes and tools, for example, through role play and group or individual exercises.

Task group members should receive the same training that is planned for delivery to the actual training audiences. Managers in the task group should be the participants for the manager training, and affected employees in the task group should serve as observers. Employee members of the task group should participate in the employee training, and the managers in the task group should serve as observers.

Observers in both situations can critique the sessions as they are being conducted, while participants should offer their critiques during content breaks in training delivery. After each training package is completed, the observers should hold an assessment session for the purpose of sharing their perceptions of the experience. Out of this session should come specific suggestions for revising the various components of the performance management process, such as plans and techniques, and the associated training. In other words, every program element should be carefully examined—both the performance management processes and the training on the processes—for both audiences. Considering the resources required to implement a competency-based performance management system, rigorous examination is a necessary investment, even though system implementation might be delayed somewhat for revisions.

Step 7: Implement the competency-based performance management system

It is essential that all persons affected by the implementation of the competency-based system are trained and fully informed of the system objectives, their responsibilities, and the timetable for administering system activities. The timetable should include activities such as competency assessment, competency development priorities, performance plans, interim performance reviews, and evaluations. Participating employees should maintain calendars of target dates for the completion of each phase of their own performance management, and managers must also have calendars for organizing their responsibilities.

The HR practitioners leading implementation of the competency-based system must provide consistent and frequent monitoring of the progress for the implementation with both managers and employees. New levels of performance assessment are sometimes necessary for effective operation with the new approach. A competency-based system works on two-way communication, and some managers are not accustomed to assuming the role of listener. Until managers are able to accept this role, difficulties can arise. Remember that implementing a competency-based performance management system is a continuous change effort—not only for the organization but for every person in the organization. This new approach is based on honest communication and mutual confidence and trust between managers and employees. The HR practitioner is key to facilitating understanding in both parties. Accordingly, the lead HR practitioner should take immediate corrective action at the first sign of difficulty while managers and employees are attempting to meet system requirements.

During implementation, participants often need assistance in completing tasks such as objectively analyzing competency assessment results, using active communication techniques to achieve mutual understanding, identifying and reaching agreement on competency acquisition needs, writing performance improvement objectives, delivering bad news to workers, and handling conflict in positive ways. Providing these services is one of HR's strengths, and HR professionals must not hesitate to fully apply those competencies when circumstances require their use.

When all parties involved in implementing a competency-based performance management system focus on the objectives of the system and maintain reasonable expectations of long-term individual and organizational performance improvement, they can act appropriately during potentially difficult situations. Open yet respectful exchanges of information will contribute a great deal toward successful implementation.

Step 8: Evaluate the implementation

Evaluations are essential to a successful implementation. Both formative and summative evaluation processes were included in the project plan developed by the performance management task group in Step 3 of this model. The HR practitioner may want to consider having task group members involved in conducting the ongoing formative evaluations.

Summative evaluations assess the long-term impact of the competency-based performance management system in terms of system objectives and organizational strategic objectives. HR practitioners must document return on investment so that senior managers will be able to recognize the value of performance managment in their organization.

One method of evaluation measures results in three areas: activity, people and business results, and the relationships between the activities of the people and the business components ("Measuring the Impact of Competencies," 1997). Another successful method is to record detailed anecdotes of successful outcomes over time. Incidents that demonstrate significant effects on the achievement of the organization's strategic objectives are of special importance. The HR practitioner must take a disciplined approach to recording and reporting these results if they are to be included in a summative evaluation of the system.

Summary

In this chapter, we defined performance management and discussed its traditional application in organizations. We explained how to make performance management competency based and examined the advantages and challenges of such a system. A competency-based approach is not appropriate in all situations, and we noted conditions under which performance management should be competency based or should be handled traditionally. We presented and discussed a model depicting competency-based performance management, steps involved in transitioning to competency-based performance management, and a model portraying implementation of a competency-based system.

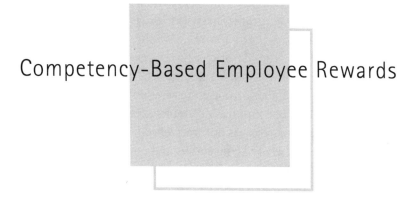

CHAPTER 8

Competency-Based Employee Rewards

Selecting rewards is an important part of any organization's overall HR strategy. The world of work is rapidly changing, and rewards must keep pace if an organization intends to attract and retain exemplary performers who can contribute to sustained competitive advantage. This is a powerful reason, it seems to us, to give attention to this topic.

Let's frame the issues as succinctly as we can, recognizing that competency-based employee rewards is a most complicated topic, that we cannot address all these issues in this chapter, and that a book could easily be written on this topic alone.

Historically in the U.S., we would argue, most compensation systems—a key part of a larger total reward system—have been focused on achieving *fair* pay. Since some work is regarded as difficult to measure, the common business practice has been to pay individuals holding the same job about the same pay. A secretary, for instance, is placed in a pay range where he or she is paid about the same as any other secretary in the organization. HR practitioners in the U.S. have been sensitive to such issues as equal pay for equal work, well-publicized gender disparities in pay practices, and compliance issues associed with the Equal Pay

Act. The tendency has been to err on the side of caution and to try to pay everyone about the same, with monor differences (small percentage differeences) recognized in so-called merit pay or pay for performance.

But competency-based rewards may provide another perspective on rewards. It recognizes that three time periods should be considered: (1) before the performance is undertaken (*incentives*); (2) during the performance (*concurrent rewards*); and (3) after the performance has been demonstrated and measurable results have been achieved (*rewards*). It reecognizes that incentives and rewards may be financially oriented or nonfinancially oriented, that competencies are only the means to the end of achieving measurable outputs or results, and that one-size-fits-all approaches to reward systems do not work effectively because individuals vary in what they perceive to be incentives and rewards of value to them. Finally, the fact is that not all individuals are equally productive if their work is measured objectively. Exemplary performers may outperform their fully successful counterparts by as much as twenty times. So, how can people be fairly incented to achieve quantum leaps in productivity improvement if everyone is paid roughly the same? How can fully successful performes be incented to become exemplary performers or at least bring their measurable performance to levels closer to those achieved by the exemplary performers? How can exemplary performers be fairly rewarded for outstanding results that may be as much as twenty times as great as those achieved by others in the same job categories? These, and similar, difficult questions are raised by competency-based employee rewards.

This chapter briefly examines reward systems by addressing the following key questions:

- What are employee rewards and total rewards?
- How are compensation, benefits, and employee rewards traditionally managed?
- How can employee rewards become competency based?
- What are the advantages and challenges of a competency-based employee reward process?
- When should an employee reward process be competency based, and when should it be handled traditionally?
- What model can guide a competency-based employee reward process, and how should it be implemented?

Employee Rewards and Total Rewards

An *employee reward* is any recognition in the form of a tangible or intangible award, prize, or incentive that acknowledges an employee's contribution to organizational success. Making decisions about employee rewards is key to establishing a total rewards strategy and aligning HR strategy with the organization's strategic objectives. It may be particularly important to reward exemplary performers, who can be as much as 20 times more productive than their fully successful counterparts.

Total rewards can be understood as an employee's salary, benefits, and short- and long-term incentives, and rewards or recognition for achieving specific performance goals (Schiffers, Young, & Shelton, 1996). Although CEOs and other senior executives are most interested in those total rewards that directly affect the financial bottom line, salary and benefits are only part of a much broader range of incentive and reward methods. Total rewards could be regarded as everything employees perceive as valuable that results from their relationship with an organization and which the organization uses to attract, retain, and motivate them. Total rewards vary greatly from one organization to another, since it is important to develop a strategy that fits within the corporate culture.

Rapid changes in the business environment have prompted many decision makers to examine the effectiveness of their reward systems. Lawler (2000) suggested moving away from a one-size-fits-all philosophy and using individualized systems, which enable organizations to offer incentives in forms that appeal to employees.

Traditional Total Rewards

The following discussion covers the components of a total rewards system: compensation, alternative compensation, incentives, and recognition and rewards.

Compensation

Compensation is critical to an organization's total rewards system. According to WorldatWork, *compensation* comprises the elements of pay—such as base pay, variable pay, and stock—that an employer provides to an employee in return for services rendered (*WorldatWork Glossary,* n.d.).

Traditional approaches to compensation rely on information about what people do, their length of employment, and the relationship between their pay and that of others in the organization. In managing compensation, employers usually weigh three factors: external equity, internal equity, and individual performance. They ensure *external equity* by considering labor market conditions that exist outside the organization and preserve *internal equity* by assessing relationships among jobs based on the relative worth to the organization. In evaluating *individual performance,* employers determine an employee's effectiveness at achieving results. This often creates a threefold challenge for HR practitioners who must establish externally competitive wages, salaries, and benefits within a system that also recognizes the different value of various jobs and provides incentives and rewards for individuals. This view was verified by a study of nearly 750 HR and compensation managers with U.S. organizations (O'Neal, 1996). The same study found, however, that employers are beginning to shift their compensation programs toward more flexible systems that allow managers to reward employees for applying competencies, achieving higher performance levels, and making more contributions to organizational success.

The existence of so many different pay plans demonstrates the widespread dissatisfaction among many managers with traditional approaches to compensation management. It also shows a great willingness to experiment with new approaches. And yet, despite so much experimentation, few managers are satisfied with any one approach.[1]

Job-based pay

There are a number of different approaches to compensation, but perhaps the most familiar is *job-based pay.* Two approaches to job-based pay, automatic step progression and the merit range, are perhaps the most traditional methods of providing pay changes within a grade (Bremen & Coil, 1999). *Automatic step progression* calls for a series of incremental increases within the pay grade. The *merit range* sets a minimum, midpoint, and maximum within a range, and workers are eligible for periodic pay increases, often on an annual basis. Merit pay is sometimes called "pay for performance," although that would not be an accurate description at most organizations, where job outputs have not been made clear or explicit. True pay for performance, which rewards genuine productivity, is not possible unless job outputs are known and measurable.

Job-based pay is not a perfect solution to compensation. One important drawback is that it often does not reward workers for improving their skills or knowledge. In addition, it does not support the corporate culture, encourage worker participation, or enhance worker flexibility (Sherman, Bohlander, & Snell, 1998).

Skill-based pay

HR practitioners have been experimenting with many new approaches to wage and salary administration. One such approach is *skill-based pay*, for which organizations create levels based on the acquisition of skills linked to the mastery of various work processes (Bremen & Coil, 1999). In this approach, pay corresponds to a worker's demonstrated ability to perform the processes. Organizations may analyze the work and then determine the knowledge and experience needed to perform it. As skills are acquired, individual pay is adjusted. This approach very often fosters an increased interest in skill acquisition and is helpful for workers who enjoy their jobs but are interested in new challenges (Tyler, 1998).

A skill-based pay system presents HR practitioners with many challenges. One centers on establishing a method of measuring skill acquisition and deciding how much to pay for it. Organizations must also determine exactly which skills should be acquired in order to receive increased pay (Tyler, 1998). Other challenges include limited advancement available for an employee who has acquired all the indicated skills, pay tied to skills that either are not used regularly or are no longer used, and the costly updates required as work processes change (Bremen & Coil, 1999).

Broadbanding

Another innovative approach to compensation is *broadbanding*, which combines many salary grades into a lesser number of wide salary bands.[2] As noted by Sherman, Bohlander, and Snell (1998), "Paying employees through broadbands enables organizations to consider job responsibilities, individual skills and competencies, and career mobility patterns in assigning employees to bands" (p. 368). Broadbanding may be used in conjunction with skill-based pay, which can add an additional dimension by linking increases in base pay to the acquisition and demonstration of new skills (Leonard, 1994). This combined approach has the potential to offer individual workers encouragement for personal and career growth (Hofrichter, 1993). Broadbanding is often linked with a performance-based approach to pay, with performance level determining the band placement for workers.

In a research study, the American Compensation Association (now WorldatWork) surveyed 116 organizations that use broadbanding. The findings suggest that broadbanding offers more flexibility, creates an interest in lateral development, provides for a focus on business goals, generates an emphasis on skill development, and enhances team focus (Abosch, 1995).

Careerbanding

Careerbanding is similar to broadbanding but emphasizes career development rather than advancement to the next grade (Tyler, 1998). This approach often establishes pay based on market surveys and does not use minimums and maximums within a range.

Alternative compensation

The meaning of this term seems to be evolving. Nadel (1998) interprets it as processes that meet the intrinsic needs of workers, develop strategies that appeal to workers while meeting strategic business needs, and communicate to workers that they are valued. He includes many initiatives within this category, such as employee training; tuition reimbursement; flexible work arrangements; worker-friendly environments, perquisites, amenities, and conveniences; and a positive management attitude (Nadel, 1998).

Incentives

Incentives, which are meant to encourage desired performance, are either monetary or nonmonetary. Monetary incentives are sometimes called "extrinsic rewards," and nonmonetary incentives are often referred to as "intrinsic rewards" (Rothwell & Kazanas, 1998).

Monetary incentives

A true pay-for-performance plan attempts to link job results with pay. Incentive pay is one such approach.

Profit sharing is a form of incentive pay in which a percentage of a company's profits is shared with workers. Another form is *gainsharing,* in which workers share in the money derived from achieving particular goals. *Small group incentive pay* and *team-based pay* apply to specific groups that attain desired results and achieve their goals. With *long-term incentive pay,* workers who reach set goals are usually rewarded through some type of stock program, and a *lump-sum payment plan* distributes incentive pay, usually to high performers, for achieving desired results. Incentive pay may also be stock based. Stock-based pay is sometimes linked to the overall performance of the organization.

Lump-sum bonuses are a one-time incentive. Bonuses can be used for a variety of reasons, including fostering skill development or encouraging workers to relocate for a lateral move (Tyler, 1998).

Nonmonetary incentives

Nonmonetary rewards for good performance include sincere praise, organizational and employee partnerships, learning and development opportunities, time off, task force or other assignments, assistance with personal chores, gifts, and recognition of achievements in company or industry publications. This type of incentive can be applied to groups, teams, or individuals and may become project based as well.

Nonmonetary awards help to create a working environment in which employees are truly engaged and feel good about themselves and their work for what is often very little cost (Coil, 1999). In the past, nonmonetary and low-cost incentives were used by a limited number of organizations, but today's workers are less inclined to want pay increases and bonuses and may prefer incentives of greater personal value. In virtually every chapter of this book, we have mentioned change and its impact on HR management systems. Change has affected workers' values and consequently their reward preferences. Organizations must recognize these changes and adapt to them.

Recognition and Rewards

Recognition can be a very effective means of rewarding behavior and emphasizing the importance of both contributions and performance. Informal employee recognition can be of little or no monetary value and includes praise, certificates, plaques, news articles, and ongoing programs such as employee of the month. Formal recognition is often more organizational in nature, usually requires management approval, and costs substantially more than informal recognition (Bowen, 2000). Gainsharing, short- and long-term incentive programs, and stock option programs are examples of formal recognition awards.[3]

Traditionally, some organizational leaders have held that a "fair" salary and a "good" benefits package are sufficient compensation for employee contributions to organizational success. In a similar manner, the traditional HR management approach—probably driven in large measure by the opinion of senior leaders—has been to focus on providing employees with a competitive compensation and benefits package. In addition, traditional reward strategies are not always well defined or geared to measurable outputs or results. Instead, leaders and their direct reports tend to become caught up in the performance of work activities. Strange as it may seem, a major success factor in any reward process is whether the organization has developed and communicated the expectation that its employees produce concrete, observable results.

A traditional system often does not single out exemplary performers for special recognition or reward. On the contrary, exemplary performers may be punished for their achievements. Exemplary performers stand out from their peers because they accept difficult challenges or achieve outstanding results with the same or less resources than others. Supervisors recognize the ability of exemplary performers and their willingness to go the extra mile and consequently assign more work to them than to their peers. A high-performing employee recently summarized this situation by saying, "The better I perform, the harder I'm expected to work. I think there's something wrong with that, don't you?" There seems to be some truth to the saying that the reward for exemplary performance is not more money but more (or harder) work! Providing more work could be seen as punishment, not reward.

Reward programs are administered in various ways by organizations that have a formal reward system in place. In some cases, and especially in team-based organizations, a committee of peers reviews accomplishments. Other reward processes may be managed by a single decision maker, a committee of decision makers, the CEO or president, or an executive committee.

Making Employee Rewards Competency Based

Every employee reward process must have a sound philosophical base that is aligned with the organization's corporate culture, business objectives, and strategies. Senior leaders must spell out specific objectives that are consistent with the organization's strategic objectives. An important issue here is the organization's reward philosophy.

Although the term *philosophy* may create the wrong impressions in some business circles—conjuring up an image of bearded philosophers contemplating how many angels can dance on the head of a pin—philosophy is critical to such fundamentally important strategic questions as the following:

- Who should allocate rewards?
- For what goals should incentives be offered, and what results should be rewarded?
- When should rewards be given?
- Why is the organization adopting a particular reward philosophy, and how does that the philosophy align with its strategic objectives?
- How will incentives and rewards be allocated?

Since allocating employee rewards in a competency framework depends on verifiable delivery of observable and measurable results, decision makers must be clear on the results they want to reward. It is not enough to reward activities. It is not enough to permit managers to decide who should receive what rewards. In a competency-based process, achievement of the desired work results is objectively measurable and verifiable. This means that competencies must also be identified and their appropriate use specified.

Before beginning a project, HR practitioners must obtain work analysis information, create performance standards, and develop metrics for determining the extent to which those standards are met. Standards could include customer or client requirements, quality level, and time frames.

A competency-based process requires an administrative infrastructure. A person must be assigned to manage, either full- or part-time, such details as completing the tasks for system development. Other functions that require support include reward decision making, a communication system that keeps all employees informed on the reward process, and ongoing evaluation of the overall outcomes of the program and its contributions to the organization's competitive success.

When an organization establishes a competency-based reward system, decision makers are declaring that rewards will be based on the following criteria:

- Meeting or exceeding the measurable standards for expected outputs or results established by the organization's leaders

- Demonstrating appropriate use of the key competencies required to achieve the outputs or results

If the goal of a competency framework is to make decisions about employee rewards, it is natural to wonder why the appropriate use of key competencies is important. What does it matter how the outcomes were achieved? To explain, we offer the following scenario.

An organization with a competency-based reward system has specified that long-term cooperative relationships must be established among the work units that are essential to achieving the desired outcome. The lead worker, a candidate for a reward, achieved the result but, in doing so, alienated several other work groups. The employee either did not have the necessary competency or did not use it appropriately, or the competency may have been poorly defined in the first place. In any case, decision makers decided not to present the reward. Under the conditions of a traditional process, this same employee probably would have been rewarded.

There are several reasons not to reward this worker under a competency-based system. First, the employee won the battle, but the organization lost the war. Relations across work units were damaged, which could compromise the organization's ability to achieve similar goals in the future. Second, had the employee been rewarded, workers might infer that the organization is interested in performance only and that senior managers have falsely endorsed competency requirements as a foundation for reward decisions. This creates the impression that they value the result more than the means or process of achieving it. Yet, competencies and their appropriate use are pivotal to both individual and organizational success beyond the major output or result.

The Advantages and Challenges of Competency-Based Employee Rewards

There are numerous advantages to using a competency-based employee reward process.

Competency-based employee rewards offer major support to other competency-based HR management practices. The approach serves as a mechanism for raising the performance bar in a fair and equitable manner, specifies clear performance requirements and the rewards for achieving them, and can easily be aligned with a competency-based performance system as defined in chapter 7. It is highly desirable to encourage everyone to perform at the level of exemplars, but since not all competencies can be developed and instead some must be acquired through selection, the goal of this approach is to raise the productivity of existing staff closer to the level of exemplars.

The unified communication strategy, which keeps employees informed of the conditions for rewarding exemplary performance, acts as an informal performance contract between the organization and its employees and encourages participation in setting higher performance standards. Under a competency-based system, employees are rewarded for achieving results in productive ways rather than simply for carrying out work activity. Job candidates who are highly motivated to do exemplary work will view this type of reward process as an employment incentive.

A competency-based approach improves an organization's bench strength. It stimulates employee development. Ultimately, clients or customers who receive exemplary-quality outputs will be more satisfied with the organization's products or services.

At the same time, a competency-based reward process also presents challenges.

The development, implementation, and maintenance of a competency-based approach demand significant commitment of organizational resources. The business benefits to be derived from a highly structured process such as the one proposed here must be weighed against the long-term investments required.

Rewards must be allocated or matched to measurable results. Organizations with secretive or untrusting corporate cultures will probably not be able to apply standards in such a way. The reason is that measurable results must be clarified and communicated to employees.

Performance requirements, competency acquisition and assessment plans, and decision-making guidelines and practices must be specified and consistently applied to employee reward decisions. An organization cannot accomplish this without first identifying and validating competencies and developing measurable specifications for the work outputs or results. The necessary technical resources must be available, sourced either internally or externally, to complete this work and maintain its accuracy as rewards are administered. Without this capability, the organization cannot operate a competency-based employee reward system.

Monetary employee rewards should be funded well before rewards are given. The organization must be able to incorporate these costs into its existing budget.

Deciding on Competency-Based or Traditional Employee Rewards

A successful competency-based approach requires senior managers who understand that competencies are a prerequisite for all performance and who are willing to embrace an innovative system for rewarding exemplary employee performance. In addition, they must be prepared to commit resources to designing, establishing, implementing, and maintaining the process even as organizational circumstances change.

A traditional process is advisable when senior managers are not interested in exploring a competency-based reward process or cannot articulate the business case for using competencies. In certain organizations, senior managers may be unable to justify the expenditure of resources because of their company's size or corporate culture or for financial reasons.

Implementing Competency-Based Employee Rewards

The model depicted in Figure 11 can be used to guide the creation and implementation of a competency-based employee reward process. It is essential that HR practitioners remain flexible in interpreting this model

Figure 11: **Competency-Based Employee Reward Process**

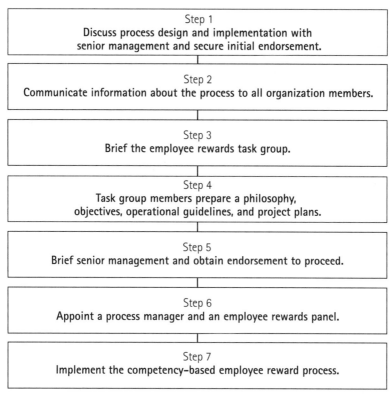

| Step 1 |
| Discuss process design and implementation with |
| senior management and secure initial endorsement. |

| Step 2 |
| Communicate information about the process to all organization members. |

| Step 3 |
| Brief the employee rewards task group. |

| Step 4 |
| Task group members prepare a philosophy, |
| objectives, operational guidelines, and project plans. |

| Step 5 |
| Brief senior management and obtain endorsement to proceed. |

| Step 6 |
| Appoint a process manager and an employee rewards panel. |

| Step 7 |
| Implement the competency-based employee reward process. |

and use the following instructions as guidelines only. Successful employee reward processes are tailored to conform to each organization's values and corporate culture.

Step 1: Discuss process design and implementation with senior management and secure initial endorsement

Typically, the organization's HR director or manager initiates this discussion as a strategic partner on the senior management leadership team. Discussions could also begin informally and evolve to a more formal basis if a manager or other respected person is willing to be a change champion. For example, an operating manager who has experienced the benefits of using competency-based HR practices to manage a work unit or division might initiate the discussion. The point is to communicate the possibilities of a competency-based approach to the organization's decision makers.

The discussion could proceed as follows:

1. Define incentives and employee rewards and explain how they fit into the organization's total rewards strategy.

2. Define the terms used in competency-based HR management and explain why a competency-based approach makes sense for the organization.

3. Explain why the organization should have a total rewards strategy and make the business case for such a process.

4. Give examples of rewards that might be valued by the organization's employees.

5. Describe the steps involved in designing and implementing a competency-based approach to employee rewards.

6. Identify some ways of implementing the new approach and offer to pilot test it.

7. Specify the time and money needed to plan and implement a pilot study and secure agreement on a method of monitoring productivity while it is being conducted.

8. Propose timelines and milestones for each stage of design, development, and implementation.

9. Ask senior managers if they support the plan. If they do, determine whether their endorsement includes provision of the necessary resources. If resources are not part of their endorsement, solicit their proposals for accomplishing the start-up phase of the initiative.

10. Double-check collective bargaining agreements to confirm the legality of conducting a pilot test with the targeted group.

11. Collect evidence, through benchmarking, of the potential benefits of competency-based HR management and communicate it to senior leaders.

Another approach is to make a formal proposal to management. The content of this kind of proposal is well known to external consultants but may be less familiar to internal practitioners. For this purpose, a good proposal identifies the key challenge or problem to be solved, including, perhaps, those associated with the current reward philosophy, and explains the business need and justification. It should contain a solution to the problem and the justification for the solution. A good proposal lists the tasks to be accomplished in implementing the reward system, deliverables or measurable outputs for each step, and accountabilities for results. It also provides a timeline for completion of each task, a budget based on the tasks, an estimate of the likely financial benefits deriving from the project, and a list of individuals who should be involved.

Upon project approval, the senior leadership team should appoint an employee rewards task group. It may be desirable to staff the task group with exemplary performers. Leaders should agree to notify the managers and supervisors of task group members and inform them of the possible benefits of these employees' participation.

Step 2: Communicate information about the process to all organization members

In this step, the HR practitioner communicates senior management's endorsement to those who will be affected by the decision. The person who prepares this information should define the implementation environment well. Introducing competency-based employee reward processes is a major undertaking for some organizations and must be handled with care. Task group members should be identified to the organization at an early stage of the project.

Step 3: Brief the employee rewards task group

Next, the HR practitioner briefs task group members on the discussion with senior managers (Step 1) and describes the group's mission. Since task group members, with extensive support from the process manager, will be responsible for completing the work described in Step 4 of this model, they should learn about the tasks they are expected to complete. The HR practitioner should present and discuss timelines for the reward processes and completion of a draft work plan with task group members.

Step 4: Task group members prepare a philosophy, objectives, operational guidelines, and project plan

The first step toward formulating a philosophy is to state the business case for having a competency-based employee reward process. Why does the organization need an employee reward process, and why must that process be based on competencies and their appropriate use in the performance environment? The objectives for any employee reward process must align with the organization's strategic plans and support achievement of its business objectives. This alignment fosters a vision of the employee reward process, its mode of operation, and the returns the organization will realize by investing in it.

Next, task group members must identify the objectives for the employee reward process and articulate these outcomes so that they can be understood clearly, especially by the organization's management. For example, objectives could be stated as strategic or tactical results, high-value-added tasks needed for improved business performance, or employee competencies that must be appropriately applied in order to achieve critical business results (Armitage, 1997). At this point, some managers may want to request information from other organizations about the costs and benefits of competency-related reward programs, but such information is not readily available and the efforts to gather such information may cause substantial delays in implementation.

In preparing operational guidelines and a project plan for the competency-based employee reward process, task group members should consider questions such as the following:

- What organizational outputs or results will be included in inaugural and later stages of implementation?

- Which employees will be included in inaugural and later stages of implementation: teams, individual contributors, supervisors, mid-level managers, support staff, or others?

- Has a competency-based employee reward decision-making process been outlined and agreed upon?

- What internal or external organizational factors now influence, or can be expected to influence, the achievement of the high-value outputs or results?

- Do the identified employees have sufficient control over their performance, or are they able to influence others who can remove performance roadblocks so that the rewards are achievable? If the environment is not conducive to achieving high performance, a reward process may be pointless.

- What measurable performance is needed, and what are the minimum requirements that must be met in order to qualify for rewards?

- Who will conduct the work analysis projects to identify the work activities, competencies, and measurable standards by which to judge the quality of work for each result?

- How will competency acquisition, assessment, and application activities be carried out?

- How will managers carry out their performance management duties to support achievement of work results?

- What rewards for exemplary performance do the organization's employees value the most?

- Are the values of the rewards proportional to the monetary and other benefits the organization will realize as a result of its investment?

- What criteria will be used for determining whether performance merits a reward? What are the conditions of the reward decision-making process?

- What is the timeline for designing, developing, implementing, and evaluating the competency-based employee reward process?

Step 5: Brief senior management and obtain endorsement to proceed

Along with the endorsement of senior management, the purpose of this briefing is to obtain commitment of resources for implementing the process. Senior managers must be given every opportunity during the briefing to clarify any of the information presented or modify the plan to meet their requirements. Maybe more so than any other HR management process, an employee reward program clearly belongs to the organization's senior managers, and their buy-in is critical because of the sizable financial investment that is involved.

Step 6: Appoint a process manager and an employee rewards panel
If a decision is made to proceed, senior managers should name a person to spearhead the effort. They should also appoint three to five exemplary performers to serve on an employee rewards panel. Panel members will represent senior managers in making decisions on rewards for exemplary performance. They will also set the standards for each employee reward and ensure that sufficient evidence to support reward decisions has been presented by the process manager.

Step 7: Implement the competency-based employee reward process
This stage will go smoothly if the process manager has developed and communicated a project plan and timetable to those individuals who will be affected by the process. At this point, the process manager acts on agreements that have been made with senior managers and confirms completion of the following major tasks:

- An employee reward decision-making process has been formulated and agreed upon.
- Work results and responsible employees have been identified.
- The employee rewards panel has established its responsibilities and duties and formulated guidelines for fulfilling them.
- Rewards panel members have been briefed and have developed the necessary operating plans.
- Work analysis data for key results have been produced and will be available when needed.
- Competency assessment procedures are in place and working effectively.
- The rewards panel has developed a nomination process that is ready to be implemented.
- A process for collecting, analyzing, and transmitting data on reward nominees to rewards panel members is ready for implementation.
- Other managers have been briefed on the implementation plan.
- A reward communication process has been reviewed by key managers and implemented across the organization.

- A calendar of reward events has been planned and integrated with the organization's major business initiatives and events calendar.
- Rewards and processes are available for immediate use.

After the process has been operating for 6 to 12 months, its internal and external workings should be evaluated.[4]

Summary

In this chapter, we introduced important ideas about competency-based employee reward strategies and the organizational requirements for formulating and implementing such strategies. Employee rewards are clearly critical to encouraging exemplary performance. The reward processes we discussed provide a means of rewarding employees not only for possessing a competency but for achieving measurable results. Conclusions regarding the design and use of competency-based compensation may not yet be definitive, but in our minds, the benefits of using a well-designed competency-based employee reward process are not in doubt. It simply makes sense to reward people in proportion to their measurable productivity, thus motivating them to become exemplary performers.

But great care should be taken to individualize rewards so as to match individual contributions while ensuring internal equity and legal compliance.

CHAPTER 9

Competency-Based Employee Development

It is difficult to discuss employee development as a formal HR initiative because applications labeled "employee development" have been so diverse. As an HR function, employee development has been somewhat of a catchall for many initiatives intended to improve employee and organizational performance. However, there is little agreement among HR professionals or organization leaders on what constitutes employee development.

Employee development, career development, career management, career planning, career guidance, career coaching, career counseling, mentoring, and initiatives with similar names and labels have been used by organizations. However, these initiatives have often lacked formal definition and specific objectives, and consequently it has been difficult to ascertain what benefits to the organization they have yielded. While some organizations have well-established and -defined employee development initiatives that are linked with business and HR strategies and are aligned with employees' life-career goals, other organizations sometimes turn to initiatives of this type in an attempt to resolve a crisis. Examples include the following situations:

- An organization is downsizing or planning layoffs and decides to provide outplacement services for its employees.
- New business outside an organization's area of core competence creates a demand for current employees to have new or different competencies.
- An organization wants to demonstrate its commitment to achieving diversity or equal employment opportunity goals.
- A merger changes or adds work roles and procedures.
- An organization wants a visible employee development function that will attract or retain exemplary performers.
- A high percentage of an organization's exemplary performers are leaving to work elsewhere.
- An organization is losing key employees due to retirement, resulting in a loss of organization knowledge.

One of the difficulties in discussing, planning, implementing, and maintaining an employee development initiative is that people have different ideas about the nature of employee development, its priority within the organization, and its goals, design, implementation, and application relative to other HR development systems. For example, competency acquisition training is sometimes offered to employees as a "career development" opportunity when, in fact, the main objective of the training is to make them competent (or more competent) in performing their current work. Since becoming more competent is a foundation outcome for employee development as we view it, the opportunity might be considered not only training but also development in that the competencies acquired could have long-term significance for employees' future marketability or life-career satisfaction. Yet the ambiguous definitions could confuse these employees, who might expect some wonderful "career opportunity" (often translated as "promotion") to follow their "employee development" experience. This could possibly damage employee morale and compromise the success of a well-defined and well-managed competency-based employee development system.

Adding to the confusion, *career development*, which is often mentioned in tandem with employee development, has meaning relative to the context in which it is used. Traditionally, career development meant upward mobility, an eventual, perhaps inevitable, promotion to a work role with greater responsibilities and increased compensation. Today, upward mobility makes little sense to many workers, as flatter and leaner organizations have become customary practice. Workers who are now in their 20s and 30s might change jobs several times, preferring better benefits to upward mobility. In other words, "up is not the only way" (Kaye, 1985). This reality has forced an evaluation and reengineering of traditional practices that are based largely on the notion that any loyal employee can move up the corporate ladder.

Leaders of organizations generally have one view of employee development, while HR and career development professionals have another. Organization leaders frequently believe that exemplary performers will automatically rise to the top, most probably without a need for organization-sponsored employee development. This belief is often bolstered by the fact that many employees look for ways to become upwardly mobile.

HR professionals and career development professionals have separate but overlapping perspectives on employee development and the purposes it should serve. On one hand, the HR camp tends to see employee development primarily as a process that increases employees' usefulness and marketability within the organization—and only secondarily as a means of encouraging employees to explore their life-career interests, values, and goals and to discover ways that the organization's employee development opportunities might help them achieve their life-career goals.

To career counselors, on the other hand, a career is the sum total of an individual's values, aptitudes, interests, motivations, education, competencies (including knowledge, skills, mind-set), training, work, and other experiences over an entire life span. Life choices are guided by the individual's personal values. In their view, it is the organization's responsibility to provide development opportunities that will help employees to achieve their life-career goals as well as improve their work performance. These two camps must join forces if employee development is to thrive and be fully integrated as a value-added HR management component.[1]

In this chapter, we address the following key questions:

- What is employee development?
- How is employee development traditionally carried out?
- How can employee development become competency-based?
- What are the advantages and challenges of a competency-based approach to employee development?
- When should employee development be competency based, and when should it be handled traditionally?

Employee Development

As is the case with most professions, vocabulary is essential to framing a context for employee development. Accordingly, we have defined several key terms that are commonly used in organizational HR practice.

Organization development consists of activities that are directed specifically toward improving the effectiveness of a total organization or its subgroups.

Employment can include an individual's self-employment, working for an organization, or volunteering, or activities such as homemaking and relationship building.

A *life-career* is the integrated progression of an individual's life- and work-related activities, including the identification, development, and pursuit of aspirations in accord with his or her personal values over an entire life span.

Training is an individually focused change effort pursued by an employee for the purpose of learning specific behaviors that are needed for immediate performance of work. After training, the employee is expected to produce outputs or results of the required quality.

Development refers to any effort to acquire competencies.

Employee development is the pursuit of any activity that leads to continuous learning and personal growth and contributes to achieving both the individual's and the organization's objectives. It is a continuous learning process that deepens an employee's understanding of his or her values, interests, skills, aptitudes, personality attributes, and competency strengths. Competencies acquired through employee development are usually intended for future application. The links to competency-based HR planning are obvious.

Employee development is thus a *process* that continues throughout an individual's life span, regardless of employers or type of employment and individual experiences. What is so interesting about this process is that it evolves and often occurs whether or not employers explicitly support it as an organizational commitment. When an employer supports employee development as a business investment, however, the organization can realize enormous benefits.

Although employee development is essential to the long-term success of organizations today, organization leaders generally classify expenditures for employee development as a cost on financial statements. Persons who intend to create an employee development process must address this incorrect mind-set from the outset. Organizations should note that they either pay now or will pay later. The "pay later" will manifest as unprepared employees, lack of talent brought on by less ability to attract and retain exemplary performers, and a reduced knowledge base across the organization. These conditions might occur at a time of crisis, when playing catch-up can have dire implications for the organization. Decision makers must understand that unless the organization invests in its future growth by making long-term improvements in its competency pool, it will pay the price for not doing so at a later time.

The philosophy, framework, and objectives of an employee development effort must be well conceived if they are to align with and support achievement of the organization's goals as well as those of its employees. Senior leaders must consider the reasons for sponsoring a developmental process from both perspectives: the organization's and the employees'. For example, an organization needs an individual who can apply a specialized competency or competency set so that it can benefit by growing, developing brand loyalty, and increasing revenues. At the same time, an employee who possesses the necessary competencies needs an arena in which to perform while addressing his or her life-career preferences. Matching these two sets of needs is at the heart of employee development.[2]

Yet, even after the development process has been tailored to organizational and employee needs, disconnects frequently occur. The organization may begin to view employees as less important than completion of work, and employees may seek upward mobility in return for their contributions. For this reason, all communications about employee development must be accompanied by a clear purpose statement *and*—of critical importance—must inform potential participants that the organization makes no guarantees of promotion. Being assigned work at a greater level of sophistication or receiving a promotion gives an employee a sense of status and personal power and traditionally represents validation by the organization. Opportunities for upward mobility are limited, however, and individuals must understand that they are being developed only for reasons consistent with the program goals. This concept of development is hard for employees to grasp and difficult for the organization to ignore. Perhaps as a reflection of employee attitudes, organizations often rate the success of development programs by the number of promotions, instead of by the degree of life-career satisfaction experienced by employees. Both employees and their organizations benefit when career planning and guidance are part of the employee development process.

Walker and Gutteridge (1979) stated that many organization leaders regard career planning and development programs as serving several purposes, such as to enhance job and work performance, enable employees to utilize the organization's HR systems more effectively, and improve the organization's ability to use its talent. Other researchers noted that an organization-sponsored career planning and development program also reduced employee turnover, supported organizational efforts to comply with diversity and equal employment opportunity requirements, and encouraged employees to assume greater responsibility for their careers (Cairo, 1985).

Traditional Employee Development

Explaining traditional employee development is challenging for a number of reasons. First, employee development may not be well defined by organizations that express an interest in it, and when definitions are given, they are usually inconsistent. Second, the leaders of some organizations do not view organization-sponsored employee development as a driver of organizational success. They do not realize that it might be necessary to provide even modest support to employees in meeting their competency or life-career development objectives or that by doing so, both the organization and their employees would reap rewards from their mutual efforts. These employers are usually surprised when employees attain development objectives on their own and then leave for jobs elsewhere. This is not to say that organizations do not have employee development approaches, but many of these applications are not part of a formal, well-defined process of development, and, consequently, the degree of success achieved through traditional practices is often unclear.

Career Telling

Typically, a supervisor asks an employee, usually during a performance review, about his or her goals and where the employee wants to be in the next 5 or 10 years. Supervisors generally direct this question to an employee's work situation and pay little or no attention to life-career issues. Because employees probably have not thought about these questions beforehand and do not have a total life-career picture in mind, they give on-the-spot responses that are not necessarily valid. In most cases, therefore, the answers are general and nebulous. Supervisors usually react by *telling* employees what would be occupationally or vocationally best for them. For example, a supervisor tells an employee, "You're really good at customer service. I think you should get a business degree with a major in sales. You'd be good at sales." The employee is flattered and develops expectations such as tuition grants, taking time off from work, obtaining child care support while pursuing his or her studies, achieving an eventual promotion, and attaining other such rewards. After the review, the employee acts on the supervisor's suggestion and obtains support to pursue the first development step, taking a sales course. The employee completes the course, discovers that two more courses are needed, and returns to the supervisor for additional support for these courses. Later, the employee returns to the supervisor and asks for a special assignment that will test the newly acquired competencies. The supervisor, who is in fact stalling for time, complies, but this still is not enough to meet the employee's expectations. Then, with no notice, the employee is terminated in a downsizing operation.

This cycle of transactions is known as the "hush puppy" effect. Think of the events described above in the context of the following analogy. A cook is frying cornmeal treats when a puppy begins to bark nearby. In order to "hush the pup," the cook throws him a cornmeal treat, and the puppy leaves the room—a hushed puppy. The puppy departs, only to return when he is hungry again. He receives another "hush puppy" (which, by this time, he has begun to expect from the cook) and is again satisfied for a while. But since cornmeal treats do not provide adequate nutrition, the puppy fails to grow and never becomes an adult dog, and he continues in this "no growth" situation. In retrospect, the cook was not doing the puppy any favors by giving him the supposed treats.

This is often the sequence of events and the outcome that results from a career telling approach to employee development. Employees fail to grow in meaningful ways and stagnate unless an appropriate employee development experience stimulates them to take responsibility for their life-careers. This unfortunate outcome could be avoided if the supervisor were aware of the employee's competence and life-career needs or preferences and the employee were aware of her responsibility for managing her own life-career. Addressing either one of the two components affects the other. The "hush puppy" is an excellent example of a procedural development process.

Choosing Work

Figure 12 illustrates a three-step process for choosing the correct work. Achieving work satisfaction begins at Step 1, when employees express an interest in exploring opportunities within the organization. At Step 2, they become engaged in understanding their options in terms of their own values. And, finally, in Step 3, they act on one or more of their options or opportunities. Career telling generally does not follow this progression.

Figure 12: **The Three-Step Process for Choosing the Correct Work**

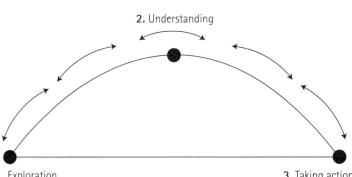

2. Understanding

1. Exploration

3. Taking action

For example, an employee approaches his career telling supervisor with a perceived need to explore his work options or opportunities and his personal values as they relate to those options. During the discussion, the supervisor starts at Step 1 but immediately moves the employee to Step 3, completely bypassing the understanding stage. Yet career telling works only when the employee understands the relationship between his values and the options or opportunities he identified in Step 1. An individual's values and their intimate connections to career choice and job satisfaction cannot be ignored. When employees do not understand their own values, or when the values of employees and organizations do not match, employees eventually leave for other positions, either within the organization or outside it (Schein, 1978). From a counseling perspective, work values are often an unnamed motive for an individual's life-career changes.

Some organizations, however, do not take their employees' value systems into consideration. A well-known example is the promotion of a technical expert to a supervisory or managerial position based on the incorrect assumption that because the employee is an excellent technical performer, she will be equally expert in a new work role. The promotion often sets the employee up for work failure, since the new role may require the use of previously unneeded competencies. The following questions should have been answered as part of Step 2:

- Is the new work role consistent with the employee's values?
- Does the employee possess the abstract, nontrainable competencies required for success in the new job? Can the employee appropriately use these competencies upon commencing the new job?
- Is the employee motivated to acquire and apply the other competencies needed for job performance success?

Moving directly from exploration (Step 1) to taking action (Step 3) predisposes the employee and the organization to failure and cheats the employee out of an opportunity to develop self-awareness and make a solid career choice—to accept the promotion or to decline it and possibly leave the organization. Bolles (2002) noted that many organizations are sometimes reluctant to provide time for developmental understanding of work opportunities because the employee might decide to leave the organization. However, as the following example illustrates, this outcome, too, can be beneficial, both for employees, who are able to pursue work that matches their values and motivations, and for organizations, which have helped potentially frustrated and unproductive employees to discover careers that are right for them.

> An individual was employed by the U.S. Postal Service as a letter carrier. The employee later realized that this type of work was not a good career fit. A *career fit* is defined as a work choice that balances the person and place with the work the person performs. In this example, the person and place were congruent, but the position was not. The letter carrier engaged in an organization-sponsored employee development planning process that placed heavy emphasis upon the use of the "explore, understand, take action" process. Following completion of the process, the letter carrier resigned and started his own business. He credited the Postal Service by saying, "I realized the position was not suited for me, and the Postal Service helped me to make a better job match. I credit the Postal Service as an organization that cares about its employees and that helped me to realize my potential. I owe the Postal Service." An excellent investment in people and a great public relations outcome for the Postal Service resulted from these transactions. Everyone won with this approach. The Postal Service does not have an unhappy, frustrated, and possibly unproductive employee, and the employee is pursuing a work path that matches his values and motivations.

It is important to keep in mind that this process does not necessarily proceed linearly. Individuals may begin at Step 1, complete Step 2, and then return to Step 1, usually because, after developing an understanding of the decision and its impact, they are not satisfied that they have chosen correctly. For similar reasons, individuals may explore, understand, take action, and then return to the understanding stage months later, seeking deeper insight into their choices or values.

Other Approaches

Some organizations have designed and implemented employee development initiatives, which are known, for example, as career, career management, or career development programs. The problem is that, in an organizational context, *program* usually means there is a beginning and an end. These programs seldom receive rigorous evaluation of their contributions to organizational and employee well-being, and, unless they are viewed as strategic to the organization's immediate success, they are frequently the first to disappear when spending is curbed. Yet many of these approaches can be not only strategically essential, but beneficial for both employees and their organizations when applied as part of a planned process of continuous employee growth. A *process* implies that there is a start with no particular end.

Many employee development programs include sessions on filling out an application, locating promotion opportunities, conducting oneself in an interview, getting a special assignment, and similar subjects related to an employee's tenure with the organization. Other programs offer education, for instance, on daily living or basic skills, team building, leadership, and visioning. In our experience, few of these programs have a long-term, significant impact on either individual development or organizational success—as some leaders have learned as cost-benefit results became more available.

Workshops

There are many topics featured in employee development workshops. Some may include, for instance, topics such as assessment of personality type (for example, the *Myers-Briggs Type Indicator®* instrument, available from CPP, Inc.); determination of interests, preferred work style, or preferences for conflict resolution; interpersonal relationships; and oral or written communication.

Individual coaching and mentoring

Supervisors, managers, or expert coworkers typically provide individual coaching for employee development activities. In organizations today, the goal is very often improved performance, which makes this type of coaching a component of the performance management process. Mentoring is closely related to coaching, but the relationship between mentor and protégé is sometimes not clear to either. Protégés may believe that their mentors will guide them toward promotions or another form of advancement in their work lives. Mentoring offers wonderful opportunities for employee growth, but misimpressions, unrealistic expectations, and other dynamics associated with mentoring may possibly ruin what can otherwise be a mutually beneficial relationship.

Toastmasters, Inc.

This group has a number of organization-based chapters throughout the United States and elsewhere. Its first objective is to support employees in acquiring presentation and public-speaking skills. This is an extremely successful developmental activity since employees initiate their own participation in this developmental process. In addition, they receive performance feedback from peers who are also participants, thereby creating an ongoing development support system. This activity can be done at little cost to the organization.

Workbook exercises

These activities are self-motivated and usually self-paced. They cover a variety of work-life topics, such as informal values assessments, occupational interest assessments, introduction to occupational areas, labor information, and sources of support for life-career management. Many exercises can be found on the Web and can be quite helpful, but it is also very beneficial to conduct life-career assessments with the guidance of qualified career counselors.

Career path systems

With this approach, employees learn about the requirements and procedures that apply to moving from one work situation to another. Although used largely in government and military settings, it may also be useful and offer tremendous value in private sector firms, especially those organizations in which upward mobility is possible. In such firms, a career path system can provide competency and performance guidelines for advancement.

Skills bank

This activity was an extremely popular form of organizational career development during the 1970s and 1980s, and despite its pitfalls, it is still used by some organizations today. An organization creates a skills bank by collecting data from employees on their education, experience, interests, knowledge, and perceived competencies (which the organization usually refers to as "skills"). After the information is returned to the skills bank manager, employees wait for the organization to take action on their career development. Unfortunately, organizations often collect the information but have no clear plans for organizing it or using it to anyone's benefit, even their own. Employees may wait years to be noticed when an organization is primarily responsible for their development.

Temporary assignments or detail job listings
Organizations sometimes post lists of employees who are seeking temporary internal assignments. As positions become available, managers consult the list and may select individuals for consideration. This does make selection a direct process, but it also raises issues of possible discrimination, favoritism, and lack of fairness since, in most cases, not every person who expresses an interest can be awarded an assignment.

Educational programs
These programs often provide college or university tuition reimbursement and support for employees who attend external seminars, workshops, conferences, and similar events. Organizations may also contract with a provider to offer an internal educational program when the program would benefit a significant number of employees.

Computer-based career guidance systems
These automated and highly sophisticated systems can be used independently by employees, with support from an employee development facilitator, to assess their values, beliefs, occupational preferences, personality type, and similar attributes via a highly structured computer program.

Competency assessment activities
Multirater competency assessment, or 360-degree feedback assessment, is increasingly being used by organizations today. With 360-degree feedback, competency assessment results are usually reviewed by the employee's manager or a performance coach, or by both. The feedback leads to development planning and a systematic employee development process. Peer review is a simplified version of the 360-degree assessment and is generally used for supervisors and higher-order managers. It helps individuals to obtain feedback on their performance from coworkers and to determine the effects of that performance on the achievement of work objectives.

Assessment centers
An assessment center is a formal, structured competency assessment mechanism. It consists of simulation and other assessment activities that use

multiple raters to determine an individual's competency strengths and performance preferences in various settings similar to the person's work situation.

Making Employee Development Competency Based

To some extent, many employee development initiatives have functioned as a response—to a crisis or a trend—rather than a strategic, long-term HR component designed to provide the organization with the necessary bench strength when the organization needs it. What is missing in many employee development efforts is a strategic link that aligns the organization's long-term success with its employees' competencies and life-career needs and preferences in ways that benefit both parties.

Why should organizations take a competency-based approach to employee development? Cafaro (2001) noted, in citing comments made by David Messinger at the 2000 WorldatWork International Conference in Seattle, "To win the proverbial war for talent, managers should focus on involving people strategically and investing in their career ambitions, even at the risk of losing them." Many workers are interested in understanding their place in the overall organization, and this fit can be defined in terms of how well each one contributes his or her talents in meaningful ways to the organization's competency pool. Cafaro in the same article singled out opportunities for advancement and challenging work as among the top reasons for joining and staying with a company, explaining that "many topflight employees are apt to be more energized by the intrinsic value and longer term payoff of education and self-improvement than the monetary value of a pay raise."

No longer is salary necessarily the reason for employees to leave one organization for another. Schein (1978) noted that individuals have unique needs and require a performance arena in which those needs can be met. If the current work setting does not provide an appropriate arena, they will seek another one, perhaps in a different work assignment in the same organization or in another organization. Consequently, it is to an organization's advantage to achieve the greatest alignment possible between its employees' work and life-career preferences and the work it needs to accomplish.

Our approach to competency-based employee development serves as the essential strategic link between organizations and their employees by emphasizing the development of worker competencies and global competence in ways that benefit the organization as well as the worker. Both workers and organization leaders must be satisfied with their answers to the question "What's in it for me?" A competency-based approach shifts the focus from job-specific training to development of competencies that can be applied in many situations.

To ensure that employee development is competency based, senior managers need to endorse employee development plans that address two key issues. First, the effort must develop those employee competencies that are aligned with achievement of the organization's strategic business objectives. Second, the plans must also address employees' issues in identifying and meeting their life-career needs.

The Advantages and Challenges of Competency-Based Employee Development

It is important to bear in mind that competency-based employee development is not a panacea for performance problems stemming from low employee morale, dysfunctional corporate culture, poor management, and other similar conditions. Organizations must separate competency-based efforts from work performance observations. Those concerns aside, there are major advantages to implementing a competency-based approach to employee development.

The process enables senior managers to communicate the organization's competency needs in a clear, straightforward manner to all employees. At the same time, its use expresses management support of employees, who are viewed as an important factor in organizational success. A comprehensive competency-based process provides employees with the tools for taking charge of their life-careers and work development by exploring and understanding their interests, values, aptitudes, personality factors, current areas of competence, and the competencies they need to build for future life-work roles and responsibilities. The concept of life-career becomes an integral part of the organization's employee development philosophy.

There are also key challenges to adopting a competency-based employee development process. A competency-based approach requires commitment to front-end competency identification and modeling, which can be a major undertaking. Competency-based employee development is intimately linked to the concepts, practices, and outputs of a competency-based HR planning system. Without such a system in place, the employee development manager might not be able to produce sound results.

Some employees may choose to leave the organization after reviewing their competency and life-career assessment results and realistically evaluating their opportunities in the organization. Employees who depart will most likely do so amicably after taking part in an employee development process. If not communicated properly, a competency-based development process could be misinterpreted by both managers and employees. For example, managers might see it as a means of providing outplacement services, while employees could view their participation as an indication of future promotion or other major advancement in the organization.

Deciding on Competency-Based or Traditional Employee Development

An appropriate organizational setting for implementing a competency-based approach requires decision makers who are willing to commit the necessary resources to the design, development, implementation, and maintenance of a competency-based process. Effective planning and implementation demand sufficient lead time as well as a competency-based HR planning system to clarify future talent needs and operate in conjunction with the development process. The organization must be prepared to invest in leaders, managers, supervisors, and others to provide ongoing support of its employees' development, for example, by coaching or offering direction and feedback. Leaders must also train and assign at least one employee to serve as an employment development facilitator.

The corporate culture must support employees in taking responsibility for identifying their life-career needs or preferences and their work-life progression. For example, leaders could provide the opportunity for employees to select and meet with a career advisory committee, consisting of the employee, his or her supervisor, an HR practitioner, and a peer. The committee might address topics such as the employee's competencies or competency needs, interests, development objectives, and plans and offer honest feedback and suggestions. Senior managers must accept employee development as a long-term process that integrates workers' life-career concerns with the organization's strategic goals and objectives and requires sustained commitment.

Implementing Competency-Based Employee Development

Implementing a competency-based approach in one component of an HR management system does not necessarily require competency-based practices throughout the organization. This is perhaps more true of employee development than of any other process. Because employee development as a key work unit is sometimes an afterthought, it frequently can be found in silos within the organization, such as operations, human resources, diversity, quality, or training. Nevertheless, the design, development, and implementation of a competency-based employee development process can be a daunting task for even the most seasoned HR professional.

Typically, an operations manager approaches an HR executive about the need for a competency-based employee development process for a particular group of workers. The manager probably does not say "competency-based" or even "employee development," but the HR professional usually understands that the request has nothing to do with short-term training.

It may be advisable to contract an external consultant if expertise in competency-based employee development is not available in the organization. The consultant's tenure in the organization and the work to be completed should be well defined and planned before work begins. The consultant can also provide oversight of the start-up process and perhaps conduct some of its activities. Employees who participate in the creation and implementation of the competency-based process will develop the sophisticated competencies needed to maintain and improve it, which makes the organization's investment well worth the cost in the long term.

Figure 13 depicts our model for creating, implementing, and maintaining a competency-based employee development process. The following step-by-step discussion provides instructions for the model.

Figure 13: **Implementing Competency-Based Employee Development**

Step 1
Identify a sponsor and develop a philosophy and a framework for the employee development process.

Step 2
Secure resources for a front-end needs assessment.

Step 3
Identify the organization's present-to-future competency needs and assess employee competencies.

Step 4
Complete preliminary competency assessments and develop estimates of competency needs for targeted employees.

Step 5
Identify employee competency development needs and life-career needs and preferences.

Step 6
Draft objectives for the employee development process and identify possible delivery methods for development services.

Step 7
Develop a plan for the start-up process.

Step 8
Brief senior managers and organize an advisory panel.

Step 9
Brief advisory panel members.

Step 10
Implement and evaluate the start-up process.

Step 11
Brief senior managers on outcomes and lessons learned.

Step 12
Institutionalize and evaluate the employee development process.

Additional suggestions on designing and implementing a competency-based employee development system can be found in Appendix B.

Step 1: Identify a sponsor and develop a philosophy and a framework for the employee development process

An organization's HR department is the logical sponsor for a competency-based employee development process. If resources are not available in the HR department, however, the manager with the most urgent need for a competency-based development initiative can also sponsor the program. A member of the HR department generally shares joint responsibility for facilitating the initiative with a representative from the sponsoring manager's staff.

The organization must decide at the outset on a philosophy for the employee development effort; the framework of the process will be built on this foundation. For example, an organization could adopt a life-career philosophy, thereby endorsing the concept that development is a holistic, continuous process. A framework consistent with this philosophy would provide initiatives that help employees to create development plans expressive of their work preferences, leisure activities, learning, families, and other dimensions of their lives.

In most organizations, the employee development process must effectively serve a diversity of persons from several generations of workers. Today, for example, baby boomers are working side-by-side with Gen-Xers and senior citizens. Consequently, organizations that create an employee development process must accommodate these generational differences in planning their service options and delivery methods.

All stakeholders must develop a clear understanding of the words used to describe the competency-based employee development process and its objectives. Vocabulary is critical to explaining how employee development will interface with other HR management initiatives and address the needs of other work units. It is also important in managing employee expectations of the process. All competency-based HR management practices are interconnected, not only within the HR function, but across the organization.

Step 2: Secure resources for a front-end needs assessment

The competency-based employee development initiative, like every effort that could have significant impact on the organization, should undergo a front-end needs assessment. Senior leaders will require considerable data about employees' competencies and life-career issues and the organization's competency needs. Without this information, obtaining their support for such an effort will be very difficult. Organizations with no competency or employee development practices in place will require resources such as the following:

- At least two computer workstations with the necessary peripheral equipment

- Office space, furniture, supplies, secure storage, telephone, fax

- Valid and reliable competencies for the work to be completed by participants

- Life-career resources such as personality assessment materials, occupational interest inventories, access to the Department of Labor's O*Net on the World-Wide Web, appropriate software systems, and values determination or clarification instruments (see Step 5 for further information on life-career issues)

- An external consultant or contractor with competency-based employee development expertise, such as a professional career counselor or certified career development facilitator, if the necessary experience is not available internally

- A research resource who can set up, administer, analyze, and report the findings of employee surveys, interviews, and similar data collection and analysis tasks

Step 3: Identify the organization's present-to-future competency needs and assess employee competencies

In identifying competency needs, it is important for the sponsor or senior leaders to specify which employees will be customers of the employee development process, as this will determine both the competency sets and the characteristics of the employee development process. It is important to keep in mind that these characteristics could become constraints when the client base for employee development is expanded to other competency sets and employee groups.

In the context of this process, the organization's competency needs and employees' competency requirements are the same. The elements to be defined are simple: Here is the work that must be done, here are the persons (or types of persons) who are available to do that work, and here are the competencies they must possess and use in appropriate ways to achieve those work objectives in a fully successful or exemplary manner. If a competency-based HR planning system is in place in the organization, then the information needed for this step is already in the planning system. Without an HR planning system, the HR practitioner must identify the competency sets that will become the foundation for the employee development process. (Competency identification is a complex topic. If necessary, review the discussion in Steps 4, 5, and 6 of Figure 3 in chapter 4.)

Identifying present-to-future competencies is challenging when work that has not yet been performed must be defined and assessed first for outputs or results and then for competencies and behavioral indicators. It can also be daunting to identify competencies and behavioral indicators for work when the current performance emphasis must be modified so as to improve the quality of the outputs. These uncertainties, of course, affect the accuracy of the predictions. When employee development targets the wrong competencies, the error can be costly in terms of resource investment and credibility. Consequently, this step must be carefully carried out.

The most direct way to identify competencies is to determine the organization's strategic goals and business objectives and, from those, the results employees must produce if they are to demonstrate successful or exemplary performance. These required work tasks should be stated in clear terms, grouped in a meaningful manner, and then analyzed for competencies and behavioral indicators.

When work elements are analyzed for competency identification purposes, three types of competencies will result. The first type consists of functional or technical competencies peculiar to the specialized nature of the work. The second type includes those required for successful daily living or basic skills, such as reading and arithmetic. The third type includes the more abstract competencies employees use in performing work, such as the capacity for patience or the ability to effectively accommodate ambiguity. Several methods of identifying competencies are currently in use, and new methods become available as the practice evolves. Each organization must select an approach that will yield comprehensive, accurate results and is also practicable, given its circumstances.

If the use of highly rigorous competency identification and modeling methods is not possible, HR practitioners might consider making a high-quality preliminary identification of competencies for the subject work and the target population. To do so, we recommend the modified DACUM process, which is one of the competency identification methods described in chapter 2. This method produces competency sets that are sufficiently accurate for needs assessment purposes. Our experience with the modified DACUM process suggests that it tends to overidentify rather than underidentify the competencies required to perform the subject work, depending on whether it is being performed at that time or is to be performed in the future.[3]

Step 4: Complete preliminary competency assessments and develop estimates of competency needs for targeted employees

Supervisors or managers judged to be experts in the work that must be performed and who are familiar with the performance of the subject employees are the best sources of information for the preliminary assessment. Assessors should evaluate only those persons about whose performance they have firsthand knowledge. The ratings could also be validated by an assessor's immediate superior, if that individual also has direct knowledge of the subject employees' performance. In short, the preliminary competency assessment data should be of the highest reliability and validity possible.[4] (See the discussion of Step 7 of Figure 3, which describes competency assessment for HR planning purposes, in chapter 4.)

Step 5: Identify employee competency development needs and life-career needs and preferences

We have already defined *employee development* as the pursuit of any activity that leads to continuous learning and personal growth and which contributes to the achievement of both individual and organizational objectives. For employees, there are two types of development needs: competency development needs and life-career needs and preferences.

These needs are assessed separately using different approaches. After data from both domains become available, HR practitioners integrate each participant's information into a competency and a life-career profile. The organization plays a major role here in designing the framework for the accomplishment of this work and thereby ensuring that data and interpretations are handled and communicated appropriately to participants. The information in the profiles should help managers to match employees with work that potentially is consistent with their needs and preferences. Because the development of this composite profile depends on the types of data collected and the purposes of the employee development process, the following suggestions should be considered general guidelines for proceeding.

We begin with competency development needs. By comparing the organization's present-to-future competency needs with the competency strengths of employees, the HR practitioner can identify and quantify competency gaps. A profile of those competencies can be easily constructed by placing the information in a two-by-two matrix composed of identical columns and rows. The rows could be assigned to participants' competencies and the columns to the competencies required by the organization. A check mark in a cell of the matrix would indicate that the employee in that row possesses the competency to the strength needed by the organization. HR practitioners can depict more detailed information by using a strength rating instead of a check mark. Keep in mind that not every participating employee needs to possess every competency and at the same strength. This information will be significant in designing competency development for individual employees.

The three types of competencies noted in Step 3—functional or technical, daily living or basic skills, and abstract—could affect the organization's ability to realize successful or exemplary work performance. HR practitioners can classify and identify competency development needs and match them to development opportunities by using these three categories. The first two types of competencies are, almost without exception, trainable, but the third type, the abstract competencies, probably cannot be acquired through training or other developmental experiences. Abstract competencies require especially creative strategies for identifying or creating development opportunities. Each organization must devise an approach that is situation specific. It is best to remain flexible and open to suggestions as start-up activities unfold. Listing the three types of competencies against needs will help the start-up process manager to determine the resources required.

Next, we consider life-career needs and preferences. The life-career dimension of employee development includes a large body of knowledge, skills, practices, and techniques and encompasses career counseling, HR development, psychotherapy, organization development, training, knowledge management, and industrial psychology. Although HR practitioners will not do in-depth life-career assessments and profiles until the start-up process is well under way, a life-career perspective on employee development will help in planning a competency-based development process that includes life-career practices as a key element. This step requires only a preliminary assessment of participants' life-career needs and preferences appropriate for pilot study purposes.

There are as many explanations of life-career needs and preferences as there are theorists. In our experience, however, the following six life-career needs have been mentioned repeatedly by clients in organizational settings and in private practice:

1. A need to achieve, motivated by the desire for personal competence and self-mastery.

2. A need to produce work results or outputs with perceived value, or, in other words, finding work that has personal meaning.

3. A need to perform work that is personally enjoyable.

4. A need to exercise a degree of control over the performance of one's work activities as well as when and under what conditions one performs work.

5. A need for quality information, time to process the information, and an arena in which employees can use the information to actively pursue their preferences.

6. A need for time away from work for activities such as, for example, hobbies, recreation, care giving, independent learning or personal growth, physical rest, and spiritual development.

This final need raises a critical point regarding the design and implementation of an employee development process. While employees are engaged in a development process, they need to understand that their total sense of satisfaction will not come from their worker roles. As Bolles (2002) noted, satisfaction comes from an integration of life roles and activities that include work, leisure, learning, and family. The life-career concept is a major philosophical change for a typical organization. It not only directs attention to facets of life other than work but also stresses that success is not confined to advancement in an employee's work-for-hire.[5]

An organization needs a collective inventory of employee life-career needs and preferences if it intends to address these issues. Probably the best suggestion we can offer, in terms of time and expense, is to organize a focus group that is representative of all the participants. This group could consist of up to 20 persons if necessary. By conducting a facilitated discussion, HR practitioners can create a comprehensive list of life-career needs and preferences as expressed by the group members. To ensure additional comprehensiveness, a panel of subject-matter experts can review both the list and the draft questionnaire assembled from the list. The final document incorporating their suggestions and revisions can then be distributed to all start-up participants, instructing them to select their five highest-priority, most critical life-career needs or preferences and to rate the importance of those five needs or preferences relative to their current or anticipated life and work circumstances.[6] The data, once analyzed, provide a very comprehensive understanding of participants' life-career needs and preferences and will be useful in making additional plans. If participants agree to place their names on their questionnaires, management will be able to consult these personalized records of their life-career preferences when considering work assignments and development opportunities. Further examples of life-career assessment exercises can be found in Appendix C.

Step 6: Draft objectives for the employee development process and identify possible delivery methods for development services
The objectives for any competency-based employee development process will differ somewhat across organizations; however, facilitators of the effort may want to include one or more of the following statements of objectives among their own:

- To ensure an adequate and balanced competency pool so that the organization can achieve its strategic goals and business objectives
- To communicate to employees the organization's support of their continuous learning and the understanding and pursuit of their life-career preferences

- To ensure that work assignments are aligned with employees' competency strengths and the successful pursuit of their life-career preferences
- To serve as an employment incentive to attract exemplary performers
- To encourage the retention of fully successful and exemplary performers
- To provide less productive employees with self-insight in an ethical and professional manner and encourage them to take responsibility for their daily work and life-career preferences, possibly including outplacement

There is an astounding range of approaches available for providing employee development services, even in geographically isolated areas. Candidates for learning opportunities include the following:

- Web-based and distance learning
- Embedded learning
- On-the-job learning with peers or site-assigned facilitators
- Coaching from a supervisor, manager, or executive
- Professional counseling, career counseling, or assistance from a certified career development facilitator
- Management discussions
- Workbooks or other self-directed learning media
- Computer-based career guidance systems
- Professional or trade conferences, seminars, and workshops
- Job or work rotation
- Learning opportunities provided by labor or other organizations
- Group-based life-career exploration or planning activities
- Community college, 4-year college, and university courses or other offerings, including adult or continuing education
- Community-based adult or continuing education
- Employee-initiated learning projects (for example, self-study projects, reading programs)

Step 7: Develop a plan for the start-up process
Competency-based employee development initiatives can be difficult to implement and may not be fully accomplished in one attempt. Those who pursue this approach must maintain a realistic mind-set and expect to learn as they go. Process milestones should be marked by reasonable objectives, taking into account the resources available and organizational attitudes toward the process and its outcomes.

The following items should be reviewed before beginning development of the start-up plan:

- The organization's strategic goals or objectives
- The competency needs to be addressed
- Competency assessment data for participating employees
- Estimates of participating employees' life-career preferences, the effect of those preferences on the achievement of work, optimal placement of employees to complete that work, and employees' competency development needs
- Estimates of the types and volume of employee development activities needed to close competency gaps
- Summary of participating employees' life-career preferences and the impact on meeting work placement and competency development needs
- The time frame for completing start-up activities
- Possible roadblocks to achieving start-up outcomes and ways in which to overcome them

A well-conceived start-up plan will go a long way toward creating a high-quality employee development process that will be valued by organization leaders. Producing a tight yet flexible plan is well worth the investment of time and effort. The start-up process manager should confirm that the plan meets the following criteria:

- Is absolutely consistent with the start-up process objectives
- Uses only those resources that management has already committed to completion of the project
- Is easy to understand

- Is automated so that it can be easily modified, annotated, and distributed

- Communicates the agreed-upon results or deliverables needed for project success

- Includes tasks required to produce administrative and other documents for key project stages (the time and effort needed to produce or acquire these items is often underestimated)

- Includes tasks and time needed to obtain, review, evaluate, or implement vendor products such as a computer-based career guidance system

- Begins identification of process evaluation activities

The start-up manager is responsible for providing ongoing internal communication on start-up design and implementation. A standardized project-planning matrix makes this task easier. Each row of the matrix states a major project task and, below the task, any key subtasks that are of critical importance for successful performance of the work. The columns of the matrix list details for each task. These details should include, at a minimum, the task output, result, deliverable, or outcome; target completion date; actual completion date; resources assigned to the task; and inputs to the task, such as earlier deliverables, materials, decisions, and so forth.

Step 8: Brief senior managers and organize an advisory panel

With the information collected and developed in the previous steps, the start-up process manager is now well prepared to brief the organization's senior leaders on the project. The main objectives of this briefing are to ensure the following:

- Senior leaders understand the need for certain employee competencies as part of the organization's talent pool. The critical data to support the need should be presented and explained in detail. Leaders must also understand the consequences if these competencies are not available when required for organizational success.

- Senior leaders understand the advantages of taking a holistic view of employee development by accommodating employees' life-career preferences while developing their competencies and making work placement decisions.

- Senior leaders are prepared to commit the resources needed for a successful start-up.

Senior leaders should also select an employee development advisory panel and compile a list of responsibilities for panel members. The advisory panel will be charged with reviewing, assessing, and reporting on the project and will make recommendations on implementation to the start-up process manager.

Step 9: Brief advisory panel members

Advisory panel members should receive the same briefing as the senior managers. It is especially important that they understand their specific responsibilities and the timetable for carrying them out. Panel members offer a no-fault environment for preliminary testing of start-up instruments, procedures, and techniques, which may then be revised as needed. They could also engage in process activities, such as life-career assessment and debriefing, that participating employees will complete after the system is implemented. Advisory panel members have an integral role in reviewing and interpreting process evaluation information and recommending improvements. They should be available to the start-up process manager on an ad hoc basis as needed.

Step 10: Implement and evaluate the start-up process

There is no one way to implement a competency-based employee development process. Each organizational setting requires its own unique approach. The following suggestions for implementing and evaluating the process therefore represent general guidelines only.

First, HR practitioners must confirm that the required resources— space, personnel, materials, and related support mechanisms—are in place and ready for immediate use. A premature launch could result in failures, employee and management dissatisfaction, inappropriate use of established employee development practices, ethical violations, compromised confidentiality, employee assessment errors, poor service delivery, and other unfortunate occurrences. Since credibility is essential in this particular HR application, it is advisable to delay implementation rather than risk a disaster.

Second, the sequence of activities should ensure that the approach is indeed systematic. Organizational circumstances must dictate when and in what manner these steps are taken, but the following are the minimum that must be completed by the start-up process manager:

- Continue to review the process philosophy and objectives and all agreements made with sponsors, organization leaders, and HR practitioners. Make changes to all agreements as circumstances warrant but be certain to communicate those changes in a timely manner to all parties with a need to know. Ensure that communications are complete and accurate.

- Review the specifications for the targeted employees and prepare an electronic participant database, using the HR information system if possible. The database should include, at a minimum, each participant's name, work unit designation, work location as a street address, telephone numbers, e-mail addresses, and position title. Collect the same information from the participants' supervisors.

- Brief participating employees, their supervisors, and employee development advisory panel members on anticipated objectives and outcomes as well as plans for start-up activities and the role each group will play in these activities. The timing and content of this preliminary briefing could be somewhat problematic. It is essential, on one hand, to build interest and enthusiasm but, on the other, to avoid creating rising expectations about project services or outcomes. Organizations today face rapid change and sometimes must accommodate business crises by modifying employee development priorities.

- If it has not yet been done, complete multirater competency assessments for the key competencies to be addressed by the participants. Valid competency assessment data are essential to project success.

- Identify the elements that will constitute the life-career component of the employee development process. For example, what life-career assessment instruments will be used, who will administer and score them, and how will the results be interpreted to participants?[7] Are certifications required? What are the requirements for maintaining the security of the assessment results? Are confidentiality agreements understood, and can they be met within organization operations?

- Develop practices for linking and analyzing competency assessment and life-career preference information and communicating the data to participants. Decide on the briefing protocol and select the persons to conduct the briefings. Should an employee need further development counseling after learning about his or her assessment information, how will these services be identified and made available in a timely and appropriate manner? What payment source will fund this support? These issues must be addressed when performance and capabilities assessments are part of an employee development effort.

- Assess participants' development needs and identify development activities for meeting those needs. Assess gaps between development needs and opportunities.[8]

- Specify work placement and assignment practices for matching employees with work that is aligned with their competencies and life-career preferences. Verify the legality of the practices before applying them.

- Announce formal implementation of start-up activities to participating employees and their supervisors. Explain the philosophy, foundation, and objectives of employee development; the approach that will be used to provide the services; employees' and supervisors' responsibilities; the benefits for employees and the organization and how they are related; and specific steps to be followed to implement the activities and the time frame for doing so. This should be a structured presentation that allows for extensive participation by employees and their supervisors.

- After the start-up process has been completed, implement the planned evaluation activities by collecting and analyzing summative evaluation data.[9] Prepare a comprehensive yet brief evaluation report and present it to the project sponsors, with recommendations for the long-term implementation of an appropriate employee development process.

Step 11: Brief senior managers on outcomes and lessons learned
Although each application has its own information requirements for senior management, the following key points should be covered:

- Review start-up process objectives and their relationship to the organization's strategic goals, business objectives, and competency needs.
- Highlight the purposes of both life-career and competency assessment, how each was completed, the results that were achieved, and the value of both to employees and the organization.
- Summarize the work completed to date.
- Identify successes and lessons learned.
- Document the impact of employee competency acquisitions that resulted directly from start-up activities.
- Provide case reports or testimonials of successes from participating employees and their managers.
- Cite unintended benefits or outcomes that were realized.
- Identify and give frank, specific reasons for process start-up objectives that were not achieved. Explore the issues with participating senior managers.
- Recommend institutionalizing a competency-based employee development process in the organization. List the resources and management support needed to create a continuous, strategically focused process that will benefit both the organization and its employees.

Step 12: Institutionalize and evaluate the employee development process
If senior leaders make the commitment to a formal, competency-based process, the successful start-up must be institutionalized, usually by extending the process to a wider audience, to greater depth with the existing audience, or both. At this stage, HR practitioners should confirm the following conditions:

- Key leaders agree on a clear philosophy and framework for a competency-based employee development process.
- The philosophy and framework are communicated throughout the organization.

- Adequate resources have been committed to institutionalize the process.
- A formal, continuous assessment mechanism is in place to track process accomplishments and identify areas for improvement.

Finally, how will evaluation be planned and conducted? Evaluation planning began earlier in this model and was included in Step 7, with the development of a start-up plan. HR practitioners should examine evaluation activities and their effectiveness and decide on any necessary modifications. We have found the CIPP (context, input, process, product) model by Stufflebeam to be a useful first resource for conceptualizing a systematic evaluation of this type of intervention.[10] The American Society for Training and Development also has available numerous evaluation resources. Return on investment should be researched and documentation made available to senior management. It is best to have an independent assessor perform comprehensive evaluations of a summative nature, when possible.

Employee Development and Succession Management

It is well worth noting that employee development plays a key role in many areas of HR management. Succession planning, for example, has become a major issue for organizations as workers from the baby boom generation are retiring or preparing to retire. Succession planning and management tend to be viewed largely from a top-down rather than a bottom-up perspective, but planning should be a priority at all levels of most organizations. Regardless of perspective, however, a competency-based process will make a substantial contribution to closing the succession-related gaps in an organization's competency pool. See Appendix D for a discussion on the interrelationship of the employee development, individual career management, and succession management processes.

Summary

In this chapter, we introduced the employee development concept from several perspectives. Because this complex area of human resources is often surrounded by confusion, we provided operational definitions of key terms. The chapter addressed ways of making employee development competency based and enumerated the advantages and challenges of competency-based practices. We explained organizational conditions that suggested the use of either a traditional or a competency-based approach. A model for creating and implementing a competency-based employee development process in an organization was presented and discussed in depth. Finally, we noted the value of a competency-based process in meeting the demands of succession management.

Part Three

TRANSITIONING
to Competency-Based HR Management

CHAPTER 10

The Transformation to Competency-Based HR Management

This book has been about transforming HR management from a traditional work- or job-based system into one that is competency based. A competency-based approach reinvents HR departments and functions, making them more organizationally responsive and aligned with strategic objectives.[1] It can help to leverage the strengths of individuals and unleash their potential in a way that is less likely to occur in a work-based system.

Traditional approaches to HR management do not seem to be effective anymore. Using activities or jobs as the foundation for work design is increasingly out of touch with the competitive needs of organizations. In contrast, competency-based HR management can focus attention on discovering, applying, and making use of the differences between exemplary and fully successful performers. That can possibly lead to quantum leaps in productivity improvement. Our approach is based on the principle that organizations should match people to work rather than vice versa.

But no change of this magnitude can be made without effort. Organizations need a plan. Developing and implementing that plan is the focus of this chapter, which addresses the following questions:

- How can the HR department become competency based?
- What model can guide this transformation, and how is it applied?
- How can HR practitioners become competent in applying this new approach?

Making the HR Function Competency Based

Managers who plan to reinvent their HR functions on a competency-based foundation have their work cut out for them. There are no textbooks to guide HR practitioners in using such an approach. And it may fly in the face of common and familiar business practices. In other words, being on the cutting edge leads to challenges that are not easily resolved.

The first place to start is with HR practitioners themselves. They must be briefed on competency identification, modeling, and assessment. They must be guided toward an understanding of the differences between competencies and work activities and between competency models and job descriptions. When they realize the possible benefits of a competency-based HR function, both to the organization and to themselves, they will lend their support to exploring and advocating such a transformation.

There are two key issues to keep in mind during early discussions on transforming the HR function. First, HR practitioners themselves are often the most vocal opponents of changing the systems in their own organization. That should not be too surprising. They have learned what to do and how to do it in a certain way. Challenging the status quo is not easy. Second, transforming HR from a work-based to a competency-based approach does not have to be an all-or-nothing proposition. HR practitioners may need to consider which functional areas will benefit most from the use of competency-based practices. Those areas should be chosen according to their strategic significance for the organization's success. It is also worth emphasizing that changing the entire HR function is much more difficult than focusing on one or two HR components, or specific job categories, work areas, or company sites. Often the most effective approach is to start small, achieve a quick success, and then leverage the credibility and measurable benefits gained from that success to demonstrate the value of the effort.

Transforming the HR Department

In other chapters, we have noted that models can help to conceptualize the implementation of competency-based processes. However, there is no one model for formulating and implementing a competency-based approach to HR management. Each organization has its unique corporate culture, and senior managers differ in their awareness of HR practices, the sophistication of their approaches, and their willingness to experiment. The model depicted in Figure 14 therefore provides only general guidelines for formulating and implementing a competency-based approach to HR management.

Step 1: Build awareness

Most HR practitioners are familiar with the traditional work-based approach to HR management. They know that work analysis, which leads to such products as job descriptions and job specifications, is the foundation for all HR efforts. From work analysis and its products, they derive recruitment and selection strategies, training needs, career paths, employee performance management systems, compensation and reward systems, and other HR efforts. But fewer practitioners are familiar with the history and techniques of competency identification, modeling, and assessment.

Consequently, an important starting point is to build awareness. HR practitioners should attend workshops, classes, or conferences on competency modeling or invite external consultants to discuss competency-based HR management in the organization. They can circulate white papers, explore the topic in department staff meetings, collect information about the benefits realized by other organizations from using a competency-based approach to HR, and encourage other stakeholders to read about competency modeling. Taking these actions does much to cast HR practitioners as true leaders for human capital in their organization.

After this step is completed, meaningful discussions can begin on the possible value of a competency-based approach to HR management.

Figure 14: **A Model for Transforming the HR Function**

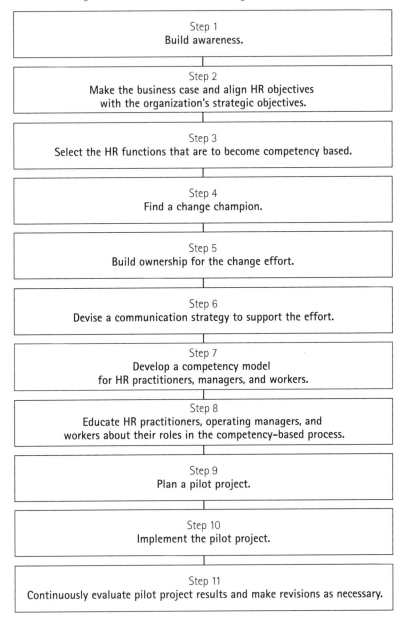

Step 1
Build awareness.

Step 2
Make the business case and align HR objectives
with the organization's strategic objectives.

Step 3
Select the HR functions that are to become competency based.

Step 4
Find a change champion.

Step 5
Build ownership for the change effort.

Step 6
Devise a communication strategy to support the effort.

Step 7
Develop a competency model
for HR practitioners, managers, and workers.

Step 8
Educate HR practitioners, operating managers, and
workers about their roles in the competency–based process.

Step 9
Plan a pilot project.

Step 10
Implement the pilot project.

Step 11
Continuously evaluate pilot project results and make revisions as necessary.

Form 4: Assessing the HR Function

Directions: Use this worksheet to collect perceptions about the HR function from managers and workers.	
1. What is the organization doing particularly well in managing its human resources?	
2. What could the organization do to improve its management of human resources?	
3. If you could magically transform the organization's HR efforts into something that meets your greatest expectations and supports the organization's strategic objectives, what would you change and why?	

Step 2: Make the business case and align HR objectives with the organization's strategic objectives

Before decision makers can be convinced to invest sizable amounts of time, money, and effort in adopting (or even experimenting with) competency-based HR management, they must see its value. It is easier to understand the business case when they see evidence of what is going well—and not going well—with the organization's approach to managing human resources. One way to do that is to ask managers and employees about the HR function. Form 4 can be used to organize their answers. The information gained through answers to these questions will provide excellent feedback on HR efforts.[2]

Step 3: Select the HR functions that are to become competency based

Large, complex organizations are usually unable to implement competency-based HR management in every HR function. It is essential to be selective and apply change efforts on a smaller scale. Use Form 5 to

Form 5: Selecting Which HR Functions Should Become Competency Based

Directions: Use this worksheet to organize your thinking and that of key stakeholders on selective implementation of competency-based HR management.	
1. Which HR functions would benefit most from a competency-based approach?	
2. Explain the reasons for your answer. Describe your vision of the newly transformed HR function if it were installed according to your ideas.	

decide which areas—for example, planning, selection, training, or development—would realize the greatest benefits from a competency-based approach.

Step 4: Find a change champion

Although the support of senior executives is important, HR practitioners should seize the initiative in reinventing their own function. They are perhaps the ones most able to recognize the signs that a department needs to be revitalized. For example, do managers complain that the HR function is not responsive to their needs? Are HR directors frequently replaced? Do employees give each other knowing glances when someone brings up the topic of HR?

If resources are not available in the HR department, however, senior leaders or operating managers can also champion the initiative.

Step 5: Build ownership for the change effort

Transforming HR management to a competency-based approach requires the support of many people. Senior executives, HR practitioners, operating managers, and workers must all feel that they own the effort.

The Whole Systems Transformation Conference is one method of developing ownership. The conference can last several days and involves a cross section of people from the organization. After a review of internal and external trends as they affect the workforce, participants form small groups, consider external trends and their organizational impact, evaluate the existing HR function, and identify the challenges involved in aligning HR practices with the organization's strategic objectives. They then prepare a written report for management in which they specify which HR components should be reinvented, explain the reasons for their choices, and clarify the role of competency-based HR management in achieving strategic objectives. HR practitioners can maintain the momentum generated at the conference by setting up electronic bulletin boards and commissioning task forces to investigate best practices, and their costs and benefits, in other organizations.[3]

Step 6: Devise a communication strategy to support the effort
A major undertaking such as this requires constant communication. Stakeholders must be informed about what is happening, why it is important, what it means, how it will affect them, and what the organization will gain from it. Ongoing communication ensures continued involvement and develops ownership in the change effort.

Step 7: Develop a competency model for
HR practitioners, managers, and workers
Many competency studies address HR management, operating management, and various employee job categories. The goal in this step is to ask all key stakeholders to consider the effects of a competency-based approach on the roles, competencies, and work outputs or results expected of HR practitioners, operating managers, and workers. Use Form 6 to organize the answers to this question.

Step 8: Educate HR practitioners, operating managers, and
workers about their roles in the competency-based process
People cannot be expected to change their performance if they do not have the knowledge, skills, or attitudes to do so. Employee education is a necessary part of the move from a work-based to a competency-based approach. Use Form 7 to organize your thinking on educating HR practitioners, operating managers, workers, and other key stakeholders.

Step 9: Plan a pilot project
Plan to pilot test the competency-based approach in one or two HR functions. Executive or management development is a good area in which to begin, for several reasons. Conducting competency modeling

Form 6: Expected Roles, Competencies, and Outputs

Directions: Use this worksheet to record the expected roles, competencies, and outputs of HR practitioners, operating managers, and workers in a competency-based HR management system. Explain how they differ from those of a traditional approach.	
1. For HR practitioners:	
2. For operating managers:	
3. For workers:	

with managers introduces an important stakeholder group to competency-based HR management, and their support is essential to extending competency-based practices to other HR efforts. Another option for pilot testing is the employee recruitment and selection function. This is a major, highly visible area of HR practice and is familiar to almost everyone in the organization. Actions taken here can be widely communicated. Developing awareness across the organization is an important part of the pilot project.

The pilot project plan should specify the following:

- What will happen
- Who will be involved and what they will do
- The timeline for accomplishing the project outputs or results
- The method of assessing the results
- The means of communicating the results to others in the organization

At this point, you should also think ahead to evaluating the pilot project. For example, what kind of information would be most persuasive to decision makers, and how should it be collected? What HR problems will be addressed by a competency-based approach? Begin collecting metrics for measuring the impact of each problem and establish a means of tracking improvements.

Step 10: Implement the pilot project
Actual implementation requires the involvement of a full-time manager who will oversee the pilot effort on a daily basis, tracking outcomes

Form 7: Educating Key Stakeholder Groups on Competency-Based HR Management

Directions: Use this worksheet to organize your ideas about educating key stakeholders.	
Question	**Describe the type of education that will enable key stakeholders to answer the questions.**
1. What is a competency?	
2. How are competencies identified? Modeled? Assessed or measured?	
3. Why should the organization adopt a competency-based approach to HR management?	
4. How is a competency-based approach different from the familiar traditional approach?	
5. What will a competency-based approach mean for the organization? For individual employees?	
6. What advantages will the organization gain from a competency-based approach? What advantages will individual employees gain?	
7. What challenges will the organization experience in adopting a competency-based approach? What challenges will employees experience?	

against project objectives and ensuring that the initiative stays on course. Failure with a pilot project will probably mean the end of the proposed competency-based effort. Therefore, the manager assigned to the project should have the credibility to command support and be given the resources needed to achieve success. The project manager should keep key stakeholders informed of measurable project results as pilot implementation proceeds and take steps to publicize the effort, within and, possibly, outside the organization.

Step 11: Continuously evaluate pilot project results and make revisions as necessary

It is not enough simply to manage the pilot project. Information about its results must be collected. Decision makers will be reluctant to devote additional resources to broadscale implementation without seeing major benefits that outweigh the costs of implementing the project. For instance, can it be shown that a pilot effort directed toward recruitment and hiring actually led to successful hiring or raised the retention rate among staff? If directed toward executive and management development, did it improve performance or increase the organization's bench strength? Be sure to keep decision makers regularly informed by using a variety of means, such as a standing committee, listserv, or Website. Success has little impact if it is not demonstrated or publicized.

Continuing evaluation is also helpful in keeping the project on track. As implementation continues, the project manager should make any midcourse corrections necessary to maintain alignment with the desired objectives and goals.

Developing Competence With the New Approach

It makes sense to reinvent the HR function through the use of a competency-based approach. Such an approach involves creating a competency model for HR practitioners, assessing individuals against that model, and identifying their developmental needs. Use Form 8 to determine the behavioral indicators linked to the required competencies. The assessment instrument in Form 9 helps to identify developmental needs for HR practitioners in your organization.

Form 8: Important HR Practitioner Competencies and Associated Behaviors

Directions: Use this worksheet to help you think through the specific behaviors associated with competencies related to competency-based HR management. Describe the observable behaviors HR practitioners would demonstrate when applying the competency outlined in the lefthand column.

HR practitioner competency	Observable behaviors
1. Revising the HR department mission to reflect a competency-based approach	
2. Rethinking the organizational structure of the HR department in terms of a competency-based approach	
3. Reviewing the qualifications of HR staff in terms of a competency-based approach	
4. Applying competency-based HR planning	
5. Applying competency-based employee recruitment	
6. Applying competency-based employee selection	
7. Applying competency-based employee training or education	
8. Applying competency-based performance management	
9. Applying competency-based employee development	
10. Applying competency-based reward processes	

Form 9: Assessing the Competency-Based HR Practitioner

Directions: Use this assessment instrument to determine how well HR practitioners in the HR function understand and can demonstrate competency-based HR. For each practitioner competency, indicate in column A its importance, using this scale:

1 = Not applicable	4 = Important
2 = Not at all important	5 = Very important
3 = Somewhat important	

Then in column B indicate the level of development needed, using this scale:

1 = Not applicable	4 = Substantial need for development
2 = No need for development	5 = Great need for development
3 = Some need for development	

HR practitioner competency	(A) Importance of ability to demonstrate this competency (1–5)	(B) Level of development needed for this competency (1–5)
1. Revising the HR department mission to reflect a competency-based approach		
2. Rethinking the organizational structure of the HR department in terms of a competency-based approach		
3. Reviewing the qualifications of HR staff in terms of a competency-based approach		
4. Applying competency-based HR planning		
5. Applying competency-based employee recruitment		
6. Applying competency-based employee selection		
7. Applying competency-based employee training or education		
8. Applying competency-based performance management		
9. Applying competency-based employee development		
10. Applying competency-based reward processes		

The same basic approach used for the roles and competencies of operating managers and workers may also be examined in relation to the new approach. Simply consider these questions:

- What roles should managers and workers play, and which competencies are required when implementing competency-based HR management?
- How can the behaviors associated with these competencies be identified?

The answers to these questions can provide a starting point for organized processes by which managers, workers, and other key stakeholder groups can participate in the successful implementation of competency-based HR management.

Summary

If an organization is to be successful in moving from traditional work-based HR management to a system that is competency based, a plan is essential. This chapter provided guidelines for preparing such a plan and for developing competence among HR practitioners in applying the new approach.

CHAPTER 11

Competency-Based HR Management: The Next Steps

Many readers may be wondering, "Where is this all headed? Everything we've heard sounds true and worthwhile, but what's next—and why?" In this chapter, we offer some predictions about the future of competency-based HR management, its possible innovations and uses, and some of the challenges that lie ahead for those who apply it.

Future Direction

We believe that competency-based HR management will become the standard approach for all or most organizations. Job descriptions, the basis of traditional work-based HR management, are no longer an effective means of making good employment decisions. There are several reasons for this. First, job descriptions tend to focus on activities or responsibilities instead of on measurable outcomes or results. Second, they do not take into account the abstract qualifications that affect customer satisfaction and are integrally related to exemplary performance. And third, in the volatile business world of today, job descriptions simply cannot be written quickly enough to keep up with work changes.

Many decision makers are looking for an alternative approach as they simultaneously attempt to retrofit existing methods and practices. Competency modeling has much to recommend it. Competency models are more flexible and more enduring than job descriptions. They are based on measurable work results and are specific to the organization's culture and success factors. Competency models are also highly effective at describing the less definable characteristics associated with exemplary individual performance. This may enhance the capability of HR practitioners to link organizational core competencies to the competencies of individual exemplary performers. Pinpointing the characteristics of exemplary performers holds out the promise of making quantum leaps in productivity improvement if HR systems are retooled such that the competencies of exemplary performers become the foundation for all HR practices.

At this time, case studies have documented HR departments with one or more competency-based HR functions within their organization. In the future, however, we expect that competency-based HR management will be used to align HR practices with the organization's strategic objectives and employee development efforts and to integrate all components of the HR function across an organization.

Future Innovations

Growing awareness of the value of competency-based HR management will lead to innovations in competency technology. For example, HR practitioners will be able to apply increasingly sophisticated electronic technologies to competency identification, modeling, and assessment. Web-based applications for competency identification and validation as well as for development and career management, already possible, will become the norm.

As more organizations conduct competency identification and modeling work, we can expect that the development and verification of innovative methods for competency identification will advance both the state of the practice and the state of the art. Increased use of competency methods will build the inventory of identified competencies, thus improving the data available for use in menu-based competency modeling activities. Organizations will then be able to define exemplary performance more precisely and with greater validity and reliability.

We anticipate that the use of competency technology will be the subject of considerable research regarding its value for improving performance—both individual and organizational—and the long-term effects of competency applications. There will be increasing focus on return on investment, return on assets, and other valuation measures that demonstrate the superiority of a competency-based approach.

Future Uses

We believe that competency-based HR management practices that enhance, encourage, and support exemplary performance will dominate the HR management scene in the future.

Organizations will most likely introduce competency-based HR management through their recruitment and selection applications. This will be a response to growing awareness of the critical need to match people to work rather than work to people. Talent will be increasingly recognized as a major competitive resource, and competency-based HR management is a more effective approach to identifying the people who are essential to sustained competitive advantage.

Performance management and rewards are the second and third HR management processes that will most likely become competency based. In the case of performance management, organizations will be responding to their need to achieve organizational success with decreased HR complements by utilizing the full potential of existing employees. In other words, managers who are expected to do more with less will turn to exemplary performers for the huge advantages they offer compared to their fully successful peers. As for rewards, exemplary performers must be given incentives and rewards that match their exceptional contributions and measurable productivity.

Because employees recognize the benefits of a wide spectrum of competencies, which makes them highly marketable both within their organizations and externally, they will expect growth and development opportunities at unprecedented levels. This will require many leaders to understand the importance of a competency-based employee development function as a key HR management strategy. Competency-based employee development defines competency acquisition needs as those that align with life-careers as well as with development. When both of these dimensions are successfully addressed, organizations will be better able to attract and retain exemplary performers.

Future Challenges

Wrongheaded application of competency identification, modeling, and assessment methods is foremost among the challenges in the widespread use of a competency-based approach. HR practitioners must take steps to distinguish the good from the bad methods of identifying competencies and constructing competency models. Too many practitioners are in a rush to develop the models so that they can move on to the next steps. Given these inadequate models, decision makers are never able to discover what sets exemplary performers apart from fully successful ones, and much of the models' value is lost.

A second challenge is the lack of HR staff capable of completing high-quality competency technology applications. In the absence of resident HR specialists who can perform this work, organizations must enlist the support of experienced contractors or consultants.

Third, it will continue to be a challenge to gain the long-term commitment of senior mangers. Senior managers must be willing to learn, become involved, and commit to objectives that might require more time to realize than they prefer. An organization's decision makers sometimes view initiatives as all-or-nothing propositions. As noted earlier, however, it is not necessary to convert all HR functions and practices to a competency-based foundation in one step. A more practical approach is to introduce the use of competency-based practices in those areas that will realize the greatest organizational benefits with the available resources.

Fourth, and finally, organizations that do not initiate and maintain continuous communication with their employees on the use of competency-based practices will find implementation of the new approach a difficult undertaking. All persons affected by the technology must be informed about its benefits, requirements, and other factors relative to the applications to be used.

Summary

In this brief chapter, we have attempted to predict the future direction of competency-based HR management and the innovations that may affect it. We discussed the particular HR functions that we believe will adopt and use competency-based HR management and identified some key challenges that lie ahead in applying a competency-based approach. We believe that the use of competencies and competency-based HR management practices are here to stay. Competency applications will revolutionize the way an organization's leaders and employees work together. To accept the value of competencies is to embrace the value of elements of the human soul. In doing so, we also recognize and nurture the concept that work is, after all, a deeply human enterprise, and without the contributions that come from human performance, nothing of great value can be accomplished.

APPENDIXES

Frequently Asked Questions About Competency-Based HR Management

While we have been talking and listening to others about competency-based human resource management, we have received numerous questions as intrigued listeners have thought about it. Here are some actual questions and answers on the issue.

Question 1: *How can HR practitioners justify the costs involved with identifying competencies, establishing competency models, and implementing these models?*

Competency identification is based on the view that exemplary performers, who exist in each job category, can be much more productive than average performers in the same job category. If it were possible to get all employees up to the level of exemplars (the so-called best-in-class workers), then an organization might be able to get the same work out with far fewer people. Alternatively, they might be able to get much more work done with the same number of people. Of course, that is only the theory. The reality is that some competencies must be hired or selected for (for example, "patience"). Only some competencies can be developed through training, coaching, experience, education, or other learning pursuits.

Question 2: *How can HR practitioners sell management on the importance of performing competency identification, competency assessment, and competency modeling?*

See our answer to question 1. In addition, the notion of "jobs" is becoming outdated. Competencies are more enduring than jobs, though it is important to remember that a competency is inherent to individuals and is not resident in the work that they do. In other words, you (as a person) have competencies. It is up to the company or employer to figure out how best to identify, quantify, and harness those talents.

Additionally, job descriptions speak only to the activities or duties that people carry out—not to the results they are intended to get. Research continually shows that workers and their organizational superiors differ on their expectations about what results should be obtained by the worker. But competency models do speak to results, working backward to the qualities that people need to obtain them. Moreover, in an age when people have grown to appreciate the value of emotional intelligence, competency models do a better job than job descriptions at helping to describe important yet intangible elements that are essential to job success. (Educators have, for some time now, called that the *affective domain* of learning.) For instance, would you like a doctor who is technically proficient but who does not treat you like a human being? The intangible part of a doctor's job is to treat you like a human being, and that's exactly what we are talking about. As work involves more relationships—that is, with customers and with coworkers—the intangible, affective domain, the emotional intelligence issue, only grows more important.

Question 3: *Do you have any case studies involving organizations that have gone through the competency implementation process?*

Many case studies have been published that involve organizations that have implemented competency-based HR in one or all facets of their HR effort. One particular work includes details of twelve cases of competency-based performance improvement applications in a variety of organization settings. See Dubois, 1998.

Question 4: *What tools should practitioners use to link competency models to the organization's core competencies and strategic strengths?*

It is better to think of methodologies (that is, approaches) than tools (which sound like "gimmicks").

The big challenge in this line of work is that everyone wants quick fixes. But there is a trade-off between rigor and speed. There are thousands of competency models that you can get for free on the Web. And some organizations have even published books full of the competency models collected from various organizations. But their value is suspect. Why? The answer is simple: To be most useful, a competency model must be based on the corporate culture in which the performer carries out his or her work; and competencies are based on the person, not on the work.

Question 5: *What does a competency-based HR management organization look like?*

All aspects of the traditional HR function are based on work analysis, which has "job descriptions" as its chief output. But a competency-based HR management organization adds and emphasizes the many competency models to updated job descriptions. All aspects of HR—from recruitment and selection through training through performance management and appraisal through employee reward systems—are based on competencies. Dubois and Rothwell (2000) covered the "how to" of competency identification, modeling, and assessment. It is now time to think of how to implement competency models across an organization or its HR functions.

Question 6: *What advice do you have for those who are interested in pursuing competency-based HR management?*

Buy this book.

Question 7: *If an organization can't afford to apply competency modeling to all its jobs, how should it determine its priorities?*

You can take a slipshod, quick, dirty, and cheap approach to competency modeling—just as you can for analyzing work to come up with job descriptions. So we think the question is not, "What do you do if you can't afford it?" but rather, "How do you do it with any value when you may be facing other pressures?" One approach is to outsource the work by hiring competent external consulting assistance.

Question 8: *What is the dynamic between individual competencies and job descriptions, and how are jobs modified based on who's in the job?*

You are asking about what is called *personalization*, which is how the person modifies the job (or corporate culture) to suit himself or herself. It is the opposite of socialization, which is how the organization modifies a person to conform to the corporate culture. Less research exists on personalization than on socialization.

In a pure competency-based system, the foundation would not be jobs but competencies. That means we would build a job to fit the person's talents with the view in mind of leveraging that individual's intellectual capital and the individual's key strengths and talents.

Question 9: *What is the dynamic between established competencies (as a kind of standard) and the unique ways that individuals get the job done that might not fit the mold—for example, an enormous strength that compensates for considerable gaps?*

We do not know what you mean by *established competencies*. Do you mean the difference between what fully successful (read "average") performers do and what exemplary performers do? Or do you mean "off-the-shelf" competencies from print or online sources?

The best competency models are corporate culture specific. Of course, many off-the-shelf competency models exist. But they do not get at the corporate cultural context in which the individual performs. That is why it is best to devise corporate culture–specific models.

Question 10: *How does the possibility of unanticipated ways in which people can be successful get taken into account in the use of competencies?*

Well, good competency models are developed directly from the people within the organization. You discover, during so-called behavioral event interviews, what they do.

Your question continues to assume that the focus is on work activities—which is how we read "ways in which people can be successful." But competency-based HR is about discovering the characteristics shared by superstar performers to get work results—and then selecting or developing other people to achieve similar quantum leaps in productivity improvement.

Imagine a job description that lists the results or outcomes expected of people instead of the duties or responsibilities (activities) they are expected to carry out. Typical job descriptions fall flat because they focus on how the work is done. Competency models, if done well, determine what results we want (results or outcomes) and work backward.

Question 11: *How do competencies in an organization at a particular time reflect organizational culture, management philosophy, and trends in management theory and education?*

Competencies are reflections of the existing culture, in most cases.

Do not confuse corporate core competencies with individual competencies. Corporate core competencies refer to strategic strengths or what the organization does better than any other and what really cannot be outsourced. Individual competencies focus on the characteristics shared by successful—or even exemplary—performers.

It is possible to invent a competency model for the future to which nobody in the current organization fits. In fact, that is one way to start to make operational a strategic plan. If that is done, people can be assessed—using competency assessment centers or 360-degree competency assessment—for the competencies from the competency model that we believe will be needed in the organization if the strategic plan is to be realized.

Question 12: *What is the range of the possible types of items that make up competencies—for example, tasks, skills, values, and so on?*

Competencies are about the characteristics individuals possess and use in appropriate ways that help them get desired results in the context of a unique corporate cultural context. These characteristics include knowledge, skills, mind-sets, thought patterns, or social roles.

Increasingly, organizations are using competency models to get results. But they are supplementing that work with value systems or value models to build in the increasingly important domain of ethics and rules.

Question 13: *What is the relative nature of competencies regarding the level of detail or comprehensiveness (scoping competencies)?*

A competency cannot be measured by itself. To do that you must establish behavioral indicators, which can be as time-consuming and expensive as doing the competency study to begin with. We believe that behaviorally anchored rating scales and their cousins, behaviorally anchored observation scales and behaviorally anchored expectations scales, are the most rigorous ways to do that.

Question 14: *Can competency systems form the basis of most or all of the HR components of an organization—such as selection, evaluation, compensation, and development?*

Yes. We call that *competency-based human resource management.* All facets of HR can be reinvented, and competencies, rather than "jobs" or "work activities," can be used as the foundation for an HR system.

Think of using competency-based HR as being like switching from a Windows-based to a UNIX-based computer. It simply runs the operating system on a different foundation.

Further Suggestions on Employee Development

In this appendix, we offer several suggestions for HR practitioners who plan to establish a competency-based employee development process in an organization. Not all suggestions will apply equally to every organization or work unit.

The person assigned to spearhead the effort must establish a process for documenting the progress of the work. Documentation should include explanations of all techniques and tools, both the ones that worked and those that did not meet expectations. Testimonials from employees, managers, supervisors, team leaders, and others should be put in writing and logged for future reference. The log will be useful for conducting public relations campaigns and justifying budget requests.

Career development efforts should always start small and grow gradually. It takes time and considerable effort to implement the competency-based process, after which employees must complete development activities before they can begin contributing to the organization's success. Certainly it would not be unusual for a full calendar year to elapse between system implementation and the production of observable, measurable results. Leaders of organizations often have difficulty realizing the value of the effort when its benefits are not readily apparent. For this reason, small expenditures that produce observable and measurable results should be the objective of every employee development effort.

Take every opportunity to inform the organization's leaders of the short- and long-term returns on their investment in the competency-based process, and do so in a timely manner. An important truism applies here: What the CEO supports, *all* support.

Career coaches can be trained as ambassadors for the competency-based employee development process. They can collect information and communicate it to the sponsoring work unit or throughout the organization, as appropriate. They can also source information for employees. Consult Simonsen (1997) for strategies for marketing an employee development system in an organizational context.

Schedule regular informational sessions for participants in the employee development process. Topics could include organization life and possible development opportunities. Senior managers could play a role by talking about the business, its current and future needs, and how employees can contribute toward meeting those needs. Senior managers should also honestly communicate the organization's succession planning and management practices to all employees. Succession planning should not be limited to senior management but should be a priority for many positions in the organization.

When employees show signs of distress while discussing their life-career issues, the HR practitioner should refer them to a qualified career counselor. It is important to understand that employees may enter the development process with issues that they portray or perceive as work related but which are instead due to personal factors. HR practitioners must recognize when this is the case and should never practice beyond their level of expertise, no matter how well they know these employees. The HR practitioner should confirm that assistance has been provided by following up with employees and, if necessary, the career counselor. Credentialed career development facilitators or counselors should be available either as employees of the organization or as contracted consultants.

Specialized seminars can be designed and presented to address specific life-work issues such as résumé development, child care or elder care needs, competency development concerns, and other topics. Systematically assess needs before taking action on this suggestion.

Helping employees to achieve their agreed-upon employee development objectives should be a job performance assessment factor for every supervisor, team leader, manager, and executive in the organization. As a part of their overall performance rating, it should affect their pay and other benefits.

An employee development process (whether competency based or traditional) can very easily fail because the organization's leaders do not understand the value of the life-career approach and will not endorse its use. The person who spearheads the employee development effort must continually work to ensure that decision makers and senior leaders accept the importance of these practices.

Examples of Life-Career Assessment Exercises

These two examples of life-career assessment exercises are typical of methods for helping employees to think in more precise terms about their life roles and their satisfaction with each role. The first exercise, Kemp's Life-Career World Wheel, was created by Linda K. Kemp. It has been used with a great deal of success in individual and group client settings for many years. The second exercise, the Quick Goal-Setting Exercise, is attributed to Carol Christen and represents another life-career assessment process.[1] However, it should be used only by persons who are trained and experienced in facilitating exercises that may be dramatically enlightening for clients. Credentialed career counselors, career facilitators, or similar professionals are probably best qualified to use this exercise in either a group or an individual setting.

These two exercises represent low- and high-impact approaches to facilitating reflection on life-career issues as part of a formal competency-based employee development process. We cannot stress too much the importance of qualified career counselors or facilitators in using these methods.

Figure 15: **An Example of the Use of Kemp's Life-Career World Wheel**

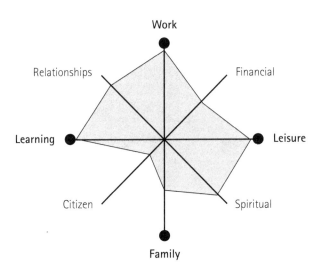

Kemp's Life-Career World Wheel

Figure 15 depicts an example of Kemp's Life-Career World Wheel. The wheel is divided into eight spokes. Each spoke represents an individual's primary life roles: work, financial, leisure, spiritual, family, citizen, learning, and relationships. Note that the structure is grounded on four key life roles: work, leisure, family, and learning.

In our example, a fictitious employee has used Kemp's Life-Career World Wheel to rate her satisfaction with the current status of each of her life roles by placing a dot at the point on the spoke that indicates her level of satisfaction. The farther out from the center, the greater the individual's satisfaction. The eight rating points were connected with straight lines to form a closed polygon. It would be extraordinarily unusual for an individual to express complete satisfaction with the status of all eight roles. Had this been the case for our fictitious employee, connecting the rating dots would have formed a regular octagon (one with eight sides of equal length and eight equal interior angles).

The employee reviewed her polygon with assistance from an HR specialist. She easily discerned her degree of satisfaction with the status of each life role and decided to increase her satisfaction with the financial and citizen roles over the next 18 months. This decision raised a host of life-work questions in her mind, including the following:

- How can I improve my financial status? What resources can I use to do so? What will be required of me? What is my target date for completing this work? What must be sacrificed? What *could* be sacrificed? What *should* be sacrificed?

- Can I reduce my emphasis on the learning role in my life? If so, what will be the impact? What consequences will result from making this change?

- Can I divert some of the energy now invested in my family to achieve my target satisfaction ratings in the other roles? If so, how much?

Quite obviously, the two roles the employee selected for improvement are related to some of her other life roles. Her work role, for example, has financial ramifications, which led to another set of questions:

- Should I volunteer for overtime work?

- Should I seek higher-paying work or work with a different compensation and benefits package with another organization?

- Should I change my residence, and if so, should I relocate to an area with a lower cost of living?

- Should I supplement my salary through part-time work or self-employment?

Since this employee is participating in a competency-based employee development process, the organization must address some of these issues. Its responses would be determined by many factors, such as the employee's perceived strategic value to the organization, her willingness to be flexible or pursue additional learning, and her performance record and competency base.

As you can tell, the life-career component of an organization's employee development process is a major one and must not be taken lightly.

Quick Goal-Setting Exercise

This exercise begins with life-career assessment and then moves to goal setting. The assessment process is essential to successful goal setting. After you have thought about your own responses to the following exercise, you will understand more clearly why career telling, which typically skips the assessment stage, can be counterproductive for both the employee and the organization.

An employee, with support from a trained and experienced career counselor or facilitator, proceeds with the goal-setting exercise by answering the following questions:

- What do you want to accomplish in your lifetime?
- What do you hope to do during the next 3 years?
- What should you have accomplished by this time in your life?
- If you found out today that you have exactly 6 months to live, what would you want to do?

This exercise can have enlightening but sometimes unsettling outcomes for employees. Individuals who complete this exercise often realize that this has been their first opportunity to honestly assess their life-career roles, achievements, and preferences in a formal and purposeful manner. It is not unusual for persons to express confusion or other strong emotions. We recommend that you consider this possibility before using this exercise. Depending on the intensity of the response, employees may require additional support with organizing their thoughts and feelings and determining their course of action. With a career counseling professional on staff or available as needed, employees can complete goal setting in a psychologically safe environment. The primary outcome of this exercise is identification of life-career goals. If several goals are identified, they must be prioritized.

Employee Development and Succession Management

Employee development also has applications in succession manage-ment. At this writing, decision makers in public, private, and nonprofit organizations are scurrying to prepare as members of the so-called baby boom generation approach retirement age. Organizations offering early retirement packages are already feeling the need to replace many of their most experienced workers.

The effects of the problem in the United States are widely known. Labor economist Douglas Braddock (1999) noted that "over the 1998–2008 period, more job openings are expected to result from replacement needs (34.7 million) than from employment growth in the economy (20.3 million)" (p. 75). By one estimate, about one-fifth of the largest U.S. companies are already beginning to lose up to 40% of their senior executives (Caudron, 1999). Perhaps not so well known is that aging-related issues, of which succession management is but one, are global in scope. Over the next 20 years, workforce replacement needs will emerge as a key concern in all nations of the developed world and in most nations in East Asia, Southeast Asia, and Latin America. This is significant for organizations that do business internationally.

Many principles that apply to employee development and individual employee career management and development, which are usually driven from the bottom up with employees taking the lead, are also applicable to succession management, which is usually a top-down process initiated by management. Employee development plays a key role in both employee life-career development and succession management. It is through employee development that individuals are prepared for a longer-term future, perhaps extending beyond the next job or position.

Rothwell (2000) supplied one conceptual model for establishing a succession management process. The model consists of a series of steps, which begins with decision makers' commitment to installing the system. Next, analyses of the work and competencies necessary for current work success are followed by evaluations of individual performance. Similar analyses are conducted for the work and competencies needed for future success, followed by evaluations of individual potential to meet those needs. This model thus reveals two gaps: one between current competencies and performance and a second between the competencies needed for the future and the individual's potential to acquire them. Gaps are pinpointed and employee development activities are planned to narrow those gaps. The last step of the model is an evaluation of the succession management effort.

Some organizations have established leadership development programs as a focal point for accelerating the development of so-called high-potential employees (Rothwell & Kazanas, 1999). High-potential employees are defined in different ways, depending on the organization, but are commonly thought of as exemplary performers who may be capable of advancing horizontally (across a continuum of professional competence) or vertically by two or more levels in 5 years or less. Competency identification, modeling, and assessment are keys to these programs.

Employee development, individual career management, and succession management processes must all work together. Employee development efforts may reveal individual goals, strengths, and areas for development, but a succession plan provides direction for productive and effective action.

Notes

Chapter 1

1. For further information on job analysis, see Zemke and Kramlinger (1982); Dubois (1993); Dubois and Rothwell (2000); and Rothwell and Kazanas (1998), pp. 116–148.
2. For further review on job roles, see, for example, Dubois (1993); Byham and Moyer (1998); and Cook and Bernthal (1998).

Chapter 2

1. For further review on Flanagan's work and the critical incident technique, see Flanagan (1954) or Flanagan in Zemke and Kramlinger (1982), pp. 277–317.
2. For further review of the background and a historical perspective on some of the events associated with the development of this approach, see Spencer, McClelland, and Spencer (1994).
3. The meanings associated with the term *competency* vary rather remarkably. See, for example, Blank (1982); Boyatzis (1982), pp. 20–23; Byham (1996), p. 2; Byham and Moyer (1998), pp. 4–7; Cooper (2000), pp. 2–3; Davies (1973); Dubois (1993), p. 5; Dubois (1996), pp. 5–13; Dubois and Rothwell (2000), Vol. 1, p. I-14; Folley (1980); Green (1999), p. 22; Klemp (1979); Kolodziejski (1991); Lucia and Lepsinger (1999), pp. 2, 5; Marlowe and Weinberg (1985); McLagan (1990); Rothwell (2000b), p. 152; Rothwell

(1996), pp. 29, 263; Rothwell and Kazanas (1994), pp. 188–189; Rothwell and Kazanas (1998), pp. 141–142; Weiss and Hartle (1997), p. 29; Wood and Payne (1998), pp. 19–38; and Zemke (1982), pp. 28–31.

4. Briscoe and Hall (1999); Cook and Bernthal (1998); and Robinson and Robinson (1995).

5. For further review on work activities and outputs, see Dubois (1993) and Dubois and Rothwell (2000).

6. See, for example, Byham and Moyer (1996); Dubois (1993); Dubois and Rothwell (2000); and Green (1999).

7. For further review on the validity of competency models, see Block and Rebell (1980); Byham (1996); Byham and Moyer (1996); Cooper (2000); Dubois (1993); Dubois and Rothwell (2000); Harlan, Klemp, and Schaalman (1980); Huff, Klemp, Spencer, and Williamson (1980); Lucia and Lepsinger (1999); Pottinger, Wiesfeld, Tochen, Cohen, and Schaalman (1980); and Spencer and Spencer (1993).

8. For more extensive discussions on competency identification methods, see Dubois (1993) and Dubois and Rothwell (2000).

9. Details of the JCAM process can be found in Dubois (1993); Spencer, McClelland, and Spencer (1994); and Spencer and Spencer (1993).

10. For an in-depth description of the competency menu method, see Dubois and Rothwell (2000).

11. For further review on establishing content-valid competency-based HR systems and subsystems, see Byham (1996). For information on reliability and validity, see Klein (1996).

12. For examples, see Dubois (1993, 1996) and Dubois and Rothwell (2000).

Chapter 3

1. The word *talent* is derived from the Latin *talenta* (units of weight or money). Fittingly enough, talent is an important source for creating value in organizations today (Michaels, Handfield-Jones, & Axelrod, 2001).

2. For information on tools for completing competency projects, see Dubois and Rothwell (2000).

3. For more detailed discussions of formative and summative evaluations and their role in competency-based HR management projects, see Dubois (1993).

Chapter 4

1. For further information on HR planning, see Rothwell and Kazanas (1994, which also offers a historical perspective; 2003) and Rothwell and Sredl (2000).

2. Much has been written on the topic of completing work analysis. See, for example, the classic by McCormick (1979); Carlisle (1998); Hartley (1999); and Schippmann (1999). For a review of issues related to defining competencies and completing competency modeling development projects through job analysis, see Byham and Moyer (1996) and Dubois (1993).

3. For further review on the use of DACUM as a tool for competency assessment, see Rothwell (2001).
4. Some of the more exhaustive works on the topic of identifying valid competencies for successful work performance are Spencer and Spencer (1993); Dubois (1993); and Dubois and Rothwell (2000).
5. See, for example, Dubois and Rothwell (2000); Edwards and Ewen (1996); and Weiss and Hartle (1998).
6. For detailed information on multirater competency assessment, see the discussion in Dubois and Rothwell (2000).
7. For further information on assessment centers, see Spencer and Spencer (1993); Spychalski, Quinones, Gaugler, and Pohley (1997); Thornton (1992); and Thornton and Byham (1982).
8. For more on competency-based information systems, see McShulskis (n.d.).

Chapter 5
1. Grensing-Pophal (2000); Kaplan (1999); and Sherman, Bohlander, and Snell (1998).
2. Other sources and their costs indicated in the SHRM survey are employee referral, $320; Internet, $444; print advertising, $943; college recruiting, $2,510; and agencies, $9,187 (Pfau and Kay, 2002).
3. For more about succession planning, see Rothwell (2001).
4. Behavioral event interviews are the foundation methodology for researching job, work, or role competencies in work settings. See Dubois (1993) and Spencer and Spencer (1993) for background and details.
5. For additional reading on the topic, see Callaghan and Thompson (2002); Harvey and Novicevic (2000); Markwood (2001); Rothwell and Kazanas (2003); Smith and Kandola (1996); and Warech (2002).

Chapter 6
1. Training types from Rothwell and Sredl (2000), pp. 9–10.
2. Many sources provide guidance on e-learning and blended learning. See, for example, Rosenberg (2001) and Rossett (2002).
3. In response to this problem, trainers have experimented with alternative approaches, including models that attempt to make training a joint venture (Rothwell & Cookson, 1997) or place greater responsibility for learning on the learner (Rothwell, 2002).
4. For additional information on the SSM, see Dubois (1993, 1998).
5. For further review on self-directed learning, see Rothwell (1996a, 1996b) and Rothwell and Sensenig (1998).
6. To learn more about these topics, consult Ciancarelli (1998); Cobb and Gibbs (1990); Crabb (n.d.); Filipowski (1991); Fleming, Oliver, and Bolton (1996); Gould et al. (1996); Meade (1998); and Ridha (1998).

Chapter 7

1. For further information about performance management concepts or practices, please consult any of the following sources: Adler and Coleman (1999);
Bowen and Lawler (1992); Greene (2000); Kanin-Lovers and Bevan (1992);
Laumeyer (1997); Lukesh (2000); McAfee and Campagne (1992); Pardue
(2000); Ripley (1999); and Weiss and Hartle (1997). For in-depth information on many of the processes and technical aspects of using competencies
in human resource management practices, please consult Dubois and
Rothwell (2000) or Dubois (1993).
2. Others have written about, and several organizations have implemented, the
use of competencies for elements of the performance process as we have
described it. You might want to consult, for example, Nolan (1998); Jones
(1995); Pickard (1996); or Orr (2002) for further information.
3. Other sources of information on implementing the use of competencies in
the performance management process include Jones (1995); Nolan (1998);
Orr (2002); and Pickard (1996). For further review on the concepts,
processes, and technical aspects of using competencies in HR management,
see also Dubois (1993); Dubois and Rothwell (2000); Harris, Huselid, and
Becker (1999); and Maccoby (2001).

Chapter 8

1. Additional resources on the fundamentals of establishing and managing
compensation systems, whether traditional or competency based, include
Flannery, Hofrichter, and Platten (1996); Hale (1998); Kochanski and LeBlanc
(1999); Manas (2000); O'Neal (1998); Risher (1999); Tropman (2001); Weiss
and Hartle (1997); WorldatWork, at http://www.worldatwork.org; and
Zingheim and Schuster (2000).
2. For more information on broadbanding, see Abosch and Gilbert (1996).
3. For more information on recognition programs, consult Bowen (2000) or
Nelson (1994). For a criticism of such programs, see Kohn (1999).
4. For more extensive discussion on planning the process evaluation, see
Stufflebeam (1974a, 1974b) and Stufflebeam et al. (1971).

Chapter 9

1. Employee development is a broad field, and those who pursue this work
must be conversant with a wide variety of concepts, ideas, and facts. We suggest the following references: Fredrickson (1982); Hafer (1992); Harris-
Bowlsbey, Dikel, and Sampson (1998); Kapes and Whitfield (2002);
Kummerow (2000); Leibowitz, Farren, and Kaye (1986); Niles (in press);
Niles, Goodman, and Pope (2001); and Pope and Minor (2000). For extensive applications of the concepts discussed in this chapter, see Anonymous
(1993, 1995); Delahoussaye (2001); and Patch (2000).

2. For information on creating a development culture in an organization, consult Simonsen (1997).
3. For a more extensive discussion of DACUM, consult Dubois and Rothwell (2000).
4. For descriptions of competency assessment procedures, consult Dubois and Rothwell (2000).
5. For more on finding personal meaning and enjoyment in work, see Eanes, Richmond, and Link (2001); and Bloch and Richmond (1997, 1998). The stages of a life-career and the competencies that individuals must possess and use in appropriate ways for successful life-career plans are identified and discussed in Dubois (2000).
6. Bolles (1981) includes a discussion for setting life-career priorities and presents a method for doing so. The instrument he recommends, the "Prioritizing Grid for 10 Items," is found in this work.
7. Assessment instruments are available to prequalified purchasers from organizations such as the Institute for Personality Assessment and CPP, Inc. (formerly Consulting Psychologists Press).
8. For detailed information on competency-based individual development planning, including useful instruments, consult Dubois and Rothwell (2000).
9. For extensive discussion on planning the process evaluation, see Stufflebeam (1974a, 1974b); and Stufflebeam et al. (1971).
10. See Dubois (1993), pp. 227–231; Stufflebeam (1974a, 1974b); and Stufflebeam et al. (1971).

Chapter 10

1. For further discussion on HR effectiveness, see Joinson (2000); and Wright McMahan, Snell, and Gerhart (2001).
2. HR audits and scorecards can also be used to obtain results. For information on HR audits, see Becker, Huselid, and Ulrich (2001); for HR scorecards, see McConnell (2000).
3. For an extensive review of the Whole Systems Transformation Conference, see Sullivan, Fairburn, and Rothwell (2002).

Appendix C

1. Carol Christen, personal communication with Linda K. Kemp, February 26, 2003.

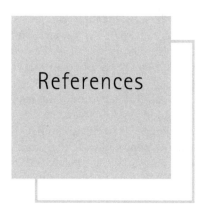

References

Chapter 1

Byham, William C., & Moyer, Reed P. (1998). *Using competencies to build a successful organization.* Pittsburgh, PA: Development Dimensions International.

Dubois, David D. (1993). *Competency-based performance improvement: A strategy for organizational change.* Amherst, MA: Human Resource Development Press.

Dubois, David D., & Rothwell, William J. (2000). *The competency toolkit* (Vol. 1). Amherst, MA: Human Resource Development Press.

Fay, C., Risher, H., & Mahony, D. (1997, Winter). The jobless organization: Survey results on the impact of new job design on compensation. *ACA Journal.*

Joinson, Carla. (2001, January). Refocusing job descriptions. *HR Magazine.*

Leonard, Sharon. (2000, August). The demise of job descriptions. Future focus: Emerging issues. *HR Magazine, 45*(8).

Rothwell, William J., & Kazanas, H. C. (1994). *Planning and managing human resources: Strategic planning for personnel management* (Rev. ed.). Amherst, MA: Human Resource Development Press.

Rothwell, William J., & Kazanas, H. C. (1998). *Mastering the instructional design process: A systematic approach* (2nd ed.). San Francisco: Jossey-Bass.

Rothwell, William J., Prescott, Robert, & Taylor, Maria. (1998). *Strategic human resource leader: How to prepare your organization for the six key trends shaping the future.* Mountain View, CA: Davies-Black Publishing.

Walker, J. (1980). *Human resource planning.* New York: McGraw-Hill.

Zemke, Ron, & Kramlinger, Thomas. (1982). *Figuring things out: A trainer's guide to needs and task analysis.* Reading, MA: Addison-Wesley.

Chapter 2

Blank, W. F. (1982). *Handbook for developing competency-based training programs.* Englewood Cliffs, NJ: Prentice-Hall.

Block, A. R., & Rebell, M. A. (1980). *The assessment of occupational competence. Competence assessment and the courts: An overview of the state of the law.* Springfield, VA: U.S. Department of Education. (ERIC Report No. ED 192 169/CE 027 168)

Boyatzis, Richard E. (1982). *The competent manager: A model for effective performance.* New York: John Wiley & Sons.

Briscoe, Jon P., & Hall, Douglas T. (1999, Autumn). Grooming and picking leaders using competency frameworks: Do they work? An alternative approach and new guidelines for practice. *Organizational Dynamics, 28*(2), 37–52.

Brockbank, Wayne. (1997). Human resources' future on the way to a presence. In Dave Ulrich, Michael R. Losey, & Gerry Lake (Eds.), *Tomorrow's HR management: 48 thought leaders call for change.* New York: John Wiley & Sons.

Byham, William C. (1996). *Developing dimensions: Competency-based human resource systems* [Monograph]. Pittsburgh, PA: Development Dimensions International.

Byham, William C., & Moyer, Reed P. (1998). *Using competencies to build a successful organization.* Pittsburgh, PA: Development Dimensions International.

Competencies and the competitive edge. (1998). Washington, DC: Watson Wyatt Worldwide. May be retrieved from http://www.watsonwyatt.com/research/printable.asp?id=W-99.

Competencies in the public service. (1998, November). Public Service Commission of Canada. Retrieved October 27, 2001, from http://www.psc-cfp.gc.ca/publications/monogra/comp_e.htm.

Cook, Kevin, & Bernthal, Paul. (1998, July). Job/role competencies practices survey report. *HR Benchmark Group, 4*(1). Pittsburgh, PA: Development Dimensions International.

Cooper, Kenneth Carlton. (2000). *Effective competency modeling and reporting: A step-by-step guide for improving individual and organizational performance.* New York: AMACOM.

Cooper, Scott, Lawrence, Eton, Kierstead, James, Lynch, Brian, & Luce, Sally. (1998). *Competencies—A brief overview of development and application to public and private sectors.* Ottawa: Public Service Commission of Canada, Research Directorate. Policy, Research and Communications Branch.

Davenport, Thomas O. (1999). *Human capital: What it is and why people invest in it.* San Francisco: Jossey-Bass.

Davies, Ivor. (1973). *Competency-based learning.* New York: McGraw-Hill.

Dewey, Barbara. (1997, March/April). Six companies share their insights: The challenges in applying competencies. *Compensation and Benefits Review, 29*(2), 64–75.

Dubois, David D. (1993). *Competency-based performance improvement: A strategy for organizational change.* Amherst, MA: Human Resource Development Press.

Dubois, David D. (1996). *The executive's guide to competency-based performance improvement.* Amherst, MA: HRD Press.

Dubois, David D., & Rothwell, William J. (2000). *The competency toolkit* (Vol. 1 of 2). Amherst, MA: Human Resource Development Press.

Fitz-enz, Jac. (2000). *The ROI of human capital: Measuring the economic value of employee performance.* New York: AMACOM.

Flanagan, John C. (1954, July). The critical incident technique. *Psychological Bulletin, 51,* 327–358. (Reprinted in Ron Zemke & Thomas Kramlinger, *Figuring things out: A trainer's guide to needs and tasks analysis* [1982], Reading, MA: Addison-Wesley.)

Flannery, Thomas P., Hofrichter, David, & Platten, Paul E. (1996). *People, pay and performance.* New York: The Free Press.

Folley, J. D., Jr. (1980). Identifying competencies. In J. W. Springer (Ed.), *Job performance standards and measures* (ASTD Research Series, Paper No. 4). Madison, WI: American Society for Training and Development.

Fuller, J. (1999). Understanding human performance improvement. In B. Sugrue & J. Fuller (Eds.), *Performance interventions: Selecting, implementing and evaluating the results.* Alexandria, VA: The American Society for Training and Development.

Green, Paul C. (1999). *Building robust competencies: Linking human resource systems to organizational strategies.* San Francisco: Jossey-Bass.

Harlan, A., Klemp, George O., Jr., & Schaalman, M. L. (1980). *The assessment of occupational competence. Competence assessment in personnel selection: Current practices and trends.* Springfield, VA: U.S. Department of Education. (ERIC Report No. ED 192 165/CE 027 160)

Huff, S. M., Klemp, George O., Jr., Spencer, Lyle M., Jr., & Williamson, S. A. (1980). *The assessment of occupational competence. Summary: A synthesis of issues.* Springfield, VA: U.S. Department of Education. (ERIC Report No. ED 192 170/CE 027 165)

Johnson Brackey, Harriet. (1998, April 6). Competency: What's behind a new buzzword. *The Miami Herald,* 15BM.

Klein, Andrew L. (1996, July/August). Validity and reliability for competency-based systems: Reducing litigation risks. *Compensation and Benefits Review, 28*(4).

Klemp, George O., Jr. (1979). Identifying, measuring and integrating competence. In P. Pottinger and J. Goldsmith (Eds.), *Defining and measuring competence.* San Francisco: Jossey-Bass.

Klemp, George O., Jr. (Ed.). (1980). *The assessment of occupational competence.* Report to the National Institute of Education. Washington, DC: National Institute of Education.

Kolodziejski, K. (1991). *Competency model? Task analysis? What do I do?* Presentation at the 1991 ASTD National Conference, San Francisco, CA. Audiotape No. 91 AST-M10. Alexandria, VA: American Society for Training and Development.

Lucia, Anntoinette D., & Lepsinger, Richard. (1999). *The art and science of competency models: Pinpointing critical success factors in organizations.* San Francisco: Jossey-Bass/Pfeiffer.

Marlowe, H. A., Jr., & Weinberg, R. B. (1985). *Competence development: Theory and practice in special populations.* Springfield, IL: Charles C. Thomas.

McClelland, David C. (1973, January). Testing for competence rather than for "intelligence." *American Psychologist, 28*(1), 1–14.

McClelland, David C. (1976). *A guide to job competency assessment.* Boston: McBer and Company.

McClelland, David C. (1985). *Human motivation.* Glenview, IL: Scott, Foresman and Company.

McClelland, David C., & Daily, Charles. (1972). *Improving officer selection for the foreign service.* Boston: McBer and Company.

McClelland, David C., & Dailey, Charles. (1973). *Evaluating new methods of measuring the qualities needed in superior Foreign Service information officers.* Boston: McBer and Company.

McDowell, Callie. (1996, September). Achieving workforce competence. *Personnel Journal* (New Product News Supplement).

McLagan, Patricia A. (1989). The models. In *Models for HRD practice* (Vol. 3). Alexandria, VA: American Society for Training and Development.

McLagan, Patricia A. (1990). Flexible job models: A productivity strategy for the information age. In J. P. Campbell & R. J. Campbell, (Eds.), *Productivity in organizations.* San Francisco: Jossey-Bass.

Miles, Matthew, & Huberman, A. Michael. (1994). *Qualitative data analysis: An expanded sourcebook.* Thousand Oaks, CA: Sage Publications.

Norton, R. (1997). *The DACUM handbook* (2nd ed.). Columbus, OH: The National Center for Research in Vocational Education.

Pickett, Les. (1998, Spring). Competencies and managerial effectiveness: Putting competencies to work. *Public Personnel Management, 27*(1), 103–115.

Pottinger, P. S., Wiesfeld, N. E., Tochen, D. K., Cohen, P. D., & Schaalman, M. L. (1980). *The assessment of occupational competence. Competence assessment for occupational certification.* Springfield, VA: U.S. Department of Education. (ERIC Report No. ED 192 167/CE 027 162)

Prahalad, C. K., & Hamel, Gary. (1990, May/June). The core competence of the corporation. *Harvard Business Review,* 81.

Pritchard, Kenneth H. (1997, August). *Introduction to competencies* (Reviewed April 1999). SHRM white paper. May be retrieved from http://www.shrm.org.

Rahbar-Daniels, Dana, Erickson, Mary Lou, & Dalik, Arden. (2001, First Quarter). Here to stay—Taking competencies to the next level. *WorldatWork Journal, 10*(1).

Raising the bar: Using competencies to enhance employee performance. (1996). Scottsdale, AZ: American Compensation Association in cooperation with Hay Group, Hewitt Associates LLC, Towers Perrin, & William M. Mercer, Inc.

Robinson, Dana Gaines, & Robinson, James C. (1995). *Performance consulting: Moving beyond training.* San Francisco: Berrett-Koehler.

Rothwell, William J. (1996). *Beyond training and development: State-of-the-art strategies for enhancing human performance.* New York: AMACOM.

Rothwell, William J. (2000a). *ASTD models for human performance improvement: Roles, competencies, outputs* (2nd ed.). Alexandria, VA: The American Society for Training and Development.

Rothwell, William J. (2000b). *Effective succession planning: Ensuring leadership continuity and building talent from within* (2nd ed.). New York: AMACOM.

Rothwell, William J., Hohne, Carolyn K., & King, Stephen B. (2000). *Human performance improvement: Building practitioner competence.* Houston, TX: Gulf Publishing.

Rothwell, William J., & Kazanas, H. C. (1994). *Human resource development: A strategic approach* (Rev. ed.). Amherst, MA: HRD Press.

Rothwell, William J., & Kazanas, H. C. (1998). *Mastering the instructional design process: A systematic approach* (2nd ed.). San Francisco: Jossey-Bass/Pfeiffer.

Schein, Edgar H. (1992). *Organizational culture and leadership* (2nd ed.). San Francisco: Jossey-Bass.

Schoonover, Stephen C., Schoonover, Helen, Nemerov, Donald, & Ehly, Christine. (2000). *Competency-based HR applications: Results of a comprehensive survey.* Falmouth, MA: Schoonover, Arthur Andersen, & SHRM.

Sherman, Arthur, Bohlander, George, & Snell, Scott. (1998). *Managing human resources* (11th ed.). Cincinnati, OH: South-Western Publishing.

Spencer, Lyle M., Jr., McClelland, David C., & Spencer, Signe M. (1994). *Competency assessment methods: History and state of the art.* Boston: Hay McBer Research Press.

Spencer, Lyle M., Jr., & Spencer, Signe M. (1993). *Competence at work.* New York: Wiley.

The state of competencies: ACA's research one year later. (1997, Autumn). *ACA Journal, 6*(3).

Ulrich, Dave, Zenger, Jack, & Smallwood, Norm. (1999). *Results-based leadership: How leaders build the business and improve the bottom line.* Boston: Harvard Business School Press.

Weiss, Tracey B., & Hartle, Franklin. (1997). *Reengineering performance management: Breakthroughs in achieving strategy through people.* Boca Raton, FL: St. Lucie Press.

White, Robert. (1959). Motivation reconsidered: The concept of competence. *Psychological Review, 66,* 279–333.

Wood, Robert, & Payne, Tim. (1998). *Competency-based recruitment and selection: A practical guide.* West Sussex, England: John Wiley & Sons.

Zemke, Ron. (1982). Job competencies: Can they help you design better training? *Training, 19*(5), 28–31.

Zemke, Ron, & Kramlinger, Thomas. (1982). *Figuring things out: A trainer's guide to needs and task analysis.* Reading, MA: Addison-Wesley.

Chapter 3

Beer, Michael. (1997). The transformation of the human resource function: Resolving the tension between a traditional administrative and a new strategic role. In Dave Ulrich, Michael R. Losey, and Gerry Lake (Eds.), *Tomorrow's HR management: 48 thought leaders call for change.* New York: John Wiley & Sons.

Bennett, John L. (2001, September). Change happens. *HR Magazine, 46*(9), 149–156.

Bernthal, Paul, Pescuric, Alice J., & Wellins, Richard S. (2000). *Workforce development practices survey report: Executive summary.* Pittsburgh, PA: Development Dimensions International. May be retrieved from http://www.ddiworld.com.

Competing in a global economy. (1997). Washington, DC: Watson Wyatt. May be retrieved from http://www.watsonwyatt.com/research/printable.asp?id=W-63.

Dubois, David D. (1993). *Competency-based performance improvement: A strategy for organizational change.* Amherst, MA: Human Resource Development Press.

Dubois, David D., & Rothwell, William J. (2000). *The competency toolkit* (2 vols.). Amherst, MA: Human Resource Development Press.

Green, Paul C. (1999). *Building robust competencies: Linking human resource systems to organizational strategies.* San Francisco: Jossey-Bass.

Greene, Robert J. (2000a, March). *Effectively managing intellectual capital: Critical challenge for human resources* (SHRM white paper). Alexandria, VA: Society for Human Resource Management. May be retrieved from http://www.shrm.org.

Greene, Robert J. (2000b, August). *Building social and intellectual capital: Critical challenge/opportunity for human resources* (SHRM white paper). Alexandria, VA: Society for Human Resource Management. May be retrieved from http://www.shrm.org.

Kerr, Steven, & Von Glinow, Mary Ann. (1997). The future of human resources: Plus ça change, plus c'est la même chose. In Dave Ulrich, Michael R. Losey, and Gerry Lake (Eds.), *Tomorrow's HR management: 48 thought leaders call for change.* New York: John Wiley & Sons.

Lawler, Edward E., III, & Mohrman, Susan A. (2000). Beyond the vision: What makes HR effective? *HR. Human Resource Planning, 23*(4), 10–20.

Lucia, Anntoinette D., & Lepsinger, Richard. (1999). *The art and science of competency models: Pinpointing critical success factors in organizations.* San Francisco: Jossey-Bass/Pfeiffer.

Michaels, Ed, Handfield-Jones, Helen, & Axelrod, Beth. (2001). *The war for talent.* Boston: Harvard Business School Press.

Orr, Brian. (1998, November 30). Competencies key in a changing world. *Canadian HR Reporter, 11*(21), 10.

Rothwell, William J. (1996). *A 21st-century vision of strategic human resource management.* Unpublished manuscript, report to the Society for Human Resource Management and CCH, Inc.

Rothwell, William J. (1999). *The action learning guidebook: A real-time strategy for problem solving, training design, and employee development.* San Francisco: Jossey-Bass/Pfeiffer.

Rothwell, William J., Prescott, Robert K., & Taylor, Maria. (1998). *Strategic human resource leader: How to prepare your organization for the six key trends shaping the future.* Mountain View, CA: Davies-Black Publishing.

Rothwell, William J., Prescott, Robert K., & Taylor, Maria. (1999, March). Transforming HR into a global powerhouse. *HR Focus, 76*(3), 7–8.

Schoonover, Stephen C. (1998). *HR competencies for the year 2000: The wake-up call!* [Monograph]. Alexandria, VA: Society for Human Resource Management Foundation.

Ulrich, Dave. (1997). *Human resource champions: The next agenda for adding value and delivering results.* Boston: Harvard Business School Press.

Yeung, Arthur, Woolcock, Patricia, & Sullivan, John. (1996). Identifying and developing HR competencies for the future: Keys to sustaining the transformation of HR functions. *Human Resource Planning, 19*(4), 48–58.

Chapter 4

Boyatzis, Richard. (1982). *The competent manager.* New York: Wiley.

Brockbank, Wayne. (1999, Winter). If HR were really strategically proactive: Present and future directions in HR's contribution to competitive advantage. *Human Resource Management, 38*(4), 337–350.

Byham, William C., & Moyer, Reed P. (1996). *Using competencies to build a successful organization* [Monograph]. Pittsburgh, PA: Development Dimensions International.

Carlisle, Kenneth E. (1998). *Analyzing jobs and tasks.* Techniques in Training and Performance Development Series. Englewood Cliffs, NJ: Educational Technology Publications.

Chowdhury, Paroma R. (1999, June 7). The right profile. *Business Today.*

Cooper, Kenneth C. (2000). *Effective competency modeling and reporting: A step-by-step guide for improving individual and organizational performance.* New York: AMACOM.

Dubois, David D. (1993). *Competency-based performance improvement: A strategy for organizational change.* Amherst, MA: Human Resource Development Press.

Dubois, David D., & Rothwell, William J. (2000). *The competency toolkit* (2 vols.). Amherst, MA: Human Resource Development Press.

Edwards, Mark, & Ewen, Ann. (1996). *360-degree feedback: The powerful new model for employee assessment and performance improvement.* New York: AMACOM.

Gendron, Marie. (1996, September). Competencies and what they mean to you. *Harvard Management Update,* 3–4.

Greengard, Samuel. (2001, November). Make smarter business decisions: Know what employees can do. *Workforce, 80*(11), 42.

Hartley, Darin E. (1999). *Job analysis at the speed of reality.* Amherst, MA: Human Resource Development Press.

Jansen, P., & Jongh, F. (1998). *Assessment centres: A practical handbook.* London: John Wiley.

Kane, J., & Lawler, E. E. (1978). Methods of peer assessment. *Psychological Bulletin, 85*(3), 555–586.

Kesler, Gregory. (2000). Four steps to building an HR agenda for growth: HR strategy revisited. *HR. Human Resource Planning, 23*(3), 24–37.

Klemp, George O. (Ed.). (1980). *The assessment of occupational competence.* Report to the National Institute of Education. Washington, DC: National Institute of Education.

Lewin, A. Y., & Zwany, A. (1976a). Peer nominations: A model, literature critique, and a paradigm for research. *Personnel Psychology, 29,* 423–447.

Lewin, A. Y., & Zwany, A. (1976b). *Peer nominations: A model, literature critique, and a paradigm for research.* Springfield, VA: National Technical Information Service.

McCormick, Ernest James. (1979). *Job analysis: Methods and applications.* New York: AMACOM.

McShulskis, Elaine. (n.d.). An argument for competency-based information systems. HR *Magazine, 41*(8), 16.

Norton, Robert. (1997). *The DACUM handbook* (2nd ed.). Columbus, OH: National Center for Research in Vocational Education.

Peters, Glen. (1996). *Beyond the next wave with scenario planning: Imagining the next generation of customers.* Englewood Cliffs, NJ: Prentice-Hall.

Raising the bar: Using competencies to enhance employee performance. (1996). Scottsdale, AZ: American Compensation Association in cooperation with Hay Group, Hewitt Associates LLC, Towers Perrin, & William M. Mercer, Inc.

Rothwell, William J. (1996). *Beyond training and development: State-of-the-art strategies for enhancing human performance.* New York: AMACOM.

Rothwell, William J. (2000). *Effective succession planning: Ensuring leadership continuity and building talent from within* (2nd ed.). New York: AMACOM.

Rothwell, William J., & Kazanas, H. C. (1994). *Human resource development: A strategic approach* (Rev. ed.). Amherst, MA: Human Resource Development Press.

Rothwell, William J., & Kazanas, H. C. (2003). *Planning and managing human resources: Strategic planning for personnel management* (2nd ed.). Amherst, MA: Human Resource Development Press.

Rothwell, William J., Prescott, Robert K., & Taylor, Maria W. (1998). *Strategic human resource leader: How to prepare your organization for the six key trends shaping the future.* Mountain View, CA: Davies-Black Publishing.

Rothwell, William J., & Sredl, Henry J. (2000). *The ASTD reference guide to workplace learning and performance* (3rd ed., 2 vols.). Amherst, MA: Human Resource Development Press.

Schippmann, Jeffrey S. (1999). *Strategic job modeling: Working at the core of integrated human resources.* Mahwah, NJ: Lawrence Erlbaum Associates.

Schoonover, Stephen C., Schoonover, Helen, Nemerov, Donald, & Ehyly, Christine. (2000). *2000 competency-based HR applications: Results of a comprehensive survey.* Alexandria, VA: Society for Human Resource Management.

Sherman, Arthur, Bohlander, George, & Snell, Scott. (1998). *Managing human resources* (11th ed.). Cincinnati, OH: South-Western College Publishing.

Spencer, Lyle, & Spencer, Signe. (1993). *Competence at work.* New York: Wiley.

Spychalski, Annette C., Quinones, Miguel A., Gaugler, Barbara B., & Pohley, Katja. (1997, Spring). A survey of assessment center practices in organizations in the United States. *Personnel Psychology, 50*(1), 71–90.

Thornton, George C. (1992). *Assessment centers in human resource management.* Reading, MA: Addison Wesley.

Thornton, George. C., & Byham, William C. (1982). *Assessment centers and managerial performance.* New York: Academic Press.

Traveling beyond 360-degree evaluations: UPS delivers feedback with role-playing, training. (1999, September). *HR Magazine, 44*(9).

Ulrich, Dave. (1992). Strategic and human resource planning: Linking customers and employees. *Human Resource Planning, 15*(2), 47.

Walker, James W. (1994). Integrating the human resource function with the business. *Human Resource Planning, 17*(2), 59.

Weiss, Terri, & Hartle, Franklin. (1998). *Reengineering performance management.* Delray Beach, FL: St. Lucie Press.

Chapter 5

Blazey, Mary E., & MacLeod, Joan A. (1996, June). Competency: A basis for the selection of staff nurses. *The Health Care Supervisor, 14*(4).

Callaghan, George, & Thompson, Paul. (2002, March). "We recruit attitude": The selection and shaping of routine call centre labour. *The Journal of Management Studies, 39*(2), n.p.

Competency-based selection: Program summary. Produced by the Consortium for Research on Emotional Intelligence in Organizations. Retrieved on April 8, 2002, from http://eiconsortium.org/model_programs/competency_based_selection.htm.

Cook, Kevin W., & Bernthal, Paul. (1998, July). Job/role competency practices survey report. *HR Benchmark Group, 4*(1). Pittsburgh, PA: Development Dimensions International.

Dubois, David D. (1993). *Competency-based performance improvement: A strategy for organizational change.* Amherst, MA: Human Resource Development Press.

Grensing-Pophal, Lynn. (2000, October). *The do's and don't's of recruiting from within.* Retrieved on April 8, 2002, from http://www.shrm.org/whitepapers/default.asp?page=61281.asp.

Guinn, Kathleen A. (1998, January/February). Transforming organizational behavior through competency-based integrated HR systems. *Journal of Compensation and Benefits, 13*(4).

Harvey, Michael G., & Novicevic, Cheri. (2000, Winter). An innovative global management staffing system: A competency-based perspective. *Human Resources Management, 39*(4), 381–394.

Kaplan, Gary. (1999, October). Now what? The pros and cons of hiring from within or without. *ACA News, 42*(9).

Knowlton, Lisa Wyatt. (2001, May/June). Study shows gaps in nonprofit management—And ways to improve. *Nonprofit World, 19*(3), 29–31.

Little, Patrick J. (1998, July/August). Selection of the fittest. *Management Review, 87*(7), 43–47.

Markwood, Susan. (2001, August). Hire power. *Security Management, 45*(8), 54–62.

Michaels, Ed, Handfield-Jones, Helen, & Axelrod, Beth. (2001). *The war for talent.* Boston: Harvard Business School Press.

1997 survey of human resource trends. (1997). Alexandria, VA: Society for Human Resource Management. May be retrieved from http://www.shrm.org

O'Daniell, Ellen E. (1999, Second Quarter). Energizing corporate culture and creating competitive advantage: A new look at workforce programs. *Benefits Quarterly, 15*(2), 18–25.

Pfau, Bruce N., & Kay, Ira T. (2002). *The human capital edge: 21 people management practices your company must implement (or avoid) to maximize shareholder value.* New York: McGraw-Hill.

The role of competencies in an integrated HR strategy. (1996, Summer). *ACA Journal, 5*(2), 6–21.

Rothwell, William J. (2000). *Effective succession planning: Ensuring leadership continuity and building talent from within* (2nd ed.). New York: AMACOM.

Rothwell, William J., & Kazanas, H. C. (2003). *Planning and managing human resources: Strategic planning for personnel management* (2nd ed.). Amherst, MA: Human Resource Development Press.

Rubin, James Peter. (2002, October 23). Breakaway (A special report)—Web workers: More small businesses are filling vacancies from an ever-growing pool of Internet candidates. *Wall Street Journal,* 8.

Schoonover, Stephen C., Schoonover, Helen, Nemerov, Donald, & Ehyly, Christine. (2000). *2000 competency-based HR applications: Results of a comprehensive survey.* Alexandria, VA: Society for Human Resource Management.

Sherman, A., Bohlander, G., & Snell, S. (1998). *Managing human resources* (11th ed.). Cincinnati, OH: South-Western College Publishing.

Smith, Tom, & Kandola, Brian. (1996, June 11). Dealing out work to the right stuff. *People Management, 2*(1), 28.

Spencer, Lyle M., Jr., & Spencer, Signe. (1993). *Competence at work.* New York: Wiley.

Vincola, Ann, & Mobley, Nancy. (1999, February). Competency-based hiring. *Executive Excellence, 16*(2), 17.

Warech, Michael A. (2002, February). Competency-based structured interviewing at Buckhead Beef Company. *Cornell Hotel and Restaurant Administration Quarterly, 43*(1), 70–77.

Wood, Robert, & Tim Payne. (1998). *Competency-based recruitment and selection.* Chichester, England: John Wiley.

Chapter 6

Ciancarelli, Agatha. (1998, June 18). Purchasing goes to school on company internets. *Purchasing, 124*(10), 525–526.

Cobb, Jeremy, & Gibbs, John. (1990). A new, competency-based, on-the-job programme for developing professional excellence in engineering. *The Journal of Management Development, 9*(3), 60.

Cook, Kevin W., & Bernthal, Paul. (1998). Job/role competency practices survey report. *HR Benchmark Group, 4*(1). Pittsburgh, PA: Development Dimensions International.

Crabb, Steve. (n.d.). Certified competent. *Personnel Management, 25*(5), 57.

Dubois, David D. (1993). *Competency-based performance improvement: A strategy for organizational change.* Amherst, MA: Human Resource Development Press.

Dubois, David D. (Ed.). (1998). *The competency casebook: Twelve studies in competency-based performance improvement.* Amherst, MA: Human Resource Development Press.

Filipowski, Diane. (1991, May). Florida Power turns training into dollars. *Personnel Journal, 70*(5), 47.

Fleming, Richard K., Oliver, Julienne R., and Bolton, Debra M. (1996). Training supervisors to train staff: A case study in a human services organization. *Journal of Organizational Behavior Management, 16*(1), 3.

Goodridge, E. (2001). Slowing economy sparks boom in e-learning. *Informationweek, 863,* 100–104.

Gould, Renee, Thompson, Robin, Rakel, Barbara, Jensen, Joelle, et al. (1996, February). Redesigning the RN and NA roles. *Nursing Management, 27*(2), 37.

Greengard, S. (2001). Make smarter business decisions: Know what employees can do. *Workforce, 80*(11), 42–46.

Industry report. (1999, October). *Training,* 46.

Kaplan-Leiserson, Eva. (n.d.). *E-learning glossary.* Retrieved from http://www. learningcircuits.org/glossary.html.

Meade, Jim. (1998, December). A solution for competency-based employee development. *HR Magazine, 43*(13), 54–58.

Raising the bar: Using competencies to enhance employee performance. (1996). Scottsdale, AZ: American Compensation Association in cooperation with Hay Group, Hewitt Associates LLC, Towers Perrin, & William M. Mercer, Inc.

Ridha, Al-Khayyat. (1998). Training and development needs assessment: A partial model for partner institutes. *Journal of European Industrial Training, 22*(1), 18–27.

Rosenberg, M. J. (2001). *Building successful online learning in your organization. E-learning strategies for delivering knowledge in the digital age.* New York: McGraw-Hill.

Rossett, A. (2002). *The ASTD e-learning handbook: Best practices, strategies, and case studies for an emerging field.* New York: McGraw-Hill.

Rothwell, William J. (1996a). *Just-in-time training assessment instrument.* Amherst, MA: Human Resource Development Press.

Rothwell, William J. (1996b). *The self-directed on-the-job learning workshop.* Amherst, MA: Human Resource Development Press.

Rothwell, William J. (2002). *The workplace learner: Aligning training initiatives with individual learning competencies.* New York: AMACOM.

Rothwell, William J., & Cookson, Peter S. (1997). *Beyond instruction: Program planning for business and education.* San Francisco: Jossey-Bass.

Rothwell, William J., Lindholm, J., & Wallick, W. (2003). *What CEOs expect from corporate training.* New York: AMACOM.

Rothwell, William J., & Sensenig, Kevin. (Eds.). (1998). *The sourcebook for self-directed learning.* Amherst, MA: Human Resource Development Press.

Rothwell, William J., & Sredl, H. J. (2000). *The ASTD reference guide to workplace learning and performance* (3rd ed., 2 vols.). Amherst, MA: Human Resource Development Press.

Van Buren, Mark E., & Erskine, William. (2002). *State of the industry: ASTD's annual review of trends in employer-provided training in the United States.* Alexandria, VA: The American Society for Training and Development.

Chapter 7

Adler, Ronald L., & Coleman, Tom. (1999, April). *Performance management profile: Example audit of an HR function* (SHRM white paper). Alexandria, VA: Society for Human Resource Management.

Bowen, David E., & Lawler, Edward E., III. (1992, Spring). Total quality-oriented human resource management. *Organizational Dynamics, 20*(4), 29–41.

Competencies drive HR practices. (1996, August). *HR Focus, 73*(8), 15.

Cripe, Edward J. (1997, November/December). Making performance management a positive experience. *ACA News, 40*(10).

Dubois, David D. (1993). *Competency-based performance improvement: A strategy for organizational change.* Amherst, MA: Human Resource Development Press.

Dubois, David D., & Rothwell, William J. (2000). *The competency toolkit* (2 vols.). Amherst, MA: Human Resource Development Press.

Greene, Robert J. (2000, March). *Effectively managing intellectual capital: Critical challenge for human resources* (SHRM white paper). Alexandria, VA: Society for Human Resource Management.

Harris, Barbara R., Huselid, Mark A., & Becker, Brian E. (1999, Winter). Strategic human resource management at Praxair. *Human Resource Management, 38*(4), 319–320.

Jones, Thomas W. (1995, Fall). Performance management in a changing context: Monsanto pioneers a competency-based, developmental approach. *Human Resource Management, 34*(3), 425.

Kanin-Lovers, Jill, & Bevan, Richard. (1992, March/April). Don't evaluate performance—Manage it. *Journal of Compensation and Benefits, 7*(5), 51–53.

Laumeyer, James A. (1997, March). *Performance management systems: What do we want to accomplish?* (SHRM white paper). Alexandria, VA: Society for Human Resource Management.

Lukesh, Richard J. (2000). *Change performance evaluations to process evaluations* (SHRM white paper). Alexandria, VA: Society for Human Resource Management.

Maccoby, Michael. (2001, May/June). Successful leaders employ strategic intelligence. *Research Technology Management, 44*(3), 58–60.

McAfee, R. Bruce, & Campagne, Paul J. (1992). Performance management: A strategy for improving employee performance and productivity. *Journal of Managerial Psychology, 8*(5), 24–32.

Measuring the impact of competencies. (1997, March/April). *Compensation and Benefits Review, 29*(2), 70–71.

Nolan, Pat. (1998, May). Competencies drive decision-making. *Nursing Management, 29*(3), 27–29.

Orr, Brian. (2002, May 20). Focus on strengths, manage weaknesses. *Canadian HR Reporter, 15*(10), 6–12.

Pardue, Howard M. (2000). *Performance appraisal as an employee development tool* (SHRM white paper). Alexandria, VA: Society for Human Resource Management.

Pickard, Jane. (1996, December 5). Playing by its own rules. *People Management, 2*(24), 25.

Ripley, David. (1999, May). *Improving employee performance: Moving beyond traditional HRM responses* (SHRM white paper). Alexandria, VA: Society for Human Resource Management.

2000 Performance Management Survey. (2000). Alexandria, VA: Society for Human Resource Management.

Weiss, Tracy B., & Hartle, Franklin. (1997). *Reengineering performance management: Breakthroughs in achieving strategy through people.* Boca Raton, FL: St. Lucie Press.

Chapter 8

Abosch, Kenan S. (1995, January/February). The promise of broadbanding. *Compensation and Benefits Review, 27*(1), 54.

Abosch, Kenan S., & Gilbert, Dan. (1996). *Improving organizational effectiveness through broadbanding.* Scottsdale, AZ: American Compensation Association.

Armitage, Amelia. (1997, Summer). The three R's of organizational performance: Reinforcement, recognition and rewards. *ACA Journal, 6*(2), 32–41.

Bowen, R. Brayton. (2000). *Recognizing and rewarding employees.* New York: McGraw-Hill.

Bremen, John M., & Coil, Maggi. (1999, June). Comparing alternative base pay methods: Which one meets your organization's needs? *ACA News, 42*(6).

Coil, Maggi. (1999, April). Making employees happy with noncash rewards. *ACA News, 42*(4).

Dzamba, Andrew. (2001, Winter). Compensation strategies to use amid organizational change. *Compensation and Benefits Management, 17*(1), 16–29.

Flannery, Thomas P., Hofrichter, David A., & Platten, Paul E. (1996). *People, performance, and pay: Dynamic compensation for changing organizations.* New York: The Free Press.

Hale, Jamie. (1998, Summer). Strategic rewards: Keeping your best talent from walking out the door. *Compensation and Benefits Management, 14*(3), 39–50.

Hofrichter, David. (1993, September/October). Broadbanding: A "second generation" approach. *Compensation and Benefits Review, 25*(5), 53.

Kochanski, James, & LeBlanc, Peter. (1999, February 22). Should firms pay for competencies? *Canadian HR Reporter, 12*(4), 10.

Kohn, Alfie. (1999). *Punished by rewards: The trouble with gold stars, incentive plans, A's, praise, and other bribes.* New York: Houghton Mifflin.

Lawler, Edward E., III. (2000, January). Pay strategy: New thinking for the new millennium. *Compensation and Benefits Review*, 7–10.

Leonard, Bill. (1994, February). New ways to pay employees. *HR Magazine, 39*(2), 61.

Manas, Todd. (2000, November/December). Combining reward elements to create the right team chemistry. *Workspan, 43*(11).

Nadel, Robert S. (1998, December). *Compensation alternatives: Changes in business strategy, plans and expectations* (SHRM white paper). Reviewed April 1999 and July 2001. Alexandria, VA: Society for Human Resource Management. Retrieved from http://www.shrm.org/whitepapers/documents/61440.asp.

Nelson, Bob. (1994). *1001 ways to reward employees.* New York: Workman.

O'Neal, Sandra. (1996, November/December). Study shows compensation programs more strategic. *ACA News, 39*(10).

O'Neal, Sandra. (1998, Autumn). The phenomenon of total rewards. *ACA Journal, 7*(3), 6–18.

Risher, Howard (Ed.). (1999). *Aligning pay and results: Compensation strategies that work from the boardroom to the shop floor.* New York: AMACOM.

Rothwell, William J., & Kazanas, H. C. (1998). *Mastering the instructional design process: A systematic approach* (2nd ed.). San Francisco: Jossey-Bass.

Schiffers, Peggy Espy, Young, Sedonia, & Shelton, Daniel L. (1996, October). *Employee recognition and award programs that work* (SHRM white paper). Reviewed April 1999 and September 2001. Alexandria, VA: Society for Human Resource Management.

Sherman, Arthur, Bohlander, George, & Snell, Scott. (1998). *Managing human resources.* Cincinnati, OH: South-Western College Publishing.

Stufflebeam, D. L. (1974a). Evaluation perspectives and procedures. In W. J. Popham (Ed.), *Evaluation in education.* Berkeley, CA: McCutchan.

Stufflebeam, D. L. (1974b). Alternative approaches to educational evaluation: A self-study guide for educators. In W. J. Popham (Ed.), *Evaluation in education: Current applications.* Berkeley, CA: McCutchan.

Stufflebeam, D. L., Foley, W. J., Gephart, W. J., Guba, E. G., Hammond, R. L., Merriman, H. O., et al. (1971). *Educational evaluation and decision making.* Itasca, IL: Peacock.

Tropman, John E. (2001). *The compensation solution: How to develop an employee-driven rewards system.* San Francisco: Jossey-Bass.

Tyler, Kathryn. (1998, April). Compensation strategies can foster lateral moves and growing in place. *HR Magazine, 43*(5), 64–71.

Weiss, Tracey B., & Hartle, Franklin. (1997). *Reengineering performance management: Breakthroughs in achieving strategy through people.* Boca Raton, FL: St. Lucie Press.

WorldatWork Glossary. Retrieved May 13, 2001, from http://www.worldatwork.org.

Zingheim, Patricia, & Schuster, Jay. (2000). *Pay people right: Breakthrough reward strategies to great companies.* San Francisco: Jossey-Bass.

Chapter 9

Anonymous. (1993, November). Catalysts for career development: Four case studies. *Training and Development, 47*(11), 26.

Anonymous. (1995, January/February). Nike pushes the limits with Life Trek. *Compensation and Benefits Review, 27*(1), 74.

Bloch, Deborah P., & Richmond, Lee J. (Eds.). (1997). *Connections between spirit and work in career development: New approaches and practical perspectives.* Mountain View, CA: Davies-Black Publishing.

Bloch, Deborah P., & Richmond, Lee J. (1998). *Soul work: Finding the work you love, loving the work you have.* Mountain View, CA: Davies-Black Publishing.

Bolles, Richard N. (1981). *The three boxes of life.* Berkeley, CA: Ten Speed Press.

Bolles, Richard N. (2002). *What color is your parachute?* Berkeley, CA: Ten Speed Press.

Cafaro, Don. (2001, February). When the honeymoon ends: Thinking in long-term solutions. *Workspan, 44*(2).

Cairo, Peter C. (1985). Career planning and development in organizations. In Zandy Leibowitz and Daniel Lea (Eds.), *Adult career development: Concepts, issues and practices.* Alexandria, VA: American Counseling Association, National Career Development Association.

Delahoussaye, Martin. (2001, March). Dennis Liberson. *Training, 38*(3), 46–52.

Dubois, David D. (2000, December). The seven stages of one's career. *Training and Development, 54*(12), 45–50.

Dubois, David D., & Rothwell, William J. (2000). *The competency toolkit* (2 vols.). Amherst, MA: Human Resource Development Press.

Eanes, Beverly E., Richmond, Lee J., & Link, Jean W. (2001). *What brings you to life: Awakening woman's spiritual essence.* Mahwah, NJ: Paulist Press.

Fredrickson, Ronald H. (1982). *Career information.* Englewood Cliffs, NJ: Prentice-Hall.

Hafer, Al A. (Ed.). (1992). *The nuts and bolts of career counseling: How to set up and succeed in private practice.* Tulsa, OK: National Career Development Association.

Harris-Bowlsbey, JoAnn, Dikel, Margaret Rile, & Sampson, James P. (1998). *The Internet: A tool for career planning.* Tulsa, OK: National Career Development Association.

Kapes, Jerome T., & Whitfield, Edwin A. (2002). *A counselor's guide to career assessment instruments* (4th ed.). Tulsa, OK: National Career Development Association.

Kaye, Beverly L. (1985). *A guide for career development practitioners: Up is not the only way.* San Diego, CA: University Associates (Pfeiffer/Jossey-Bass).

Kummerow, Jean M. (Ed.). 2000. *New directions in career planning and the workplace: Practical strategies for career management professionals* (2nd ed.). Mountain View, CA: Davies-Black Publishing.

Leibowitz, Zandy, Farren, Caela, & Kaye, Beverly. (1986). *Designing career development systems.* San Francisco: Jossey-Bass.

Niles, Spencer G. (Ed.). (In press). *Adult career development: Concepts, issues, and practices* (3rd ed.). Tulsa, OK: National Career Development Association.

Niles, Spencer G., Goodman, Jane, & Pope, Mark. (2001). *The career counseling casebook: A resource for practitioners, students, and counselor educators.* Tulsa, OK: National Career Development Association.

O*Net On-Line. (2002). Washington, DC: U.S. Department of Labor. Available online at http://online.onetcenter.org and also at http://www.doleta.gov.

Patch, Kenneth. (2000, Summer). Innovations in corporate career centers. *Career Planning and Adult Development Journal, 16*(2), 5–6.

Pope, Mark, & Minor, Carole W. (2000). *Experiential activities for teaching career counseling classes and facilitating career groups.* Tulsa, OK: National Career Development Association.

Schein, Edgar H. (1978). *Career dynamics: Matching individual and organizational needs.* Reading, MA: Addison-Wesley.

Simonsen, Peggy. (1997). *Promoting a development culture in your organization: Using career development as a change agent.* Mountain View, CA: Davies-Black Publishing.

Stufflebeam, D. L. (1974a). Evaluation perspectives and procedures. In W. J. Popham (Ed.), *Evaluation in education.* Berkeley, CA: McCutchan.

Stufflebeam, D. L. (1974b). Alternative approaches to educational evaluation: A self-study guide for educators. In W. J. Popham (Ed.), *Evaluation in education: Current applications.* Berkeley, CA: McCutchan.

Stufflebeam, D. L., Foley, W. J., Gephart, W. J., Guba, E. G., Hammond, R. L., Merriman, H. O., et al. (1971). *Educational evaluation and decision making.* Itasca, IL: Peacock.

Walker, J. W., & Gutteridge, T. (1979). *Career planning practices: An AMA report.* New York: AMACOM/American Management Association.

Chapter 10

Becker, B., Huselid, M., & Ulrich, D. (2001). *The HR scorecard: Linking people, strategy, and performance.* Boston: Harvard Business School Press.

Joinson, C. (2000). Public sector HR: Leaving bureaucracy behind. *HR Magazine, 45*(6), 78–85.

McConnell, J. (2000). *Auditing your human resources department: A step-by-step guide.* New York: AMACOM.

Sullivan, R., Fairburn, L., & Rothwell, W. (2002). The whole system transformation conference: Fast change for the 21st century. In S. Herman (Ed.), *Rewiring organizations for the networked economy: Organizing, managing, and leading in the information age.* San Francisco: Jossey-Bass/Pfeiffer.

Wright, P., McMahan, G., Snell, S., & Gerhart, B. (2001). Comparing line and HR executives' perceptions of HR effectiveness: Services, roles, and contributions. *Human Resource Management, 40*(2), 111–123.

Appendix A

Dubois, David D. (Ed.). (1998). *The competency casebook: Twelve studies in competency-based performance improvement.* Amherst, MA: Human Resource Development Press.

Dubois, David D., & Rothwell, William J. (2000). *The competency toolkit* (2 vols.). Amherst, MA: Human Resource Development Press.

Appendix B

Simonsen, Peggy. (1997). *Promoting a development culture in your organization: Using career development as a change agent.* Mountain View, CA: Davies-Black Publishing.

Appendix D

Braddock, Douglas (1999, November). Employment outlook: 1998–2008: Occupational employment projections to 2008. *Monthly Labor Review,* 51–77.

Caudron, S. (1999). The Looming Leadership Crisis. *Workforce, 78*(10), 72–79.

Rothwell, William J. (2000). *Effective succession planning: Ensuring leadership continuity and building talent from within* (2nd ed.). New York: AMACOM.

Rothwell, William J., & Kazanas, H. C. (1999). *Building in-house leadership and management development programs.* Westport, CT: Quorum Books.

Index

action plan, 52–53
activities, 20
affective domain of learning, 242
assessment centers, 91–92, 195–196
automatic step progression, for job-based pay, 166

behavior, 20
behavioral event interview/interviewing: competency-based employee selection using, 106–107, 118–119; description of, 28–29; time allotment for, 119
behavioral indicators, 20
behavioral language, 19
behaviorally anchored scales: expectation scales, 246; observation scales, 246; rating scales, 246
benchmarking, 54–55
blended learning, 128
broadbanding, 167–168

business objectives: alignment with needs of HR customer, 55–56; competency-based HR planning and, 65–66; definition of, 39; employee's role in achieving, 66; identifying of, 53, 82–83; implementation role of, 53, 55–56
business plans, 39
business strategies: competencies and, 37, 39–40; definition of, 39
businesses. *See* organization

CAP. *See* competency assessment process
capital: human, 33–34, 55; knowledge, 49–50
career coach, 248
career counselors, 185, 251
career development, 184–185, 247–248
career fit, 192

career path systems, 194
career planning, 188
career telling, 189–190
careerbanding, 168
certification programs, 90
change: champion of, 224; competency-based HR planning benefits for, 74; magnitude of, 50–52; negative effects of, 51; ownership development for, 224–225; rate of, 50–52; resistance to, 51; trends that cause, 52
coaching, 193
commitment: to competency identification, 25; by senior management, 236
compensation systems: alternative types of, 168; broadbanding, 167–168; careerbanding, 168; definition of, 165; employer considerations in designing, 166; fair pay standards for, 163–164; job-based pay, 166–167; negotiation of, 120–121; skill-based pay, 167; traditional approaches, 163, 166. *See also* competency-based employee rewards; rewards
competencies: abstract types of, 86, 205; acquisition training, 184; attributes of, 17–18; background of, 16–19; barriers to using, 25–26; business strategies and, 37, 39–40; classification of, 19; for completing employees' work, 148; comprehensiveness of, 246; core, 39–40; corporate culture influences on, 20, 245; definition of, 16–18, 86; employee development for, 186; for exemplary performers vs. fully successful performers, 87; experience with, 32; human capital characterized by, 55; for HR practitioners,

228–231; identification of. *See* competency identification; individual, 132–135; interpretation of, 19; job description vs., 233, 242, 244–245; knowledge, 18; level of detail of, 246; measurement methods, 19–20; nontechnical, 19, 203; organizational role of, 37–38, 135; personal functioning, 19, 72, 203; present-to-future, 202–203; reasons for applying, 38; self-assessments of, 88–89; skills, 18; sources of, 32; spectrum of, 235; studies of, 38; supply and demand, 87–92; tasks and, 21; technical, 19, 72, 203; tracking of, 66; types of, 16, 205, 245–246; worker characteristics as, 86
competency assessment process: assessment centers, 91–92; baseline, 151; certification programs, 90; customer-based, 90; data organization after, 92–93; definition of, 88; employee development, 195; expert work performers for, 89–90; multirater systems, 90–91, 195; peer-based, 90; for performance managers, 151; performance requirements and, 151; self-assessments, 88–89; supervisors, 89
competency development needs, 204–207
competency identification: challenges of, 24–27; competency menu method for, 29–31; for competency-based HR planning, 85–87; costs of, 241; definition of, 24, 28; employee benefits, 36; information necessary for, 86; job competence assessment method (JCAM) for, 28–30; lack

of commitment to, 25; management endorsement of, 87; methods of, 28–32, 203; modified DACUM method for, 31–32; principles of, 241; resources for, 24–25, 27; rigor of, 24, 27; sources for, 32; speed of, 24; studies of, 25–26

competency inventory questionnaire: data compilation, 93; description of, 70–73, 92

competency menu method, 29–31

competency models: advantages of, 234; business needs achieved by using, 35–36; competency menu for building, 30; core competencies linked with, 243; corporate culture-specific, 244; costs of, 241; definition of, 23; development of, 244; future of, 233–237; studies of, 38; types of, 23–24

competency pool, 50, 88

competency projects: facilitation of, 27; outcomes alignment for, 27; problems associated with, 26–27

competency-based employee development: advantages of, 197; challenges of, 197–198; characteristics of, 13; competency acquisition needs, 236; creation of, 196–197; reasons for, 196; senior manager's role in, 197; traditional employee development vs., 198–199

competency-based employee development process: advisory panel for, 211; competency needs assessment, 202–204; evaluation of, 214–215; external consultant for, 199; front-end needs assessment, 201–202; implementation of, 199–215; initiation of, 199; institutionalizing of, 214–215; learning opportunities, 208; life-career needs and preferences, 204–207; objectives for, 207–208; outcomes, 214; philosophy for, 201; present-to-future competencies, 202–203; senior management briefings, 210–211, 214; sponsor for, 201; start-up plan, 209–213; steps for, 200

competency-based employee recruitment: advantages of, 108–109; challenges of, 109–110; creation of, 102–104; description of, 12; identifying needs, 112, 114; indications for, 110–112; initiation of, 103; job analysis information, 114; job descriptions and specifications determined, 103; materials for, 115–116; model for, 112–116; nondiscrimination in, 108; organizational demands of, 103; sources for, 115

competency-based employee rewards: advantages of, 173; allocation of, 171; challenges of, 173–174; creation of, 171–173; criteria for, 172; description of, 13; implementation of. *See* competency-based employee rewards process; key competencies as criteria for, 172; results matched with, 173–174; time periods in, 164; traditional employee rewards vs., 174

competency-based employee rewards process: communication regarding, 177; implementation of, 174–181, 180–181; objectives for, 178; panel for, 180; philosophy for, 177–178; process manager for, 180; senior management endorsement of, 175–177, 179; task group, 177–179 competency-based employee selection: advantages of, 108–109; applicant pool quality using, 111; behavioral event interviews for, 106–107, 118–119; challenges of, 109–110; compensation and benefits package negotiations, 120–121; competency assessments, 119–120; creation of, 104–106; indications for, 110–112; interviewer training, 118–119; model for, 116–123; nondiscrimination in, 108; organizational demands of, 103; organizational fit of applicant, 108, 122; performance evaluations after, 121–122; recommendation list, 119–120; screening of applicants, 117–118; selection criteria and methods, 104–105, 116–117; traditional employee selection vs., 105–108; turnover rates reduced by, 112; validation of, 121–123; verification of competencies, 107, 120

competency-based employee training: advantages of, 133–134; challenges of, 133–134; characteristics of, 13; competency-based performance management systems and, 150; delivery methods for, 128, 137; description of, 129–130; evaluation of, 137–138; formative evaluations, 137; indications for, 134–135; individual competence building focus of, 133; instructional systems design model reinvented for, 130–131, 132–133, 135–138; self-directed training and development, 138; strategic systems model, 131–132; summative evaluations, 137; traditional employee training vs.,

134–135; training needs assessment for, 130; work teams for, 132

competency-based hiring. *See* competency-based employee recruitment; competency-based employee selection

competency-based HR management: advantages of, 36, 234; awareness of, 221–222; business needs achieved by, 34–39; case studies of, 242; challenges for, 236; characteristics of, 243; creation of, 220–221; description of, 34, 219–220; exemplary performance goals, 34; future of, 233–237; goals for, 53; HR practitioner's involvement in, 220; implementation of, 52–59; innovations for, 234–235; organization benefits of using, 34–35; outcomes produced by, 35; pilot testing of, 225–228; questions frequently asked in, 241–246; reasons for using, 35–37; stakeholder groups in, 227; techniques for introducing, 27; traditional HR management vs., 11–13, 221–228; transformation to, 221–228; uses of, 235–236; vignette about, 43–46

competency-based HR management projects: benchmarking, 54–55; business objectives, 53, 55–56; conditions that affect completion of, 57; diagram of, 54; environmental scanning, 53–55; formative evaluations, 58–59; HR customer needs, 53; implementation steps for, 52–59; management plan for, 57–58; objectives of, 55–57; overview of, 52–53; project management plan, 57–58; summative evaluations, 59 competency-based HR planning: advantages of, 67; business objectives understood before, 65–66; challenges of, 67–70; implementation of, 65; indications for, 73–74; specificity of, 67; studies of, 65; system for. *See* competency-based HR planning system

competency-based HR planning system: competency identification, 85–87; development plan for, 76–79; implementation of, 75–93; leadership's role in, 67, 75; model for, 75; operations managers and users briefed about, 80–82; organization's goals, business objectives, and outputs or results identified, 82–83; organizations that require, 74–75; pilot testing of, 93; plan for, 76–79; project manager's responsibilities, 77; project objectives identified, 77; senior management briefing about, 79–80; tasks, 83–84; traditional HR planning vs., 64–65, 70, 73–75; work activities, 83–84

competency-based instructional systems design model: advantages of, 132–133; application of, 135–137; challenges of, 133; description of, 130–131; individual competence, 135; model for, 135–138; and organizational competence, 135–136; and performance analysis, 135

competency-based interviews, 111, 118

competency-based performance management: advantages of, 152–153; challenges of, 153–154; characteristics of, 13; communication requirements, 152; description of, 235; employees' work results, 148, 153; factors that affect, 145; HR focus in, 149–150; indications for, 154–155; model for, 146–152; outputs or results expectations clarified for, 153; performance monitoring in, 149; performance reviews in, 149–152; process reinventions for, 146; roadblocks to, 154; success of, 154; system for. *See* competency-based performance management system; traditional performance management vs., 145–146, 154–155

competency-based performance management system: blueprint for, 157–158; communication requirements of, 160; evaluation of, 161; formative evaluations of, 161; implementation of, 159–161; materials for, 158; pilot testing of, 159; planning for, 157–158; senior management involvement in, 157–158; steps for implementing, 155–161; summative evaluations of, 161; and task completion, 160; and task group members, 159; training for, 158–159

competency-based work teams, 138–139

competent performance, 85–86

computer-based career guidance systems, 195

concurrent rewards, 164

core competencies: competency models linked with, 243; employee, 40, 245; organizational, 39–40, 243, 245

corporate culture: competencies and, 20, 244–245; definition of, 20; employee support by, 198

cost containment, 48–49
creativity, 50
critical incident technique, 16–17
cross training, 126
culture: corporate, 20, 198, 244–245;
    definition of, 20
customer assessments of worker
    competencies, 90

DACUM method, for competency
    identification, 31–32, 84
dimensions, 19
downsizing, 63

e-learning, 128
employee(s): in achieving business
    objectives, 66; competency
    assessments. *See* competency
    assessment process; competency
    identification benefits for, 36;
    competency inventory question-
    naire for, 70–73, 92; core compe-
    tencies of, 40; corporate culture
    support of, 198; disconnection
    from organization, 187; high-
    potential, 256; promotion of, 98;
    reactions to change by, 50–51;
    reasons for leaving organization,
    196; recognition of, 169–170;
    skills inventory questionnaire for,
    68–69; temporary assignments
    for, 195; values of, 191
employee development: approaches
    for, 192–196; assessment centers,
    195–196; career development
    professionals' view of, 185; career
    path systems for, 194; and career
    telling, 189–190; choosing work
    and, 190–192; coaching for, 193;
    communication about, 187–188;
    competencies acquired through,
    186; competency assessment
    activities, 195; competency-

based. *See* competency-based
    employee development; com-
    puter-based career guidance
    systems for, 195; definition of,
    186–188, 204; description of,
    183–186; documentation of, 247;
    educational programs for, 195;
    failure of, 249; information ses-
    sions for participants in, 248; ini-
    tiative for, 184, 196; leadership
    view of, 185; life-career develop-
    ment and, 256; mentoring for,
    193; objectives of, 187; ongoing
    nature of, 187; organization suc-
    cess and, 187; perspectives of,
    187; programs for, 193; purposes
    of, 188; seminars for, 248–249;
    skills bank activity for, 194–195;
    succession management and,
    215, 255–256; suggestions for,
    247–249; temporary assignments
    for, 195; Toastmasters, Inc., for,
    194; traditional approach to, 13,
    188–196, 198–199; workbook
    exercises for, 194
employee recruitment: applicants for,
    98–99; competency-based. *See*
    competency-based employee
    recruitment; costs of, 99; defini-
    tion of, 96; external methods for,
    98; internal, 98; and job descrip-
    tions, 97; and job specifications,
    97; methods for, 98–99; on-line
    methods of, 99; from specially
    based groups, 99; traditional
    approach to, 12, 96–99, 110,
    165–170
employee rewards: allocation of, 171;
    competency-based. *See* compe-
    tency-based employee rewards;
    definition of, 165; traditional
    approach to, 13, 174. *See also*
    rewards

employee selection: competency-based. *See* competency-based employee selection; definition of, 96; methods for, 101; process for, 99–100; traditional approach vs., 99–102, 105–106, 110

employee training: competency-based. *See* competency-based employee training; cross training, 126; definition of, 126; delivery methods for, 128, 137; expenditures on, 126; orientation training, 126; outplacement training, 126; qualifying training, 126; remedial training, 126; traditional approach to, 13, 127–131, 134; training needs assessment for, 127–128; types of, 126

employment, 186

environmental scanning, 53–55

equity, 166

evaluations. *See* formative evaluations; summative evaluations

exemplars, 22

exemplary performers, 21–23, 48, 87, 164, 235–236

focus groups, 31

formative evaluations: competency-based employee training system, 137; competency-based performance management system, 161; description of, 58–59

fully successful performers, 21–23, 87

globalization, 48

goal setting, 253–254

grandstanding, 31

groupthink, 31

head count, 64

high-potential employees, 256

human capital, 33–34

human resource customer: areas of concern for, 53–54; needs of, 53, 55; project objectives, 55–57

human resource functions: assessing of, 223; selection of functions to be competency based, 223–224

human resource management: competency-based. *See* competency-based HR management; definition of, 33; division of, 9; functional organization of, 9; functions of, 12, 223; point-of-contact organization of, 9; structuring of, 9–10; subsystems of, 9–10, 12; technology effects on, 8; traditional approach to, 11–13, 219; transformation of, 52, 221–228; trends that affect, 46–59; work-based, 34

human resource planning: business plan view of, 62; competency-based. *See* competency-based HR planning; definition of, 62; downsizing effects on, 63; history of, 63; interest in, 62–63; overview of, 61–62; purpose of, 62; system development plan for transformation of, 76–79; technology effects on, 63; traditional approach to, 62–64, 70, 73–75; trends in, 63–64

human resource practitioners: assessment of, 230; awareness by, 221; competencies of, 228–231; competency model for, 225; in competency-based HR management, 220; educating of, 225

"hush puppy" effect, 189–190

implementation: benchmarking, 54–55; of business objectives, 53, 55–56; of competency-based employee development process,

implementation *(cont'd)*
199–215; of competency-based
employee rewards process,
174–181, 180–181; of competency-based HR management,
52–59; of competency-based HR
management projects, 52–59; of
competency-based HR planning,
65; of competency-based HR
planning model, 75–93; of competency-based performance
management system, 155–161,
159–161; diagram of, 54; environmental scanning and, 53–55;
formative evaluations and,
58–59; HR customer needs, 53;
overview of, 52–53; of project
management plan, 57–58; summative evaluations and, 59
incentives: definition of, 168; description of, 164; monetary, 168–169;
nonmonetary, 169
incident: critical incident technique,
16–17; definition of, 17
individual competence: advantages of,
133–134; challenges of, 133–134;
definition of, 135; training to
build, 131–132; in work team
context, 132
individual development plans, 138
information management system, 66
institutional memory, 50
instructional systems design (ISD)
model: competency-based, 130–131,
132–138; reinventing of, 130–131,
132–133; steps involved in, 127–129
intellectual capital, 50
interviews: behavioral event. *See*
behavioral event interview;
competency-based, 111, 118;
job applicant, 118
ISD model. *See* instructional systems
design model

job activity, 20
job analysis: description of, 5–6, 109;
information, 114; purposes of, 6
job applications, 105
job competence assessment method
(JCAM), 28–30
job competency, 18, 21. *See also* competencies
job description: clarity of, 9; competencies vs., 233, 242, 244–245;
confusion regarding, 8; definition
of, 6, 96; outdating of, 8, 233;
problems associated with, 6, 242;
sample, 7; surveys of, 8–9; traditional, 6–7; updating of, 97
job interview: description of, 118;
interviewer training for, 118–119;
traditional, 118
job output, 20
job requisition, 96
job specification: definition of, 6, 96;
sample, 7; updating of, 97
job task, 20
job-based pay, 166–167

Kemp's Life-Career World Wheel,
252–253
knowledge, 18
knowledge capital, 49–50

labor forecasts, 64
leaders: competency-based HR planning role of, 67, 75; development
programs for, 256; employee
development as viewed by,
185
learning: affective domain of, 242;
blended, 128; e-learning, 128;
opportunities, 208; technology
for, 128
life-career: assessments, 206, 251–254;
description of, 186–187, 198,
212, 248; development of, 256;

goals for, 254; needs and preferences, 204–207
lump-sum bonuses, 169

managers: performance, 151; senior. *See* senior management
market change, speed in, 49
matrix management, 74
mentoring, 193
merit range, for job-based pay, 166
modified DACUM method, for competency identification, 31–32
multirater competency assessment systems, 90–91

nontechnical competencies, 19

objectives: business. *See* business objectives; project, 55–57
operational analysis, 53
organization: business objectives for, 82–83, 223; change in, 50–52; common language in, 19; competency-based HR management, 34–35, 243; competency-based HR planning, 74–75; core competencies of, 39, 243, 245; cost containment for, 48–49; employee development effects on, 187; employee disconnection from, 187; employee values considered in, 191; globalization effects on, 48; goals for, 82–83; knowledge capital management by, 49–50; marketing to job applicants by, 99; prioritizing in, 243–244; speed in market change for, 49; technology effects on, 47; trends that affect, 46–59
organization development, 186
orientation training, 126
outplacement training, 126

outputs: clarification of, for competency-based performance management, 153; definition of, 6, 21; identifying of, 82–83; job recruitment materials description of, 115

peer-based competency assessments, 90
performance: competent, 85–86; evaluations of after job applicant selection, 121–122; exemplary, 21–23, 48; roadblocks to, 154
performance evaluation, 142
performance management: competency-based. *See* competency-based performance management; definition of, 142; employee complaints regarding, 142–143; and performance plans, 144; studies of, 144; traditional approach to, 13, 142–145, 154–155
performance managers, 151
performance monitoring, 149
performance plans, 144
performance reviews, 149–152
personalization, 244
point-of-contact method, of HR management organization, 9
profit sharing, 168–169
project management plan, 57–58
project tasks, 78
promotion, 98

qualifying training, 126
questionnaires: competency inventory, 70–73, 92; skills inventory, 68–69

recruitment: applicants for, 98–99; competency-based. *See* competency-based employee recruitment; costs of, 99; definition of, 96,

recruitment *(cont'd)*
    external methods of, 98; internal, 98; job descriptions and, 97; job specifications and, 97; methods of, 98–99; on-line methods of, 99; from specially based groups, 99; traditional approach to, 12, 96–99, 110
reliability, 30
remedial training, 126
results, 6
rewards: compensation. *See* compensation systems; employee. *See* employee rewards; organization's philosophy regarding, 171; recognition as form of, 169–170; total. *See* total rewards
rigor of competency identification, 24, 27

screening of job applicants, 117–118
selection: competency-based. *See* competency-based employee selection; definition of, 96; methods for, 101; process for, 99–100; traditional approach to, 99–102, 105–106, 110
self-awareness, 191
senior management: commitment by, 236; competency-based employee rewards system and, 175–177, 179; competency-based HR planning system and, 79–80; competency-based performance management and, 157–158
skill-based pay, 167
skills: compensation based on, 167; description of, 18; inventory questionnaire for, 68–69
skills bank activity, 194–195
Society for Human Resource Management (SHRM), 26, 144
speed of competency identification, 24

speed in market change, 49
stakeholders, 201, 227
strategic systems model, 131–132
succession management: conceptual model for, 256; employee development and, 215, 255–256
summative evaluations: competency-based employee training system, 137; competency-based performance management system, 161; description of, 59
supervisor assessments, of worker competencies, 89

talent pool, 50
task(s): competencies and, 21; definition of, 20; identifying of, 83–84; project, 78
task groups: competency-based employee rewards, 177–179; competency-based performance management system, 159
technical competencies, 19
technical expert, 191
technology: categories of, 47; competitive advantage of, 47; definition of, 47; employee training using, 128; HR planning affected by, 63; HR profession affected by, 8; ongoing change in, 63
Toastmasters, Inc., 194
total rewards: definition of, 165; traditional, 165–170
training: definition of, 186; employee. *See* employee training
training needs assessment: for competency-based employee training, 130; description of, 127–128

validity, 30
vignettes: analysis of, 5; of competency-related issues, 43–46; description of, 3–5

Whole Systems Transformation
   Conference, 224–225
work: choosing of, 190–192; opportunities for, 191
work activities: DACUM method for
   identifying, 84; description of,
   20; identification of, 83–84
work analysis, 148
work teams: competency-based,
   138–139; individual competence
   building in, 132, 134

workbook exercises, for employee
   development, 194
workers: exemplary vs. fully successful
   performers, 21–23; individual
   differences in, 21–22
workshops, 193